EVE'S RENEG

Also by Valerie Sanders

HARRIET MARTINEAU: Selected Letters (*editor*)
THE PRIVATE LIVES OF VICTORIAN WOMEN: Autobiography in Nineteenth-Century England
REASON OVER PASSION: Harriet Martineau and the Victorian Novel

Eve's Renegades

Victorian Anti-Feminist Women Novelists

Valerie Sanders
*Senior Lecturer in English
University of Buckingham*

© Valerie Sanders 1996

All rights reserved. No reproduction, copy or transmission of this publication may be made without written permission.

No paragraph of this publication may be reproduced, copied or transmitted save with written permission or in accordance with the provisions of the Copyright, Designs and Patents Act 1988, or under the terms of any licence permitting limited copying issued by the Copyright Licensing Agency, 90 Tottenham Court Road, London W1P 9HE.

Any person who does any unauthorised act in relation to this publication may be liable to criminal prosecution and civil claims for damages.

First published 1996 by
MACMILLAN PRESS LTD
Houndmills, Basingstoke, Hampshire RG21 6XS
and London
Companies and representatives
throughout the world

ISBN 0–333–59563–7 hardcover
ISBN 0–333–66313–6 paperback

A catalogue record for this book is available from the British Library.

10	9	8	7	6	5	4	3	2	1
05	04	03	02	01	00	99	98	97	96

Printed and bound in Great Britain by
Ipswich Book Company, Suffolk

Published in the United States of America 1996 by
ST. MARTIN'S PRESS, INC.,
Scholarly and Reference Division
175 Fifth Avenue, New York, N.Y. 10010

ISBN 0–312–16057–7

For my grandmother, Florrie Salinsky, who has seen a century of feminist campaigns and backlashes

Contents

Acknowledgements		viii
Introduction		1
1	The Anti-Feminist Woman 1792–1850	10
2	Anti-Feminist Women and Women's Writing	36
3	'Ardour and Submission': Heroines	56
4	'Goody Men and Brutes': Heroes	91
5	'Work that Influences the World': Journalism	126
6	The Anti-Feminist Woman and Religion	160
Conclusion		199
Biographical Appendix		206
Notes		210
Bibliography		225
Index		240

Acknowledgements

The idea for this book came from a review article by Martha Vicinus in *Victorian Studies* in 1981, suggesting there was room for a study of the 'enemies of feminism' in the nineteenth century. As it happens, the time of writing the book coincided with the so-called anti-feminist backlash of the 1990s, which provided a stimulating background for rethinking the phenomenon. Elisabeth Jay's biography of Mrs Oliphant came out after I had completed my first draft, so I have not responded to it as fully as I should have liked. It is, however, the most comprehensive discussion of Oliphant's novels there is likely to be, and she is to be congratulated on having read so many of them. I can't claim to have been quite so thorough.

I am grateful to Margaret Bartley and Charmian Hearne of Macmillan for encouraging this project, and to their anonymous reader who gave excellent advice on tightening the argument. Bruce Collins and Linda Nash read early sections of the book, and my sister-in-law, Susan Sanders, invented the title. Special thanks are due to Anne Miller and Angela Brown for humouring my fear of word-processors and reducing my straggling typescript to a disk three inches square.

For permission to quote from the manuscript letters in their collection thanks are due to the Trustees of the National Library of Scotland, and the Principal and Chapter of Pusey House, Oxford.

'Girls are very different from what they were when I was young,' Mrs Parlby put in meekly.

'Yes, poor things; but didn't you all have a dismal time, playing croquet in tight stays and a hoop, and reading "The Heir of Redcliffe" [sic]?'

'There was a refining influence in our literature when Mrs Oliphant and Anthony Trollope were writing that is sadly wanting now, Mary. And nice young women were really nice,' Mrs Parlby concluded stiffly.

> Mary Elizabeth Braddon, *Miranda* (1913)[1]

'No woman does think much of her own sex, although few of them confess it as freely as I do.'

> Marian Halcombe in Wilkie Collins,
> *The Woman in White* (1860)[2]

Introduction

I'm not a feminist, quite the contrary, because it seems to me it's not feminism we need, it's the feminine, it's the woman. All this business of women trying to get high positions as executives is all so irrelevant. It's not what we need, it's the restoration of love in its full sense.

These words were spoken by the poet and critic Kathleen Raine in an interview for *The Guardian* in 1993. Regretting that she had not been a good mother, she added that 'women should love first of all'; she even felt guilty about being a writer and betraying not only her parents and children, but 'women' in general.[1] Her words could have been expressed in much the same way a hundred years earlier by Eliza Lynn Linton, but are familiar enough anyway, along with the argument that women can't paint, women can't write; the frequency with which women begin a sentence, 'I'm not a feminist, but...'; or, like Mrs Wilcox in Forster's *Howards End*, have said, 'I sometimes think that it is wiser to leave action and discussion to men.... I am only too thankful not to have a vote myself.'[2]

Why have women been so keen to distance themselves from feminism? This is not a book about political correctness, but the publicity surrounding the latest 'anti-feminist backlash' has given the controversy fresh energy, and made us think more deeply about the unpopularity of the women's movement, both now and in the past. While Victorian feminism has had considerable attention, less has been said about the other side of the debate: the resistance offered by women themselves to some aspects of their liberation – the vote, increased employment opportunities, easier arrangements for divorce, the availability of birth control, freer dress, or even higher education. Of course, these campaigns encompass a wide range of moral issues, so that an anti-abortionist, for example, may favour women going into politics, but have religious scruples about destroying human embryos. The situation has become more complex in the twentieth century, with the advancement of science and technology, but even in the nineteenth, it was often difficult for a woman to decide where she stood in many debates about women's rights. In a 1981 review of Herbert van Thal's biography of Eliza Lynn Linton, Martha Vicinus, in *Victorian Studies*, suggested that 'a good book needs to be written on the "enemies of feminism," women who fought vigorously against the advance of their sex, yet who often supported parts of the feminist cause and also insisted on their own independence'.[3] Although there have been a number of highly-acclaimed biographies of Victorian anti-feminist women – for instance Nancy Fix Anderson on Eliza Lynn Linton in 1987, John Sutherland on Mrs Humphry Ward in 1990, and Elisabeth Jay on Mrs Oliphant in 1995[4] – there is still no one critical work, apart from Vineta Colby's survey book *The Singular Anomaly* (1970),[5] which includes chapters on Linton and Ward – that brings together the main anti-feminist women novelists and examines the patterns of self-contradiction and debate in their writing. Apart from Jay's, the biographies have not attempted detailed analyses of the novels and journalism written by this group of authors, nor addressed the issue of how novelists express anti-feminist opinions. In novelists, as opposed to pure theorists, the interplay of ideas is more unstable, exposed by ambiguous characterization and dialogue, uncertain endings, and an undertow of dissent from the apparent ideological direction of the work as a whole, opening up deeper fissures of self-contradiction.

In any case, the term 'anti-feminist' is itself problematic as is the original designation of 'feminist', which was not officially used until 1894. 'Anti-feminist' emerged thirty years later, in the preface to Shaw's *Saint Joan* (1924).[6] From the outset, I am therefore using the latter term anachronistically and as used before it was properly defined for public argument. Although both terms are now commonly used, they are still difficult to theorize, partly because they are often dependent on each other and on their historical context, but also because each is essentially an 'umbrella' word, used more for convenience than with accuracy. The Oxford English Dictionary interestingly defines an anti-feminist as 'a person (usu. a man) who is hostile to sexual equality or the advocacy of women's rights': the notion of an anti-feminist woman apparently seeming bizarre or unlikely. Many women are merely indifferent to feminism and dismiss it as irrelevant to their particular needs. Yet as Margaret Forster has shown, 'the plain truth is that not only do large numbers of women feel apathetic, but many more actively hate feminism'.[7] This she attributes to the misunderstanding and misrepresentation of what feminism stands for, and indeed this has all along been part of the problem. The definition of anti-feminism naturally hinges on how we perceive feminism, and a specific anti-feminist upsurge generally arises in response to a specific feminist campaign, such as for the suffrage or the legalization of abortion. Although it can be active and take the initiative, anti-feminism, as implied by its name, is usually a resistance movement against the advancement of women's rights. It tries to halt the development of new liberal attitudes towards the boundaries between the sexes, insisting that there are fundamental differences in sexual characteristics and roles which women should accept. Like feminism, it tries to envisage a better society, but one based on tradition or status; it tries to put the brake on change, unless it is a return to family values.

Andrea Dworkin has offered perhaps the most hard-hitting political definitions of anti-feminism. At its simplest, she says, 'Anti-feminism is always an expression of hating women' (a view, incidentally, many anti-feminists might contest); more specifically, it 'holds that the social and sexual condition of women essentially (one way or another) embodies the nature of women, that the way women are treated in sex and in society is congruent with what women are...'. Unlike feminism, which insists on a single standard of human freedom, it 'proposes two standards for rights and responsibilities: two standards determined strictly by and applied strictly to sex.'[8] Anti-feminism attracts thinkers from both ends of the political spectrum (it should not be regarded as exclusively a right-wing phenomenon) and is frequently popular and fashionable. It may co-exist with feminism at times of active campaigning for women's rights, as in the second half of the nineteenth century, or it may activate backlashes after a temporary resurgence of feminist activity, as in the period immediately following the French Revolution, or after the winning of the vote in 1918. It may even share some of feminism's attitudes, especially the glorification of motherhood as the apogee of female development, and a concern for the welfare of children. Far from sympathizing with misogyny, anti-feminism may celebrate femininity and so-called 'female values' as long as they are confined to the home. If anything, anti-feminism has often been an undercurrent to British and American thought, and may often appear the 'normal' or 'natural' way of thinking.

Anti-feminism is difficult enough to define in the twentieth century, but in the nineteenth, it suffers from additional complications.

At first glance, it appears to entail support of the 'separate spheres' ideology, which reached the peak of its popularity in the 1860s: an active decade for all the writers in this study except Mary Ward, who was still a teenager. 'Separate spheres' decreed that while men worked outside the home and were exposed to the worldly temptations of the market-place, women, whether married or single, watched over the house and preserved their own purity and integrity. The picture is complicated, however, by evidence that 'separate spheres' operated more as an ideal than as a fact, especially towards the end of the century, when women were breaking into the workforce and higher education. As Philippa Levine argues, 'the ideal division between domestic woman and public man was never realized in many homes, and never became the dominant reality'.[9] In her view, the concept is best seen psychologically, as influencing the way men and women felt they ought to behave. Such division of roles was often a luxury that working-class women were unable to afford, though it might push their wages down and make them second-class citizens in the workforce; as for middle-class women, the ideology had developed when the industrial revolution took home-based crafts, such as spinning, weaving and brewing, out of the home and into the factory, leaving them with time on their hands and a new cult of gentility to maintain. In practice, many women still needed work outside the home, as the 1851 Census proved so dramatically; while the sheer number of women who broke the rules and made public appearances is proof of the fragility of 'separate spheres' as a binding construct. Florence Nightingale in nursing, Elizabeth Garrett Anderson and Sophia Jex-Blake in medicine, Caroline Norton in reform of the marriage laws, Emily Davies in education, Harriet Martineau in anti-slavery, and Josephine Butler in the field of sexual morality are just the most obvious examples of women who led an active public life; while Linda Colley, Malcolm I. Thomis and Jennifer Grimmett have noted the widespread participation of women in public demonstrations and protests in the first fifty years of the nineteenth century, when the 'separate spheres' ideology was being formulated. 'If British women were being urged to remain at home more stridently in this period than ever before,' argues Colley, 'it was largely because so many of them were finding an increasing amount to do outside the home.'[10]

Still more was this the case after the 1860s, when the issues of education, work, the suffrage, divorce, married women's property, and sexual morality were widely debated, and the official orthodoxies hotly contested. With evidence of women's need to work, and the exposure of the underground world of prostitution (publicized especially by the arguments over the Contagious Diseases Acts of the 1860s), it was becoming harder to insist that 'separate spheres' was the practised norm, however desirable it might be. It was also naïve to maintain that marriage guaranteed happiness and singleness ensured penury and deprivation. Death in childbirth or after a long series of pregnancies was a real danger, quite apart from the temperamental differences that must have made the cohabitation of working husbands and housebound wives frequently stressful. Novelists such as Dickens in *Dombey and Son* (1848) and George Eliot in *Middlemarch* (1871–2) were breaking the old taboos in showing how an unsuccessful marriage could gnaw at the souls of both partners through years of silent misery. Middle-class ideology, according to Mary Poovey, 'was both contested and always under construction; because it was always in the making, it was always open to revision, dispute, and the emergence of oppositional formulations'.[11]

It is against this background of unstable ideology and the slippage of terms that the notion of 'anti-feminism' needs to be defined. At a purely emotional level, it may be a resistance to the term 'feminist' or to the popular stereotyped image of the feminist as a lesbian with a hacked haircut and sour attitudes. It may not involve much careful thought, but may be more like a reflex action. In addition, the debate must take account of the wide grey area between feminism and anti-feminism, where women who are indifferent to the whole controversy would place themselves ideologically. For the purposes of this book, however, I have taken 'anti-feminism' to mean a conviction that women were designed (whether by 'God' or 'Nature') to be first and foremost wives and mothers, and that their social and political subordination is the proper corollary of that position. Anti-feminists expect women to accept their subordinacy as a fact, and to do nothing to undermine the ideal construct which decrees distinct social functions for women. They oppose the efforts of women who quarrel with this clearly-stated position, though of course anti-feminism, like all other ideologies, is subject to the impact of historical change. Whereas an anti-feminist now might not object to women attending university if taking a degree would make them better mothers, an anti-feminist a century ago would think the idea outrageously unfeminine and likely to ruin a girl's chances of marriage. What seems antifeminist in one century does not necessarily carry the same reverberations in another. Nevertheless, the broad anti-feminist position opposes the crossing of domestic boundaries into direct competition with men at men's work, and upholds wifehood and motherhood as feminine ideals to which every woman should aspire.

Above all, as anti-feminism meant adherence to an ideal, rather than an actual, state of affairs, it was particularly liable to lurches of self-doubt, alternating with outbreaks of backlash. Its purpose was both to make home life seem attractive, and to castigate those who stepped outside it: it therefore had a dual intention, which it sometimes had difficulty in balancing, especially if too much sympathy was generated for the rebel-heroine. In reality, the anti-feminist women novelists I have chosen to discuss uniformly fail to idealize family life, however important this was to the impact of their beliefs. Much as in the 1990s, the family is seen as a place of disunity, anxiety, hidden stresses and personal tragedy. Usually fragmented by sudden death and sometimes by religious disagreement, the family simply fails as a practicable ideal in many of these novels, and further confuses the anti-feminist agenda for domestic revival. As will be seen from my discussion, the anti-feminist position becomes well-nigh impossible for any of the novelists to maintain consistently, not least because that 'position' itself was built on shifting sands. Their principles often disintegrate into emotionalism: a feeling that women *ought* to stay at home and be happy with it, and an impatience with all the signs that they want something more. Arguing against the tide of ambition and discontent in the next generation, they force their heroines back into traditional roles, but with decreasing conviction: in many cases avoiding extended pictures of their successful married lives. Extracting a clear 'message' from these novels has become still harder since the development of a sophisticated feminist literary criticism in the 1980s and 1990s, which has had the effect of deepening their importance as social documents, while magnifying their ambiguity as forms of entertainment, rather than direct propaganda. In the context of the 1990s backlash, readers may find fruitful comparisons between two *fins de siècle*.

Like feminism both in the nineteenth century and today, antifeminism is better known by its personalities than by a consistent set of values to which supporters can subscribe. Feminism has had John Stuart Mill, Barbara Bodichon, Emmeline Pankhurst and

Germaine Greer; anti-feminism Eliza Lynn Linton, Mrs Humphry Ward, Queen Victoria and Victoria Gillick. Yet even here we have a problem. Many apparently anti-feminist women, such as Florence Nightingale, have campaigned successfully to open the professions or alter the law in women's favour. Many apparently feminist women, such as Caroline Norton, have dissociated themselves from any fundamental review of the state of their own sex. Moreover, Margaret Forster has suggested, the issue was further confused by women's loyalty to men. 'What made so many women think they were *not* feminists was their hostility to the idea of being against men. If feminism meant being anti-male then they had no time for it.'[12] Feminists have always had to accept the fact that most women marry and put men first in their personal lives: something anti-feminists have employed as a trump-card in appealing to the natural sense of rightness in human relations and the organization of society along instinctual lines. Others again were opposed to the public expression of feminism, but were not necessarily anti-feminist, either in their private attitudes, or in their public statements. Moreover, anti-feminism in the nineteenth century was not, except for the anti-suffrage organizations that formed in response to pro-suffrage activity, a movement that mobilized in cohesive and enduring groups. The women novelists discussed in this book were not personally known to one another, though Mrs Humphry Ward, the youngest, grew up on the novels of Charlotte M. Yonge, one of the oldest. Their brands of anti-feminism were differently accented. Eliza Lynn Linton focused on the strident appearance and behaviour of the 'New Woman' while Charlotte Yonge tried to counteract improper ambition in intellectual women and inculcate domestic values. They and other anti-feminists regard women both as cleverer than men and as more stupid; as morally superior to men, and as morally inferior; as regenerators of the race and as destroyers of it; as angels in the house and as devils.

What unites the women in this book, however, is a professed commitment to the ideology of the home, undermined by a muted undercurrent of personal ambition and impatience with the limitations of a woman's life. The home is the arena of their heroines' adventures, their moral testing-ground, and natural habitat. From this stems the novelists' shared conviction that a woman's place is in the home; that marriage and motherhood are her natural roles; and above all, that true happiness is to be found only in obeying the dictates of nature which reinforce women's common instincts.

Where their convictions look less certain is in their way of showing that domestic life leads to happiness. Here the lesson is taught with varying degrees of success and growing self-contradiction; but then self-contradiction has been a hallmark of anti-feminism since it began, and is especially a symptom of the late nineteenth century's revision of gender roles.

This study focuses on four key women writers: Charlotte M. Yonge, Margaret Oliphant, Eliza Lynn Linton, and Mary Augusta Ward: all respected figures who, through their journalism as well as their novels, guided women's (and to some extent men's) opinions on the great controversies of the day: particularly women's role in public life and religion, their appearance and behaviour, and the relationship between their emotional fulfilment and their sense of vocation and personal worth. Besides influencing public opinion, they were responsive to it, and thus offer a variable register of contemporary social and cultural life. Focusing on those of their novels currently in print (except in Linton's case, where none has been reissued), the aim of this book is to look more closely at Victorian women's discomfort with the idea of their own emancipation, and to explore the rhetorical complexities of their position. I have concentrated less on the suffrage issue because so much has already been written about it;[13] but also because I am less concerned with activism and more with attitudes. Instead, the emphasis is on daily life within the home, and the kinds of conflict faced by heroines with aspirations to do something beyond what their mothers had done before them. In this respect these novelists continue the tradition established first by Jane Austen, and continued by Charlotte Brontë and George Eliot. After an initial chapter providing the historical background to anti-feminism up to around 1850, the novelists' responses to their better-known predecessors are discussed. The chapters on heroines and heroes examine their concepts of femininity and masculinity, and ask whether they diverge significantly from the traditional norms, and in the heroines' case, assess the disruptive impact of a more pro-feminist impulse running through the story. When the heroes are discussed, their tendency to weakness and disease is explored in the light of Victorian theories of masculinity. Chapter 5 considers why their journalism tends to be more overtly anti-feminist than their fiction, and what kinds of personae they projected, as early professionals in a largely male-dominated calling. The final chapter queries the assumption that anti-feminism usually goes with religious conservatism, and demonstrates the extent to which these novelists attacked both the Church of England and Catholicism as they were conducted in the second half of the century.

The methodological approach is literary and sociological, rather than psychoanalytic or deconstructionist. As much of this material is unfamiliar, it seemed sensible to focus on the texts themselves and investigate what is really going on in them, rather than force them to fit a complex theoretical framework. These women themselves distrusted theory, and were interested in actual experiences: hence the (at times) overwhelming domestic detail of their writing. In the 1990s, the tendency is all the other way: towards theoretical abstraction, with little reference to the actualities of lived experience as portrayed by creative writers. Naomi Wolf has recently criticized the feminist academy for withdrawing into élitism and exclusivity by practising elaborate forms of wordplay based on deconstructivist theory and psychoanalysis.[14] Withdrawal from the 'real world' as experienced by 'ordinary women' is a luxury even academic feminism cannot afford. This book therefore uses feminist theory, but never (I hope) loses sight of the fact that the novels discussed were about the painful frustrations and confused allegiances of daily domestic life in Victorian and Edwardian England. Its intention is to explore their depth, and measure its effect on women who claimed to be satisfied with the extent of their freedom.

1

The Anti-Feminist Woman 1792–1850

'How I loathe and detest women,' wrote Harold Nicolson in 1966. '...I am feeling very anti-feminist tonight. I *loathe* women. The only thing that will make them behave decently is to give them complete equality and no privileges.'[1] The perverse logic of this statement highlights the contradictions on which anti-feminism is based. Nicolson loathes women: therefore he wants equality for them, so that they will cease to ask for special treatment. Cynically, perhaps, he arrives at the same practical solution as a feminist, and in his belief that equality would make women 'behave decently', he would have found himself in agreement with John Stuart Mill, author of *The Subjection of Women* (1869), and one of the most radical nineteenth-century exponents of women's emancipation. Feminism and anti-feminism are essentially two sides of the same coin. They are both preoccupied with the question of what women already do, and what they might do; they both view woman in terms of her gender-role in society, focusing chiefly on the conflict between her responsibilities as a mother (actual or potential) and her participation in the workforce. In the nineteenth century, feminists and anti-feminists might easily find themselves on the same side of a campaign: for example, in working to improve standards of education in girls' schools. Whether a girl was being educated to fulfil herself, go to Girton College, or become an intelligent wife and mother (perhaps all three) was unimportant. Theorists on both sides of the debate, since Hannah More and Mary Wollstonecraft, could at least agree that girls should be less frivolous and more rational: in other words, they should 'behave decently'.

Since 1792, the year when Mary Wollstonecraft published her *Vindication of the Rights of Woman*, Britain has experienced a series of 'gender crises', when the traditional roles of men as well as women have been challenged, revised, and occasionally adjusted by law. The issue is as much alive in the 1990s as it was a century ago, with a spate of books examining gender crises past and present. The journalist Neil Lyndon's attack on feminism in 1992 generated a public debate between historians, philosophers and theorists, both in *The Times* and in a live discussion; Susan Faludi's *Backlash: The Undeclared War Against Women* (1991) prompted a similar public debate at the Institute of Contemporary Arts in London; and scarcely a women's magazine failed to run an article on the crisis in feminism. In May 1990 *Elle* asked 'The Big Question: Is Feminism Finished?' On both sides of the issue a sense of fresh discovery and urgency was felt, filling observers with the feeling that this was a sociological development of startling proportions.[2] Not for the first time feminism seemed to be used up. Forced into a defensive position by anti-feminist theories about women's unhappiness in their overcrowded, liberated lifestyles, feminist writers have, in a sense, swapped roles with anti-feminists, and begun to experience something of the latter's position in the late nineteenth century during the suffrage debate.

During the period 1792–1850, anti-feminist women writers had gradually to shift their ground as they responded to the changing expectations of their audience, and slow percolation of proto-feminist ideas through society. What began as an *ad feminam* attack on Mary Wollstonecraft evolved into a xenophobic, pro-British programme urging women to stay by the fireside, and then into a moral crusade for family values, akin to the kind of backlash experienced in the United States and England in the 1990s. Anti-feminist writers broadened their approach to pump up women's sense of their own importance, and to make their work in the home sound vital and exciting; so that, in effect, they moved from an aggressive attitude to their backsliding sisters, to one that was more positive and stimulating. What may be seen as a period of reaction, with few legal changes in women's position compared with the second half of the century, in fact experienced crosscurrents of dissent and impatience, which the anti-feminist lobby (essentially disparate and disorganized) was kept busy correcting. The fact that so much anti-feminist activity went on at this time, especially in the form of caricatures in novels and journals, as well as in reactionary advice manuals, constantly changing their approach to cope with new manifestations of the problem, shows that women's discontent with the limitations of their lives was persistently evident, if still relatively unfocused. Male-authored anti-feminism was generally cruder and emphasized the disjunction between traditional feminine softness and the harsh angularity of women in public life. The biological slant, taken up more by anti-feminists in the second half of the nineteenth century, was for the time being less popular than the positive programme of moral regeneration.

The year 1792, so often cited as the beginning of modern feminism, is also the date when anti-feminism begins to mobilize against a specific, rather than a generalized target. Opposition to the *Vindication of the Rights of Woman* soon became characterized by disapproval of Mary Wollstonecraft's personal life, especially following the publication of William Godwin's *Memoir* of her in 1798.[3] The *British Critic* of 1803 was typical in asking: 'Did she not, in private life, disdain almost every regulation by which society is held together, and erect her own caprice, inclinations, and passions as the unerring standard of right?' – a view that was still being echoed over fifty years later by Harriet Martineau in her *Autobiography*, written in 1855. 'Mary Wollstonecraft was,' she declared, 'with all her powers, a poor victim of passion, with no control over her own peace, and no calmness or content except when the needs of her individual nature were satisfied.'[4] Martineau was by no means anti-feminist, yet as the century wore on, commentators on both sides of the feminist/anti-feminist divide agreed in feeling at the least embarrassed by Wollstonecraft, and more often dismissive of her achievements. Even William Thompson, author of *Appeal of One half the human race, Women, against the Pretensions of the other Half, Men* (1825), censured her 'narrow views', while the largely sympathetic Anne Elwood, in her *Memoirs of the Literary Ladies of England* (1843), regretted that Wollstonecraft, so lavishly endowed with ladylike virtues that should have made her 'a bright pattern of perfection of her sex', should 'by her erroneous theories and false principles, have rendered herself instead, rather the beacon by which to warn the woman of similar endowments with herself, of the rocks upon which enthusiasm and imagination are too apt to wreck their possessor.'[5]

Initially associated with Jacobinism and the dangerous doctrines of the French Revolution, Wollstonecraft's name came to stand for the wild emotionalism that anti-feminists have often attributed to feminist campaigners, the 'shrieking sisterhood' as they were known in the second half of the nineteenth century. This was deeply ironic, given Wollstonecraft's emphasis in the *Vindication* on the need to make women more rational, to strengthen them in mind and body so that they would become useful members of society. In castigating her own sex for their follies, she spares no harsh epithets, and many passages in her book, if read out of context, might easily be mistaken for Hannah More's. She accuses women of indolence, frivolity, passivity, weakness and timidity. 'In the most trifling danger,' she complains, 'they cling to their support, with parasitical tenacity, piteously demanding succour; and their *natural* protector extends his arm, or lifts up his voice, to guard the lovely trembler – from what? Perhaps the frown of an old cow, or the jump of a mouse.'[6] Furthermore, in arguing for an improvement in girls' education, Wollstonecraft was at one with her arch-enemy, Hannah More, as even their contemporaries noticed. Mary Berry, who was reading Wollstonecraft's *Thoughts on the Education of Daughters* in 1799, found it both 'amazing' and 'impossible' that the two writers should agree on 'all the great points of female education', though she was prepared to bet money that More had never read the book. Given More's celebrated boast that she was resolved never to read the *Vindication*, despite being much pestered to do so, this was probably a safe bet: nevertheless, one of her biographers believes that she relented, and read the book some years later.[7]

The book of Hannah More's that the *Vindication* and *Thoughts* most resemble is *Strictures on the Modern System of Education* (1799), in which she blames the educational system for exciting the emotions of girls too early, and attaching too much importance to their tastes and feelings. Unlike Wollstonecraft, however, More approached her subject from the standpoint of Evangelical morality; nor could she resist a passing gibe at those who discuss, 'with more presumption than prudence *the rights of woman*'.[8] Both women found themselves in an awkward position regarding their friendship towards their own sex and were accused of being either too harsh or too radical, and both do some awkward explaining and apologizing. Wollstonecraft assured the readers of her 'Author's Introduction' that she had no intention of violently agitating 'the contested question respecting the quality or inferiority of the sex', nor had she any improper admiration for 'masculine women' in the crudest sense of the term (p. 80). More meanwhile asked herself:

> Is the author then undervaluing her own sex? – No. It is her zeal for their true *interests* which leads her to oppose their imaginary *rights*. It is her regard for their happiness which makes her endeavour to cure them of a feverish thirst for fame. (vol. II, p. 23)

More felt particularly uncomfortable writing about women and apparently betraying their interests by exposing their defects; nor did she exempt herself from a share of criticism. The *Strictures*, she claimed, were written 'with a deep self-abasement arising from a strong conviction of being indeed a partaker in the same corrupt nature' (vol. I, p. xvii).

Hannah More was here raising a problem that was to dog anti-feminists for at least the next hundred years. In criticizing their own sex for weakness and frivolity were they also including themselves? Or were they commenting somehow from outside the enclosure, seeing themselves (as many were to do, both feminists and anti-feminists) as atypical women whose lives were so unusual that they were entitled to measure themselves by different standards? Certainly large numbers of Victorian women, including George Eliot, Florence Nightingale, Harriet Martineau, Eliza Lynn Linton and Elizabeth Blackwell, who were all childless, and most of them unmarried, habitually discussed women in the mass as being quite different from themselves, especially in their need to marry and have children. Most accepted that women would find it difficult to devote themselves to a career at the expense of their personal lives: a view that Florence Nightingale despised, and Eliza Linton approved. Meanwhile there remained the problem of reforming the sex from within, which Hannah More believed should be done by educating women not for individual eminence, but for devotion to the higher Christian ideal. Christianity, she argued, had brought women true dignity, and ultimately it was better to have God's reward than man's. In crying down all desire for ambition, More was establishing a pattern of anti-feminist teaching that Charlotte Yonge was to continue in novels such as *The Daisy Chain*. For both, the church provided fulfilling work among the poor, through which a woman's individual achievements were subsumed by the efforts of a wider group.

Within a few years of Mary Wollstonecraft's death, her influence was evaporating under the stronger presence of Hannah More's. Although the *Vindication* was mentioned from time to time in periodical articles, only four editions were printed between 1833 and 1856, then no more until 1890. Elizabeth Barrett got hold of one at the age of twelve, but told Mary Mitford many years later that she was '*not*, as you are perhaps aware, a very strong partisan of the Rights-of-woman side of the argument – at least I have not been, since I was twelve years old'.[9] More surprising was a rejection of her mother's ideals by Mary Wollstonecraft Shelley, who, by the 1830s, was tired of being criticized for her apathy in the 'Good

Cause', as she called it. Besides lacking argumentative powers, she felt 'the counter arguments too strongly' – evidence, perhaps, that in the early decades of the nineteenth century these were more frequently and persuasively aired than the case for women's rights. Her reasons for eschewing a strong feminist line were partly idiosyncratic and personal. Since Shelley's death, she confessed, she had avoided formal association with the radicals, finding them 'violent without any sense of justice – selfish in the extreme – talking without knowledge – rude, envious & intolerant –'.[10] But her attitudes were very much in accord with the general equation of feminism with strident selfishness, and the desire to find an alternative mission that would direct women's best qualities and efforts towards an altruistic end.

Hannah More's predominance in the debate is partly a mere matter of chance. Although she wrote little after 1819, she did at least outlive Mary Wollstonecraft by over thirty years, and so gained an advantage purely by longevity. Moreover, she caught the mood of the times by realizing that women needed something to do other than wait to be married or pass the day in a round of meaningless pursuits. Here again the anti-feminist woman of the early nineteenth century appears to be working for the same ends as her more feminist successor fifty or sixty years later. Domesticity and motherhood have each been commandeered for propagandist purposes by women on both sides of the debate, with anti-feminist and feminist theorists alike attempting to win respect and recognition for women who choose to stay at home and make a serious job of raising their children. Central to both philosophies is a glorification of women's ability to reproduce, and the nurturing qualities this experience fosters. Even Mary Wollstonecraft assumed most women would stay at home and look after their families; and from this virtuous practice, conscientiously carried out, it was only a short step to the wider application of feminine principles. As Jane Rendall has shown in *The Origins of Modern Feminism* (1985), Evangelical leaders preached a religion of the heart that exalted what were seen as women's special qualities and gave them a dynamic role in the church's mission to regenerate society.[11] A popular strand in anti-feminist thinking has always been the 'superiority' argument: that women's superiority to men makes them uniquely suited to remaining outside the male sphere of work and worldliness and directs them instead to a purely ethical role in raising the moral tone of society. This was very much the predominant attitude in the

1830s and 1840s when the second generation of women moralists extended the mission already established in the 1790s and early 1800s by Hannah More and Jane West. In both generations the purpose of women's education was linked to the question of their eventual role in life, with the second generation shifting the emphasis, via Evangelicalism, towards the notion of an enhanced role within the family. The sense of crisis which had sharpened the debate in the 1790s, gradually softened, and was replaced by a feeling of confidence in Britain's stability as a sensible and Christian nation.

In her *Letters to a Young Lady* (1806), Jane West establishes a clear division between politics and religion in the lives of middle-class women, and warns her readers to shun the first as eagerly as they embrace the second. This, too, was to become a staple theme of Victorian anti-feminism, ensuring that the suffrage was ceded more reluctantly than any other single claim made by women collectively. Jane West was also convinced of a direct link between female 'depravity' and invasion by foreign states. 'No nation', she claimed, 'has preserved its political independence for any long period after its women became dissipated and licentious.'[12] By suggesting, as she did, that women could avert wars by running contented households, she was giving middle-class mothers and wives a role in the preservation of their country that remained a popular image for many succeeding generations. Increasingly, women, more than men, were seen as being responsible for the moral wellbeing of the nation, and ultimately its safety in the world at large. In Jane West's writing, a demagogue lurks round every corner, tempting the very household servants, unless the wife and mother of the family remains watchful and performs her duty to the home and state.

Above all, anti-feminist women writers of the period 1790–1850 were committed to the preservation of clear borderlines, whether between the sexes, the classes, or different countries. A growing respect for 'Britishness' as emblematic of all that was virtuous and respectable developed alongside the theory of separate spheres and a belief in firm demarcations between servants and employers. After the French Revolution, and with the outbreak of further revolutions on the Continent in 1830 and 1848, the need for these demarcations seemed all the more urgent. As Linda Colley has shown, it was common to contrast the characteristics of French and English women, and to argue that the French were less trustworthy as a nation because they allowed their women too much prominence in public life.[13] Jane West saw voluptuousness as distinctly un-British, and ascribed the fall of France 'in a great measure to the dissipated indelicate behaviour and loose morals of its women'.[14] In her *Letters to a Young Lady*, she confessed: 'I plead guilty to the charge of wishing to keep my fair countrywomen *entirely* British. I think that epithet infinitely more desirable than philosopher or cosmopolite' (vol. III, p. 441), both terms that might be applied to Mary Wollstonecraft and the members of the Godwin circle. Sarah Ellis's *Women of England* series opened in 1839 with a paean of praise for Britishness as fostering the 'domestic character of England – the home comforts, and fireside virtues for which she is so justly celebrated'. Afraid that the women of England were deteriorating in their moral character, she issued her rallying cry specifically to the middle classes as 'the pillar of our nation's strength'. 'In no other country is society thus beautifully proportioned,' she maintained, 'and England should beware of any deviation from the order and symmetry of her national column.'[15] Her imagery curiously conflates the shape of English society with that of the female body, before subsuming it in the military terminology with which her sentence ends. Female values are thus absorbed into an overarching ideology of male patriotism and orderliness. When in the 1880s Eliza Lynn Linton came to write her articles on 'The Characteristics of English Women', she was following directly in the tradition of Sarah Ellis and Jane West before her. In all three the link between Britishness and anti-feminism was well established.

On the other hand, the call to Britishness could also be interpreted as giving women a clear patriotic role in the support of their country, as happened subsequently during the First and Second World Wars. Although both these events liberated women from circumscribed domestic roles and gave them work outside the home that was often physically demanding, they were followed by periods of stagnation or backlash in the development of feminism. Similarly, as Linda Colley argues, the Napoleonic Wars stimulated women into patriotic activism and concern for the plights of two wronged queens, Marie Antoinette of France, and George IV's Queen Caroline in England. Although the ideology of 'separate spheres' was supposed to keep men and women committed to their distinctive roles, it had the additional effect of reinforcing gender loyalties, and giving women a stronger collective identity. Anti-feminist writers in the first half of the new century capitalized on this to make their programmes sound more positive and appealing. The coronation of a new young queen helped to glamorize the woman's function as empress over the dominions of her own home.

The demarcation line between servants and employers was also firmly drawn. Jane West suspected improvident and disaffected servants of being particularly susceptible to revolutionary ideas and in need of special vigilance from their employers. 'Affability and condescension' she felt were the right notes for the mistress of a household to adopt towards her employees (vol. III, p. 300). The vocabulary of many anti-feminist theorists of the post-French Revolutionary period is markedly political as they try to infuse domestic management with a sense of governmental responsibility. The household thus becomes a mini-state – as it was for John Stuart Mill in *The Subjection of Women*[16] – and the housewife–governor a mini Queen Victoria commanding her subjects. The accession of a young queen in 1837 was a highly symbolic event to Sarah Ellis, and one that she lost no time in making an example to her female readers. What might have been proof that women were capable of high office in a political sphere was instead interpreted as evidence of female moral 'influence', of which all women were exemplars, however humble their role. In her *Strictures*, written, as she put it, in 'this moment of alarm and peril' (p. 4), Hannah More called on women to exercise self-restraint and abstain from a 'struggle for power' (p. 14). The new term of 'rights', which had been made so notorious by Tom Paine and Mary Wollstonecraft (not named, but clearly implied), gave women what she considered a wholly bogus claim to privileges that were never meant to be theirs, and she compared them to 'pretenders' to undeserved thrones (p. 20). Many anti-feminist writers, from Hannah More to John Ruskin, did their best to persuade women against usurping 'pretenders'' roles, and flatter them into being gracious 'Queens', the fount of all domestic virtue and kindliness.

Against the notion of 'rights' was upheld the greater worth of 'interests' or 'influence', or, better still, 'duties'. All these terms were discussed earnestly from the 1790s and throughout the nineteenth century, as anti-feminist writers tried to enthuse women with their moral mission. 'It is her zeal for their true *interests* which leads her to oppose their imaginary rights,' pleaded Hannah More; while Sarah Lewis, in *Woman's Mission* (1839), insisted that 'influence' was far more valuable than the 'power' which belonged to men. 'Men frequently resist power,' she argued, 'while they yield to influence an unconscious acquiescence.' Sarah Lewis explained in her preface that the book, which came out anonymously and was based on Aimé

Martin's *Sur l'Éducation des Mères*, was not a manual of female duties, but something far more exciting and uplifting, that would convince women of their importance to society. 'We claim for them no less an office than that of instruments (under God) for the regeneration of the world, – restorers of God's image in the human soul.'[17]

Anti-feminist writers at this time were astute enough to sense that women were dissatisfied with their unimportant roles and that they aspired to political activity because domestic life seemed repetitive and unappealing. Much of their mission hinges on the desire to make domesticity sound exciting; they were also afraid that if women did enter the sphere of work and politics they would have an even lower opinion of the British fireside than they had before. Afraid, too, of the inevitable slide into depravity if women were not at home diffusing a sound moral influence, theorists constructed a two-stage programme of recovery, by which wives and mothers first disciplined themselves to endure and forbear, and then ensured that their husbands and sons did the same. They were often vague about the exact nature of this nebulous but powerful 'influence', but Sarah Lewis, for one, was prepared to let women interfere even in politics as 'moral agents' (p. 51). A more sophisticated thinker than More and West, with a feel for emotional rapture, Lewis tried to spell out exactly what she meant her readers to do. 'If called upon to give a definition of the peculiar mission of woman, and the peculiar source of her influence,' she explained, treading carefully, 'I should say it is the application of large principles to small duties, – the agency of comprehensive intelligence on details' (p. 108). This remained the programme for anti-feminist writers throughout the century, a programme fraught with risks because of her admission at the outset that the duties involved were 'small'. Novelists such as Margaret Oliphant and Charlotte Yonge seem to have acted unconsciously on Sarah Lewis's principles, filling their tales with the densest domestic detail, and magnifying the importance of every household incident; but whereas Yonge takes it seriously, Oliphant treats her characters' involvement in tea-parties, 'Thursday evenings' and domestic manoeuvrings with equivocal humour, while offering them no alternative sphere of activity, and claiming to admire their clever management.

Meanwhile, other writers preferred to concentrate on the 'large principles' and treated the home arena as a severe moral testing ground. The imaginative appeal of this idea extended from Sarah

Ellis to George Eliot and Elizabeth Gaskell, so that women were able to find adventures in the middle-class home as demanding of their powers of endurance as those they had experienced in the Gothic castle the century before. Henceforth the task of the anti-feminist theorist was to make women see their work in the home as a serious scientific craft of government, a highly skilled job of far greater importance to the country than anything they could do in the outside world. Following in Hannah More's wake, they urged their readers to be successful women rather than failed men.

Furthermore, they considered 'being' more important than 'knowing'. What a woman *was*, in terms of her personality and moral standards, was of far greater significance than what she knew, in terms of mere accomplishments. A woman was essentially a contingent presence, whose meaning depended on her relationships with other people, and her ethical atmosphere. Women were constantly reminded by anti-feminist writers of their best virtues: their eye for detail ('small duties' again), their powers of observation, their docility and sensibility. Many theorists were convinced that women were unable to analyse information or make comparisons: hence their unfitness for 'masculine' studies such as history and science. Hannah More concluded that women 'have equal *parts*, but are inferior in *wholeness* of mind in the integral understanding' (*Strictures*, vol. II, p. 26). Sarah Lewis, forty years later, dismissed both an intellectual education and training in accomplishments as a waste of time for women: it was better to prepare them for their 'duties' by developing their conscience, heart and affections. Sarah Ellis, similarly, stressed the importance of training the temperament. She had read *Woman's Mission*, to which she refers in her *Daughters of England* (1842), and described woman's whole life from the cradle to the grave as 'one of feeling, rather than of action; whose highest duty is so often to suffer, and be still; whose deepest enjoyments are all relative; who has nothing, and is nothing of herself; whose experience, if unparticipated, is a total blank'.[18] This is perhaps the most extreme statement of woman's position as a 'relative creature' (another of Mrs Ellis's terms) to be found in anti-feminist writing of the nineteenth century. The type of education required by such a cipher must inevitably be one which taught her only to sympathize with the tastes of others. For women writers (although she was one herself) she had little fellow-feeling. This apparent inconsistency of principle only faintly troubled anti-feminist women writers, who either glossed over the fact of their own authorship, or else made themselves honourable exceptions to the general rule. The public, moreover, seemed to accept that some women were needed as guardians of the country's moral standards, and that the most effective way they could do this was by writing advice manuals.

A further contradiction in Mrs Ellis's theory of women's education and conduct was her emphasis on the cultivation of the feelings, and her concern that women lived too exclusively in their own sensibilities. The answer, of course, was to develop the 'heart,' the higher, finer feelings that would contribute to the wellbeing of the family; but there are places in Mrs Ellis's writing where the self-absorbed George Eliot heroine (such as Rosamond Vincy) seems to be prefigured. 'To love, is woman's duty,' declares Mrs Ellis in *The Daughters of England*, '– to be beloved, is her reward' (p. 12). 'Beyond the sphere of her affections, she has nothing, and is nothing' she adds (p. 260), insisting that women are 'never so happy as when feeling grateful' (p. 259). At the point where this lap-dog philosophy might become too abject, however, Mrs Ellis describes love as 'woman's all – her wealth, her power, her very being' (p. 315). The notion of love as 'power' cleverly turned a concept of female vulnerability into a vague suggestion of strength. Armed with the power of love, a woman might do anything – provided she did it within her own family. Mrs Ellis did her best to make her women readers feel sorry for men as somehow deprived of all this mystical power, and obliged to mix in the dull or corrupting world of work. She advised the wives and daughters who read her books to be largely silent in company, accept the social restrictions imposed by good society, and avoid any desire for distinction. Her methods seem to have worked, if the reactions of Flora Tristan, a French visitor to England in the late 1830s, are anything to go by. Feeling that English women were raised by an educational system based on false principles and in an atmosphere of hypocrisy, Tristan was amazed at the difference between the ordinary woman at the hearthside and the successful woman writer: 'Quel révoltant contraste en Angleterre que l'extrême servitude des femmes et la supériorité intellectuelle des femmes auteurs!'[19]

Yet the difference between ordinary women and authors was perhaps less noticeable than Flora Tristan assumed. While it may be difficult to gauge the 'real' attitudes of successful women in the first half of the nineteenth century from reading their published articles or even their letters (most repeated the accepted views of women's conduct), their diaries, at least, might be expected to tell a different story. But Harriet Blodgett has cautioned against an assumption that early Victorian women's diaries were surging with rebellion and discontent. Over the centuries, she says, women's diaries 'show how conservative women were of the male power system and its values, how inclined as a rule to keep themselves and their sisters in check'. It is not until the later nineteenth century that they become less acquiescent and more overtly rebellious.[20] Mary Shelley's diary of the 1830s is a classic example of this internalized conservatism, as is the art critic and journalist's, Elizabeth Rigby, Lady Eastlake (1809–93). Perhaps both these women could afford to be conservative, in that their lives had been unusually adventurous. Mary Shelley's teenage elopement had been followed by several years of bohemian literary life in Europe, while Lady Eastlake had spent a year studying literature and art in the British Museum and National Gallery, before making long visits to Germany and Russia. Yet in 1840 she was still asking herself: 'Why do men invariably judge better than women?' and replying: 'Simply because their feelings have less interference.' She concluded that 'woman is made to lean, man to support', a view that must have contributed to her attack on *Jane Eyre* in the *Quarterly Review* of 1848, where she singled out for criticism Jane's rebelliousness and independence. Moreover, she began to applaud the negative virtues available to women and see them as being far more honourable than the active ones. 'There is more moral courage in refusing than in accepting,' she states sententiously, 'and more merit in restricting genius than in indulging it.'[21] Eastlake accepted that what a woman did not attempt to gain she was not qualified to use, and it was wrong of her advisors to try and make her discontented.

In the first half of the nineteenth century issues of 'power' and 'protection' were at the heart of debates about women's public and private roles in society. Nina Auerbach has shown that 'woman's very aura of exclusion gave her imaginative centrality in a culture increasingly alienated from itself': a position that explains the novelists' fascination with outsiders and the buried lives of women.[22] Did woman's exclusion give her more or less power? Once there was a queen on the throne, women moralists such as Mrs Ellis looked to her for further inspiration and a general increase in the importance of female 'influence'. Yet in her own letters in the early 1850s Queen Victoria was recoiling from the need to involve herself in European politics and marvelling at Prince Albert's more natural aptitude for government. Even so, she was concerned that 'it takes a little off from the gentleness of his character', disturbing evidence of what an interest in politics might do to a woman; 'but I am every day more convinced', she told her uncle Leopold, King of the Belgians, in 1852, 'that *we women*, if we *are* to be *good* women, *feminine* and *amiable* and *domestic*, are *not fitted to reign*; at least it is *contre gré* that they drive themselves to the *work* which it entails'.[23] Opposed to the general 'unsexing' of women, women's rights, and later the campaign to let women qualify as doctors, Victoria saw her position as anomalous, and gave little help to the burgeoning women's movement of her day.

Most early nineteenth-century women accepted their general inferiority to men (except where the moralists allowed them some spiritual superiority) and asked only for their 'protection', a term employed by Caroline Norton in her campaigns against the marriage laws for women. Norton was a classic example of someone who had suffered notoriously at the hands of a brutal husband, but who stayed well clear of any outright commitment to what she called 'the wild and ridiculous doctrine of equality'.[24] If anything, women in the 1830s and 1840s seemed ashamed of the low reputation of their own sex, and urged their readers to help repair their battered image. By 1831, when Mrs John Sandford published her *Woman, in her Social and Domestic Character*, there appeared to have been a change in attitude to women that made it necessary for them to prove their unimpeachable behaviour. Mrs Sandford, a clergyman's wife and one of many anti-feminist women to conceal her identity completely behind her husband's name (Mrs Humphry Ward and Mrs Henry Wood are other examples), sensed a decline in the chivalric, romantic idealization of women. A woman was appreciated in a different way from before, she felt: chiefly by her ability to make those around her happy. 'There is less of enthusiasm entertained for her,' claimed Mrs Sandford, 'but the regard is more rational, and, perhaps, equally sincere; since it is in relation to happiness that she is principally appreciated.' Aware that some women would find housework uninteresting, she advised them to win their family's praise by proving their powers of adaptation to their lot, and seeking comfort from religion. Ultimately, she concluded, 'what a woman knows is comparatively of little importance to what a woman *is*'.[25]

An anonymous woman writer who published a two-volume work on *Woman's Rights and Duties* in 1840 wondered why distinguished women of the age produced so little effect on 'the tastes and manners of their own sex', and concluded that 'not being disposed to become apostles of a new system, they usually make themselves cyphers in general society'. Either they feel 'stupified [sic] by the insipidity of what is commonly called small talk', or 'they are absorbed by the current'.[26] Although this writer believed in the subordination of women as a law of nature, she felt that they should at least be better educated to improve their failing vigour; Mrs Sandford, however, jeered at the feminist disciple who 'threw off her hat, and called for a bootjack; and imagined that by affecting the manners of the other sex, she should best assert her equality with them' (p. 22). In 1831 the Wollstonecraft bogey was still a valuable weapon in anti-feminist hands, especially those who were developing a taste for caricature of bluestockings and 'strong-minded women'.

The anti-feminist caricature, whether in a written or cartoon form, was produced both by men and by women, and was particularly popular at the turn of the eighteenth/nineteenth century, and again in the 1830s, when Harriet Martineau's rise to literary stardom attracted many gibes at her prudishness, angularity and unfeminine looks. But this was nothing new. In 1800 Elizabeth Hamilton's novel *Memoirs of Modern Philosophers* ridiculed the doctrines of Mary Wollstonecraft and William Godwin in the person of its anti-heroine, Bridgetina Botherim, who, in the opening chapter, rejects a compliment on the pudding with the words:'I do assure you, sir, you are very much mistaken, if you think that I employ my time in such a manner.' Too learned to trouble herself about doing anything useful, Bridgetina first read Godwin's *Political Justice* when her mother's order of brown snuff arrived from London wrapped in two proof-sheets of that notorious work: 'I read and sneezed, and sneezed and read, till the germ of philosophy began to fructify my soul,' Bridgetina reports in an autobiographical history of her mind.[27] Hamilton makes her undergo all the miseries and humiliations of unrequited passion before abandoning her, unwed, to her mother's forgiving mercies at the end of the novel. From the beginning of the caricaturing tradition, the liberated woman was either seen as unmarriageable, or was rewarded at the last moment for her recantation of feminist ideals by an honourable marriage and children. The caricaturists always stressed the incompatibility of scholarship with normal marriage and motherhood, notwithstanding the well-known examples of women such as Mrs Somerville, the mathematician and scientist.

Amelia Opie's *Adeline Mowbray*, of 1802, is an attack on free thought and free love, stressing the damage done to daughters by egotistical mothers who live for their own pleasures. Towards the end of the novel, Adeline's mother, Mrs Mowbray, is taught by a Quaker woman, Mrs Pemberton, to review her past conduct to her daughter, who has practised free love and been ostracized by society:

> Mrs Mowbray was silent: she recollected that, while she was gratifying her own vanity in composing her system of education, Adeline was almost banished her presence; and, but for the humble instruction of her grandmother, would, at the age of fifteen, have run a great risk of being both an ignorant and useless being.[28]

Her grandmother, indeed, rescued her in chapter 2 by turning her granddaughter into a useful and happy expert at household management, but had herself been at fault in the upbringing of her own daughter, Adeline's mother. Regarding her as a 'genius' her parents had excused her from all knowledge of domestic affairs, with the disastrous results recounted in the novel. Adeline herself is very far from being caricatured, and in fact impresses the reader with her sweetness and virtue, both duly rewarded at the end with a graceful death. The harshest criticism is reserved for Mrs Mowbray, a Mary Wollstonecraft figure, whose educational theory is seen as being irrelevant and harmful to the welfare of her beautiful and virtuous daughter. Mrs Opie, a former friend of Wollstonecraft's, who reacted against her, preferred the simple domestic values of Mrs Woodville, the grandmother, whose eighteenth-century household skills might have saved Adeline a life of misery and poverty. When Mrs Opie's letters and diaries were edited in 1854 by Cecilia Lucy Brightwell, the editor apologized for Opie's enthusiasm for politics in 1794: 'but there was too much of the pure womanly character in her, to suffer her ever to sympathize with the assertors of "woman's rights," (so called;) and she was not to be so spoiled even though exposed to the influence of Horace Walpole's "philosophising serpents, the Paines, the Tookes, and the Woollstonecrofts [sic]."'[29]

Nor was Maria Edgeworth, a woman writer who usually managed to avoid the gibes of anti-feminists, perhaps because she co-operated with her father in writing books for children, and led a blameless life as an unmarried daughter at home. In 1801 she joined the public reaction against Mary Wollstonecraft by including in her novel *Belinda* a caricature of a 'woman's rights' woman, Harriott Freke, whose boisterous cries of 'I hate slavery! Vive la Liberté' and 'I'm a champion for the Rights of Woman,' shatter the nerves of her more refined companions.[30] Mrs Freke seems primarily concerned with the relations between the sexes, which she thinks are too inhibited: 'why, when a woman likes a man, does not she go and tell him so honestly?' She is punished for her outlandishness by being found dressed as a man and caught in a spring-trap in Lady Delacour's garden, convinced that Lady Delacour (her friend) is having an affair: proof, perhaps, of women's prurient interest, however uninhibited, in the private lives of other women. As a loud and boisterous feminist with a complete disregard for normal drawing-room courtesies, Harriott Freke prefigures Bell Blount, the caricatured emancipated woman of Eliza Lynn Linton's *The Rebel of the Family* (1880): except that Bell Blount is a good deal more outrageous (she is both a divorcee and a lesbian) and has a larger role in the novel as the heroine's temptress. Perdita Winstanley, the rebel-heroine of the title, feels both 'repulsion and fascination' for her, but successfully evades her clutches by marrying a respectable chemist.[31]

Caricatures of 'strong-minded women' by women writers in the first forty years of the nineteenth century tended to be kinder to younger women, who were considered still redeemable, or at least less hardened: older ones, such as Harriott Freke, and later Bell Blount, were treated more harshly because they were more dangerous to naïve young heroines who might be taken in by their extravagant theories of liberty. Caricatures by male writers tended to be crueller still, with more allusions to their victims' supposed personal immorality. The most famous attack on Mary Wollstonecraft was probably Richard Polwhele's poem *The Unsex'd Females* (1798), which saw her 'the intrepid champion of her sex', triumphing over 'humbled man' and inspiring a host of followers in women such as Mrs Barbauld, Helen Maria Williams and Mary Hays. Outside the poem he commented that 'a woman who has broken through all religious restraints, will commonly be found ripe for every species of licentiousness'; inside it, he recommends his female readers to cluster round the graver women moralists, Hannah More, Hester Chapone, Elizabeth Montagu and Elizabeth Carter.[32] He also attacks Wollstonecraft's approval of lessons on sexual reproduction, mentioned in her 'Introductory Address to Parents' in her *Elements of Morality for the Use of Children* (1790), a translation of a German work by C.G. Salzmann. Male anti-feminist satirists writing between 1793 and 1850 tended to concentrate on two main aspects of women's behaviour: their bluestockingism, and their 'unnatural' rejection of childbearing in favour of writing. The two were not infrequently connected.

In general, however, men writing in the established journals tended not so much to be anti-feminist, as simply to accept women's inferiority as a matter of fact. Between 1820 and 1850 the major periodicals carried relatively few articles on women and their situation: so-called 'masculine' subjects, such as political economy, the state of the nation, travels, the church, the army, and industrialization, held the day, with few women enlisting as reviewers. Most women writers were treated courteously but with condescension by male critics, who praised their sensitivity and truth to life while implying that their concerns were essentially trivial. When a woman stepped outside the usual boundaries, and produced, as Mrs Somerville did, a work of science, it was comfortably accepted as an aberration too extreme to be worrying. A review of her *Mechanism of the Heavens* appearing in 1832 began with the extravagant claim that

> This unquestionably is one of the most remarkable works that female intellect ever produced, in any age or country; and with respect to the present day, we hazard little in saying, that Mrs Somerville is the only individual of her sex in the world who could have written it.[33]

Joanna Baillie, in the field of drama, was also treated largely as an exception, who could be chivalrously praised and gently criticized: a position that the ageing Romantic poets Wordsworth and Southey adopted towards aspirant women writers. Southey's dismissal of Charlotte Brontë is well known, while Wordsworth, according to Susan Levin, regarded women poets, at best, with 'amused tolerance'.[34] This is not entirely fair. Wordsworth read the works sent to him by women poets, and often encouraged them by saying which ones he had particularly enjoyed; he even considered writing 'an Account of the Deceased Poetesses of Great Britain – with an Estimate of their Works', but on further reflection decided that it was not 'sufficiently interesting for a separate subject'. He did, however, profess liking for the Countess of Winchilsea's poetry.[35] On the other hand, Wordsworth rebuked contemporary women poets for their lack of logic or poor handling of blank verse. He warned the brother of Eliza Hamilton, who had sent him some verses, that:

> Female Authorship is to be shunned as bringing in its train more and heavier evils than have presented themselves to your sister's ingenuous mind. No true friend, I am sure, will endeavour to shake her resolution to remain in her own quiet and healthful obscurity. This is not said with a view to discourage her from writing, nor have the remarks made above any aim of the kind; they are rather intended to assist her in writing with more permanent satisfaction to herself. She will probably write less in proportion as she subjects her feelings to logical forms, but the range of her sensibilities, so far from being narrowed, will extend as she improves in the habit of looking at things through the steady light of words . . .[36]

Wordsworth's criticism maintains the conventional split between male logic and female sensibility, with every suggestion that Eliza Hamilton should write only occasionally, and perhaps only for herself. Neither he nor Southey found it easy to accept the idea of a professional woman poet, bearing in mind the lack of formal training in classical verse forms, and the dangers to which a public life would expose a woman's 'natural' simplicity (not to mention her domestic usefulness). Norma Clarke has shown how Wordsworth was very happy to encourage a household full of intelligent female assistants, adding to them by association writers such as Felicia Hemans and Maria Jane Jewsbury: but as soon as they began to show signs of literary independence, he started to criticize them and belittle their achievements. By 1830, she suggests, intellectuality and womanliness had become opposites. 'The word "feminine" could not longer contain intellectual achievement.'[37]

Those women who did trespass on male preserves quickly attracted fire. If Mary Wollstonecraft was the popular 'hate figure' of the first ten years of the nineteenth century, Harriet Martineau succeeded her, among male commentators, at least, in the 1830s. There was little they could say against Martineau's personal life, which remained impeccable, but she could be attacked for venturing into political economy, and recommending the most 'unfeminine' of philosophies in Malthusianism. While the *Quarterly* 'tomahawked' her, Thomas Moore parodied 'Come live with me and be my love' into a Malthusian love-song, claiming 'Chas'd from our classic souls shall be / All thought of vulgar progeny.' *Fraser's Magazine* quoted Moore's parody in its own 'Gallery of Literary Characters', which also included a picture of 'Miss Harriet in the full enjoyment of economical philosophy', surrounded by 'Utilitarian' tea-things, and regretted by 'all those who feel respect for the female sex'.[38]

It is easy enough to trace the critical reception of any one woman writer whose work first appeared in the 1830s or 1840s, and recognize the crucial centrality of her gender. Whether critics were enthusiastic or negative, they rarely failed to mention that the author was a woman, and to qualify their views accordingly. One such critic, Henry Nelson Coleridge, was married to a woman writer, Samuel Coleridge's daughter Sara, and yet even he began his 1840 survey of 'Modern English Poetesses' for the *Quarterly* with a gush of chivalrous sentimentality:

> It is easy to be critical on men; but when we venture to lift a pen against women, straightway *apparent facies*; the weapon drops pointless on the marked passage; and whilst the mind is bent on praise or censure of the poem, the eye swims too deep in tears and mist over the poetess herself in the frontispiece, to let it see its way to either.[39]

The *Quarterly* was thus capable of both extremes in its treatment of women writers, within the space of a very few years. The 'poetesses', being gentler and with less impact on public life (at the end of his article Henry Coleridge compared each of them to different flowers) were treated more kindly than Martineau, whose unfeminine study had more disturbing implications; but little seemed to have changed by 1856 when Marian Evans, writing for the *Westminster Review*, complained of the way women writers were treated by male reviewers. 'No sooner does a woman show that she has genius or effective talent, than she receives the tribute of being moderately praised and severely criticized,' she objected. 'Harriet Martineau, Currer Bell, and Mrs Gaskell have been treated as cavalierly as if they had been men.'[40] This did not, however, indicate that their works were being considered impartially: and the range of names cited by the future George Eliot – one a male pseudonym long since uncovered, one a bold full name, and the third a discreet married name – proves that the options for concealment or image-making offered no long-term protection.

One further example from the 1850s should be enough to show how male anti-feminism was developing with the century. By this time the public were used to Harriet Martineau, the novelty of a queen on the throne, and the furore caused by the publication of *Jane Eyre*. They had followed the success of Caroline Norton's campaign to obtain child custody for mothers, and some had sent their daughters to the new 'lectures for ladies' at Queen's and Bedford Colleges. Yet in 1851 new shock waves were caused by Amelia Bloomer and her outlandish but comfortable knickerbocker costume for women: shock waves that were kept in motion by Charles Dickens, among others, and the anti-feminist *Punch*. Dickens dealt with the subject himself in an article for *Household Words*, seeing Bloomerism as merely a symptom of a ludicrous feminism that would wreck the domestic comfort of all homes afflicted by a woman with a mission. Using techniques similar to those he would give to Mr Bounderby three years later in *Hard Times*, Dickens envisaged his liberated woman 'behind a small table ornamented with a water-bottle and tumbler', much as Bounderby assumed that all working men with a grievance wanted turtle soup and venison with a gold spoon. 'Should we', asked Dickens, 'love our Julia better, if she were a Member of Parliament, a Parochial Guardian, a High Sheriff, a Grand Juror, or a woman distinguished for her able conduct in the chair? Do we not, on the contrary, rather seek in the society of our Julia, a haven of refuge from Members of Parliament, Parochial Guardians, High Sheriffs, Grand Jurors, and able chairmen?'[41] Once again, the blurring of boundaries was the outcome most feared by an anti-feminist man, who dreaded, above all else, to find that his wife had abandoned her private sphere for the public, and lost her name in a forbidding title. In this article he rehearses much of the ridicule he uses on Miss Wisk in *Bleak House* (1853) – Miss Wisk who informs her companions that 'the idea of woman's mission lying chiefly in the narrow sphere of Home was an outrageous slander on the part of her Tyrant, Man'.[42] In a novel teeming with careless mothers and neglected homes and children, Dickens had no further need to labour the point.

Punch meanwhile carried a letter professing to be from a 'strong-minded American Woman', Theodosia E. Bang, on the progress of the American female who delivers lectures and edits newspapers, leaving her domestic chores to the helpers of her boarding house. American women, she pointed out, were also emancipating themselves from 'the inconvenient dress of the European female', and taking not only to trousers, but also to 'the hat, the cigar, the paletot or round jacket'. An accompanying illustration shows six women exhibiting varieties of the new dress, some wearing bonnets and frilly bustles with their knickerbockers, to emphasize the incongruity, and others top hats. Some smoke cigars and carry riding crops, and most stand in a swaggering masculine posture with their hands on their hips or in their pockets.[43] The cartoon embodies all the key characteristics of mid-century male anti-feminism: mockery of female pretensions to equality and their ludicrousness, mixed with horror and even a slight touch of titillation. If a woman wanted a man's job, the fear throughout the century was that she would soon begin to look and behave like a man, removing all the pleasures of sexual difference, for women themselves, as well as for men. Although feminist women were usually depicted as brisk and self-sufficient, the implication was always that their lives lacked something: essentially the tenderness and fulfilment of married love and motherhood.

It is beyond the scope of this study to offer a comprehensive chronological account of male anti-feminism in the nineteenth century. The examples cited were chosen to illustrate the underlying attitudes of men (and therefore of society in general) during the first fifty years of the new century following Mary Wollstonecraft's death, and thus to provide a context for the growth of female anti-feminism. Male anti-feminism is a more varied, though not necessarily more complex phenomenon than the female equivalent. During the nineteenth century, and continuing today, it takes many forms. At its simplest it may be an opposition to extremists: masculine 'women's libbers' who go about proclaiming the destruction of the nuclear family and a woman's right to control her own body. Nineteenth-century men like Dickens recoiled from the image of the woman campaigner who neglected her family while dedicating herself to an abstract cause; but women of this kind were easy targets and sufficiently absurd to be unalarming. The quieter and more ladylike campaigners, such as Josephine Butler, were in some ways more dangerous, because their example implied that any other happily married wife and mother might mount a platform and start making speeches. Male anti-feminists thus continued to focus on the disjunction between a woman's natural softness and delicacy, and the harsh public roles she was trying to adopt. Apart from the age-old accusations of irrationality and emotionalism, there was little overt (and ungentlemanly) criticism of what were regarded as typically feminine characteristics. Motivating male anti-feminism at this time seemed to be resistance to change, insecurity about gender roles, and emotional recoil from apparently 'unnatural' female behaviour.

Women's anti-feminism is inevitably more complex, psychologically, than men's, in that it must entail some element of self-hate and shame, akin to a woman's dislike of her own body, and perhaps some envy of the other sex. It may be passive and reactionary, wanting things to stay as they are, with women in the home and men at work; it may focus on the emotional fulfilment of falling in love and having babies (so often assumed to be what all 'normal' women really want); it may fear the devaluation of the housewife and of the importance of having children; it may recoil from the assumption that all women who are not 'cabbages' want jobs outside the home. Alternatively, it may be active and aggressive, opposing movements that would give women more authority in the professions (an example would be women against the ordination of women in the Church of England – though their opposition might also be from deeply-held religious convictions). Whatever its variety, women's anti-feminism, more than men's, usually involves a degree of self-reflection: a reassessment of the self in relation to other women and their achievements. Later chapters will therefore consider the Victorian anti-feminist women novelists in the context of the female culture of the age, showing both what they learnt from the anti-feminist tradition, and what they contributed to it, in what was very much a two-way exchange. It was also a partial exchange with the ideas of feminism: no novelist discussed being impervious to the feminist debates that were going on around her in the journals, newspapers and social gatherings.

Anti-feminism, for both sexes, became sharper, brutal and more outspoken as the nineteenth century advanced: largely because women were clearly making progress, and encroaching on the privileges of middle-class men: the most articulate spokesmen of the backlash. If opposition to Mary Wollstonecraft was strident in the decade following her death, it quickly subsided, and was replaced by the chivalrous assumption that women compensated for their delicacy by being more perceptive and pure than men. Both male and female writers subscribed to this view from about 1820 to the late 1840s, and though individuals might dissent, the general opinion was widely accepted. Women who transgressed the proper boundaries were jeered at, more rudely by men than by women –

female anti-feminism being relatively quiescent from 1820 to 1850, when the conduct-book writers were designing a meaningful domestic crusade of attention to details and organized unselfishness. Male critics were left to pick off the errant sisters and lampoon them in the public press.

It was at this point – at what might be deemed the lull before the anti-feminist storm, that Elizabeth Lynn, a clergyman's daughter from the Lake District, who had won the freedom to live in London, read in the British Museum, and write novels, published an article on Mary Wollstonecraft in the radical journal *The English Republic* (1854). Perhaps, as her biographer Nancy Fix Anderson suggests, the significance of this article should not be overstressed, since her support for Wollstonecraft is implicitly cancelled out by an anti-feminist article, 'Rights and Wrongs of Women', published the same year in *Household Words*. Moreover, as Anderson shows, the future Mrs Linton was adept at changing her tone and ideological position to suit the journal for which she was at that moment writing.[44] Nevertheless, the historical moment of the Wollstonecraft article remains crucial. Wollstonecraft was still regarded as a dangerous radical, unadmired even by those women who were campaigning for limited improvements in their rights; yet Linton appears to be enlisting under her banner. Hailing the *Vindication* as 'one of the boldest and bravest things ever published', she argues that women in the mid-nineteenth century have 'the same fight to fight that she had, and the same things remain undone that she would fain have forwarded with a helping hand'. She particularly admired Wollstonecraft's fight against domestic tyranny and fine-ladyism – battles that Linton had also fought and won – and saw in her a perfect combination of male and female characteristics. Curiously she endows her with all the virtues of the domestic angel so praised by Sarah Ellis and other advocates of the separate spheres philosophy. Where many earlier commentators had attacked Wollstonecraft as selfish and unwomanly, Linton saw her as being beautiful, sensitive, true, and markedly unselfish, yet no submissive conformist. 'Mary Wollstonecraft's whole life proved her character in its dutiful self-sacrifice and its strong independent will, in its noble adherence to principle and its brave assertion of unbiassed judgement.' Linton here brings together what were normally seen as incompatible characteristics for women: 'dutiful self-sacrifice' and a 'strong independent will': characteristics often found in the heroines of novels by Victorian anti-feminist writers, Eliza Lynn Linton among them. Linton's language includes several battle images and many references to Wollstonecraft's 'courage' as she storms 'the citadel of selfishness'. Anti-feminist women's heroines are as frequently fighters as meek traditionalists who accept the status quo, and the novelists' fissured attraction to the two types of woman reflects their own divided loyalties in the debate about women's roles.

Linton was also interested in the response of anti-feminist women in Wollstonecraft's own time. Noting that other women turned against her, Linton conceded that this was 'but natural, from those in whom long habits of slavery have eaten out all independence and all moral dignity, in whose hearts oppression has strangled the very instinct of justice'. This, to her, was 'the obedience of the harem', and a form of anti-feminism she herself never espoused. What is significant for her own anti-feminism is the attitude she contrasts with slavish obedience: 'intelligent compliance with the will of the nobler'.[45] This phrase offers the most succinct summary of Linton's ideological position: and the essay on Mary Wollstonecraft shows her working through her response to feminism's most radical figure, to arrive at a carefully discriminated anti-feminist standpoint.

All the anti-feminist women writers in this study were aware of their female predecessors in literary history, and all, to a greater or lesser degree, positioned themselves in relation to them. From the beginning, they were pulled in conflicting directions by the examples around them: an experience that would have differing effects on the evolution of their anti-feminisms. Even Eliza Linton, the most reactionary of the four, came to realize that 'intelligence' in a young woman (and it was the young who mainly interested them) was rarely compatible with automatic 'compliance'. Their collective theme becomes female rebellion: rebellion against male autonomy, against parental authority, and against the precepts of traditional patriarchal religion. In the process of writing about them, the four anti-feminist women were also rebelling against their predecessors, Jane Austen, Charlotte Brontë and George Eliot, who treated female rebellion in different ways. The later group sympathized with their female rebels, but also wished to reassert the worth of traditional values, generally upheld by fictional descendants of *Emma*'s Mr Knightley. More than their predecessors, however, these writers betray, to varying extents, an underlying dissent from the authoritarian position they establish, inaugurating a complex rhetorical debate within the bounds of an apparently fortified ideological standpoint. The succeeding chapters will examine this debate, and try to discriminate between the different positions occupied by the debaters, showing also how they responded to changes of emphasis in the anti-feminist controversy.

What had been at the beginning of the century largely an anti-French, anti-intellectual movement, became, by the second half of Victoria's reign, a more emotional, self-divided attempt, in effect, to save the innocence of the young English girl: to keep her sexually pure in mind and body, devoted to her family, and obedient to the teachings of the Christianity she had learnt as a child. The young English girl was seen as pure, perfect and fragile: as susceptible to flaw as a piece of crystal. How to keep her that way while the girl herself was restless, active, inquiring, and anxious to get out, constituted the challenge faced by this group of novelists. Why they themselves remained so popular when their views were not, is the conundrum faced by the literary historian.

2
Anti-Feminist Women and Women's Writing

In a famous passage of *A Room of One's Own* Virginia Woolf notes that the early nineteenth-century women writers had no tradition behind them: 'For we think back through our mothers if we are women. It is useless to go to the great men writers for help, however much one may go to them for pleasure.'[1] The question to be asked about the anti-feminist writers was whether they did think back through their mothers, or whether, as Elizabeth Kowaleski-Wallace has argued of Hannah More and Maria Edgeworth, they were more strongly influenced by complicity with patriarchal traditions and dominant male writers, such as Milton and Dr Johnson. Apart from Mrs Oliphant, who lacked strong male influences in her life, the anti-feminist women discussed here were emotionally or intellectually dependent on certain key men. For Linton it was Walter Savage Landor, her idealized father-figure; for Yonge both her father and John Keble, who read her work, censored it where necessary, and gave permission for it to be published. 'It does want papa very much,' she commented on her novel *Heartsease*, which was written after Mr Yonge's death; 'but then, he did set it going, and there is mamma to gloat over it.'[2] By then she was in her thirties, but her relationship with her parents never really developed from one of childish dependency, and her work seemed meaningless without their approval. Mary Ward, moreover, inherited the intensely intellectual, male-dominated Arnold ambience for at least part of her upbringing, besides the equally formidable atmosphere of Oxford in the 1860s, and her writing constantly tackled the abstruser aspects of theology, economics and socialism traditionally considered too taxing for a woman's intellect. Both Ward and Linton were accorded free access to major research libraries, and mixed early in male-dominated, literary and academic circles. As reviewers, all four women discussed what men as well as women were writing, and admired selectively. Oliphant, for example, wrote approvingly of Dickens, Thackeray, Trollope and Reade in her articles for *Blackwood's*, and her *Chronicles of Carlingford* have often been compared with Trollope's *Barchester Chronicles*. At Mark Pattison's suggestion Ward translated the Swiss philosopher Henri Frédéric Amiel's *Journal Intime* (1885); she was friendly with Henry James for thirty-five years, and twice met Gladstone at Keble College, Oxford, for a stand-up argument about her novel *Robert Elsmere*.

Nevertheless, it is in their relationships with their female predecessors that all four anti-feminist novelists are seen at their most emotionally involved, and it is through these relationships that they came to define themselves most acutely as women writers. Oliphant's *Autobiography* was directly inspired by her reading of George Eliot's *Life* by John Cross, which made her more painfully aware of her own disadvantages (p. 4), but for any woman writing in the second half of the nineteenth century both George Eliot and Charlotte Brontë were, as Elaine Showalter has pointed out, forces to be reckoned with: 'the objects of both feminine adulation and resentment'.[3] Behind these two formidable figures was a third, Jane Austen, so often approved by male critics such as G.H. Lewes and R.H. Hutton, who associated her with small-scale perfection, perceptive delineation of character, and English ladyhood. Like their contemporaries, Yonge, Linton, Oliphant and Ward needed to come to terms with their literary foremothers as their careers developed, and as their relationships with their own real mothers became less prominent in their lives. How they read their foremothers throws light on their evolution as women writers and on their contradictory responses to the different aspects of the women's movement as it developed during their lifetimes.

Brian Southam has shown that Jane Austen was 'welcomed by Victorian feminists as a fellow-spirit', who was doubly acceptable because her writing lacked overtly feminist intent. At the same time she was a favourite of literary men; though her reputation developed slowly before 1870 when the Austen-Leigh *Memoir* was published.[4] One might have expected the anti-feminist women to admire her, but in fact they were grudging in their praise. 'A small, thin classic,' was Mary Ward's opinion, while Margaret Oliphant saw her as 'that keen and clear-eyed little cynic'.[5] The least grudging was Charlotte Yonge, who told Elizabeth Wordsworth: 'I always read Miss Austen to people of the present generation who don't appreciate her.' Even so, what chiefly struck her was the contrast in moral standards between Austen's day and her own: 'Lydia [in *Pride and Prejudice*] going off without ever having been married –'.[6]

Full-length articles were written on Austen by Oliphant and Ward, who both emphasized her conventionality and passionlessness: characteristics they saw as being dull and out of date by the second half of the nineteenth century.

Oliphant's, the earlier of the two articles, compared Austen with Mary Mitford, appearing in *Blackwood's* in 1870, after the Austen-Leigh *Memoir* had been published.[7] Although she rated Austen more highly than Mitford, Oliphant felt she had 'not inducement to come down from her pedestal and go out into the bitter arena where the strong triumph and the needy struggle'. It would be hard to find in either of them 'that (let our readers pardon us the horrible word) sexual unrest and discontent', which had been so widespread since Charlotte Brontë and *Jane Eyre*; yet although Oliphant hoped the examples of Mitford and Austen might restore moral standards, and help the public to accept the quiet existence of women writers, she clearly regretted the low status of humanity in Austen's writing. Much as she admired Mr Collins as amusing characterization, she found little to love among the heroes and heroines, dismissing even Elizabeth Bennet as 'ordinary'. However much she deplored a post-Brontë preoccupation with passion, Oliphant seemed to miss it in Austen's restricted tales of courtship, which, in any case, evade confronting the disadvantages of marriage, of which Oliphant was more aware. She also looked in vain for an ideal figure, male or female, among Austen's characters: a point she raised again in her *Literary History of England* (1882). Except in Elizabeth and Jane Bennet, she complained, 'no ideal figure finds a place in this young woman's work'.[8] Finding little of interest in Austen's life, which was so unlike her own, Oliphant was more intrigued by Miss Mitford's, ruined as it was by a selfish father who relied on his daughter for economic support. In effect, many of Oliphant's novels combine the Mitford story with the Austen cynicism, and it is surprising to find Oliphant less openly indebted to her first predecessor's example. The lives of Brontë and Eliot impinged on hers with more emotional immediacy, and aroused in her more complex responses.

Ward's essay, 'Style and Miss Austen', which appeared in *Macmillan's* in 1884, was prompted by the publication of Austen's letters, edited by Lord Brabourne.[9] Ward found them trivial – 'she was practically a stranger to what one may call, without pedantry, the world of ideas' – and could not help contrasting her with George Sand and Madame de Staël. Already she was noting the absence in Austen's writing of all the ingredients she would consider most essential to her own. 'Though the letters extend from 1796 to 1817, there is barely a mention of politics in them, except in some small personal connection, and of the literary forces of the time – Goethe, Byron, Wordsworth – there is hardly a trace.' Both Oliphant and Ward were impatient with Austen's limitations, showing how much fuller they assumed a woman's experience ought to be. Like Oliphant too, Ward noticed the 'lack of passion' in her novels, though she did not confine its meaning to the relationships between lovers. The 'wrestle of the artist with experience', she concluded, is 'the source of all the labours and all the trials of art'. Austen seemed to belong to an irrecoverably distant age where women were as yet unaware of the coming turbulence of ideas and responsibilities which preoccupied her successors.

When they read other women's lives, the anti-feminist women novelists hoped to find inspiring role-models whose example would have more personal relevance to them than those of their male contemporaries. What they were looking for was in many ways an impossible mixture of passion and propriety: a woman whose life was conventional, while her writing somehow acknowledged the perplexities of women's experiences without sinking into immorality. They were disappointed by the failure of Austen, Brontë and Eliot to live a 'normal' married life, spinsterhood being an unsatisfactory response to the emotional needs of women, at least as far as Ward and Linton were concerned. They also found other aspects of their predecessors' lives demoralizing, especially George Eliot's clinging dependence on G.H. Lewes, and lofty separation from the struggling lives of her contemporaries. The Brontës seemed more attractive if only because they were less cosseted, and there was nothing hypocritical about their morality. Far from seeing Eliot, Austen and Brontë as unattainable ideals, the anti-feminist women writers felt they could see through their façade of greatness, and afford to criticize, or even patronize. Above all, their predecessors were not 'great minds', but rather vulnerable women who had failed to discover the best way to live. It was hardly likely that their female characters would offer more convincing role-models, though they might appear more likeable, and might more honestly expose the demands and contradictions of a young woman's position in society.

To Ward and Linton, who were most concerned with the notion of crisis in women's lives (affecting choice of vocation, relationships and spiritual guidance), the apparent lack of crisis in Austen's and even Eliot's lives made them still less congenial. 'It seems as if this woman had no such disturbances in her life as ordinary people have,' Oliphant noted of Eliot;[10] yet it was common knowledge that Eliot had experienced at least two major crises: her loss of faith, and the ostracism resulting from her decision to live unmarried with Lewes. Oliphant looked in vain for a response to these events, both catastrophic to most Victorians; indeed it was difficult for any of her contemporaries, especially women, to consider Eliot's writing apart from the events of her life, and to regard her morality as being anything but coloured by her extraordinary experiences. For most Victorians the tone of sibylline wisdom and Christian resignation in the novels was impossible to reconcile with the known facts of her scandalous liaison with Lewes. Oliphant was surprised and disappointed to find that she embodied the most commonplace characteristics of womanhood, as she imagined how a (male) reader would respond to her work:

> The strongest of all female writers, he will find in her what is almost the conventional type of a woman – a creature all conjugal love and dependence, to whom something to lean upon is a necessity, who is sure of nothing until her god has vouched for it, not even of her own powers. (p. 551)

Oliphant here appropriates a masculine misogynist voice to express what might be read as a scornful condemnation of the typical woman. Alternatively, it could be read as a feminist's impatience with a strong woman who collapses into pitiable helplessness where anything outside her work is concerned – or even resorts to a 'masquerade' of femininity, in Joan Riviere's terms. Riviere, a Freudian psychoanalyst, discussed in 1929 the case history of a successful academic woman who, immediately after any public display of her intellectual abilities, became a parodic version of womanliness, flirting with her male colleagues, and trying to distract them from any purely academic appreciation of her abilities.[11] There is no reason to suppose that George Eliot was performing such a conscious masquerade, yet Oliphant felt there was something artificial about her behaviour, which she found degrading to women. Again, she was clearly influenced by the events in her own life, which had left Oliphant the sole breadwinner, not only for her own children, but also for her brother's. Oliphant's literary criticism is frequently complicated by the dual pulls of her self-identification as the most womanly of women (as shown throughout her *Autobiography*), and her lifelong performance of a masculine professional role as full-time novelist and reviewer. It is rarely clear whether she writes her criticism of other novelists as a reviewer who is male or female-identified: whether she sees the woman writer as 'the Other', or as an aspect of herself. This ambiguous stance, highly characteristic of all Oliphant's writing, blurs the distinction between what might be seen as a pro-feminist position, and an anti-feminist one, in her response to the key women writers of the age. Here, and in her novels, she seems to admire 'feminine' women (in the sense of those who are graceful, elegant and well-mannered) who somehow transcend the limitations (especially the emotional ones) of femininity. Hence Oliphant respects women who look feminine, but are towers of strength within the family; women who are efficient managers, unafraid of practicalities, and with enough self-control to take charge of other people besides themselves. The spectacle of a George Eliot terrified of reviews (which Lewes had to censor for her) aroused her strongest contempt.

Oliphant's reviews make no claims to the 'masculine' ideal of objectivity, as practised by the influential critics R.H. Hutton and Matthew Arnold. Still less is this the case in her *Autobiography*, where she meditates uncomfortably on a comparison between her achievement and George Eliot's. Even here, the sex-role is oddly inverted, as Oliphant compares her experience, not just with Eliot's, but also with that of Browning's Andrea del Sarto, and wonders whether she would have done better if she had been taken care of and kept in a 'mental greenhouse':

> In all likelihood our minds and our circumstances are so arranged that, after all, the possible way is the way that is best; yet it is a little hard sometimes not to feel with Browning's Andrea, that the men who have no wives, who have given themselves up to their art, have had an almost unfair advantage over us who have been given perhaps more than one Lucrezia to take care of. (*Autobiography*, pp. 5–6)

Oliphant here imagines herself as a man saddled with a burdensome wife, and envies George Eliot her protected status, with Lewes fussing round her and guarding her from upset. 'I think she must have been a dull woman with a great genius distinct from herself,' Oliphant decided, 'something like the gift of the old prophets, which they sometimes exercised with only a dim sort of perception what it meant' (p. 7). Oliphant constantly judges her as a woman, and finds her an embarrassment to the sex: too feeble to look after herself, and yet so convinced of her own wisdom that she presumes to advise other people in a tone of deep-souled sagacity. She falls far short of Oliphant's ideal of effective participation in mature family life.

Like so many of her contemporaries she preferred the early novels: partly, perhaps, because the author was still unknown and unspoilt. Disappointment set in with *Felix Holt*, which, she told John Blackwood, left an impression on her mind 'as of Hamlet played by six sets of gravediggers'. In another letter she urged:

> I hope you don't think me so utterly stupid as to have any doubt about the perfection of George Eliot's writing – I don't suppose she could express herself otherwise than exquisitely if she were to try – and there are a thousand turns of expressions which nobody else could have hit upon, and which gave me a positive thrill of pleasure to read them – all that is fully well implied in her name – but I am mightily disappointed in the book all the same – one feels as if a great contempt had seized her for the public and her critics (quite legitimate in some respects I think) and she had concluded that it was not worth her while to put forth her thoughts – that this would please them just as well as if it were twenty times better –[12]

What Oliphant repeatedly disliked about her rival was the remoteness and superior aura which coloured her later work, and made her own stance as critic one of reluctant admiration for her style, coupled with jealous criticism of her as a woman.

Eliza Lynn Linton also found it impossible to separate George Eliot's achievement from her own, and to judge her objectively. They had met in 1859, at John Chapman's house in London, when both women were embarking on professional literary careers (Linton's a few years ahead of Eliot's), and Linton was quickly repelled by her. 'From first to last she put up my mental bristles, so that I rejected then and there what might have become a closer acquaintance had I not been so blind, and so much influenced by her want of conventional graces.'[13] In its unexpected twist at the end, this comment reveals Linton's momentary doubts about the worth of her prejudices: if she had not been so put off by Eliot's uncouth and unkempt appearance she might have sought her friendship; on the other hand, it is again Eliot's failings as a woman that count most of all. As it was, she remained suspicious of her more successful contemporary, even though Eliot invited her to visit after her 'elopement' with Lewes, and Linton, for once, found her 'frank, genial, natural, and brimful of happiness' (p. 96). Linton most admired her when she was most like an ordinary happy woman in love. Unlike Oliphant, she positively approved of what was commonplace in Eliot, and disliked her only when she gave herself airs, as she did once adulation spoilt her, destroying the spontaneity of her work in the process. Linton found the fundamental paradox of her rival's life incomprehensible:

> in her endeavour to harmonise two irreconcilables – to be at once conventional and insurgent – the upholder of the sanctity of marriage while living as the wife of a married man – the self-reliant law-breaker and the eager postulant for the recognition granted only to the covenanted – she lost every trace of that finer freedom and whole-heartedness which had been so remarkable in the beginning of her connection with Lewes. (pp. 97–8)

Yet by this stage of her life, Linton's own experiences had made her both an upholder of conventional married ties, and the separated wife of a man whose disorderly habits jarred against her obsession with tidiness and regularity.

Throughout her life Linton compensated for her own failures and disappointments by insisting ever more loudly on other women's conformity to high domestic standards. She also, like Oliphant, resented Eliot's special status, conferred on her first by Lewes, and then by a society prepared to overlook her lived immorality out of respect for her written high-mindedness. Both Linton and Oliphant were conscious of having worked much harder than Eliot for their much smaller reputations; and Linton, constantly preoccupied by issues of female behaviour and lack of self-restraint in particular, noted Eliot's lapses from the ideal of moderation and naturalness. Attacking the 'Angel in the House' concept of womanliness, Linton felt that 'the silly idea of their own quasi-sacredness has to be first overcome before any real good can be done'.[14] Eliot embodied, to the highest degree, this idea of her own 'quasi-sacredness', which Linton deplored as not only degrading, but ultimately damaging to women. She thus rejects what might be seen as the most traditional form of woman-worship, and with it the ultra-feminine ideal of the angelic woman. Like Margaret Oliphant, Linton, in her critique of George Eliot, gestures more widely towards harmful images of femininity, encouraged by male adulation, which turn a woman into a spectacle, an artificial construct of those who worship her.

Conscious that her dislike of the woman and her goddess-like image had perhaps distorted her response to the novels, Linton devoted her chapter on Eliot in Mrs Oliphant's *Women Novelists of Queen Victoria's Reign* (1897) to a detailed appraisal of her literary achievement. Although the collection's subtitle was 'A Book of Appreciations', Linton made no bones about attacking Eliot's anachronisms and faulty scholarship, as well as her increasing ponderousness; and though she discusses each of the novels in detail, she remains convinced of the damage done to them by too much undiscriminating praise. Grudgingly, she admitted that Eliot 'stands out as the finest woman writer we have had or probably shall have' (superior to Charlotte Brontë, for instance), but 'she was not a flexible writer and her range was limited'. Because her life and principles worked at cross-purposes, Linton concluded that the sense of inharmoniousness 'between what she was and what she would have been did, to some degree, react on her work, to the extent of killing in it all passion and spontaneity'.[15] Nancy Fix Anderson notes that Linton had wanted to write on Gaskell instead, but was assigned her old rival (Anderson, p. 224); Gaskell had certainly been kinder to her when they first met, and impressed Linton with her pleasant, traditional womanliness. Moreover, Linton was herself at the time of first meeting George Eliot a shy and awkward novice, 'brought up on the old lines of childish effacement and womanly self-suppression, and taught that I ought to have no opinion of my own' (*My Literary Life*, p. 36). The later spectacle of George Eliot surrounded by adoring male admirers waiting for her next words of wisdom, offended all Linton's ideas of correct womanly behaviour, and society's proper estimation of female worth: a point she also made in her *Temple Bar* review of John Cross's biography of Eliot in 1885, where she concluded that 'with an unhappy and morbid, anxious and worrying temperament, she was singularly blessed in her affections and fortunate in her life'.[16]

Charlotte Yonge also responded in the same year to the same book, but shaped her review (in the *Monthly Packet*) into a fictitious correspondence between 'Arachne' and 'Una' (half written by herself and half by Maria Trench, 'the Author of "Charles Lowder"').

The dialogue, predictably, focuses less on Eliot's personal life than on her spiritual experiences; though whereas Oliphant and Linton thought Eliot's work as a novelist had benefited (perhaps unfairly) from Lewes's encouragement and emotional support, 'Una' believed her genius 'would have gained, had she possessed courage to refuse happiness apart from duty'. She also felt Eliot suffered in her spiritual life by not knowing an intelligent clergyman: in other words, a religious male authority equivalent to John Keble, and with an equally strong influence. For Yonge, Eliot fell short of her potential as a novelist because she was an agnostic; and although she admired the characterization of Adam Bede, Lydgate, the Garths and Mr Brooke, Yonge complained that there were no elevating ideas in Eliot's novels. In her biography of Yonge, written a few years after her death, Ethel Romanes quotes a letter on Cross's *Life* of Eliot, which reiterates many of the points made in the dialogue-article, proving that even if the authorship of the essay was shared, it ultimately represented Yonge's views on her formidably successful contemporary. 'The underlying feeling in all her books seems to be fatalism,' Yonge told Miss Ireland Blackburne, 'and the further she drifted away from the training of her youth, the more they failed as works of art.' She blamed Lewes as a bad influence, feeling again that 'a good man could have made her do grandly good work'.[17]

Yonge's criticism is the most reactionary of the group's, and the most closely tied to the religious standpoint of her childhood, which she, unlike the others, did not reject. Yet her cast of mind is not entirely different from George Eliot's. Both take as heroines misguided girls with deep spiritual yearnings, and a naïveté about worldly, practical matters, which ensures they make a series of misjudgements before being rewarded with a happy marriage (or, where this is impossible, with an appropriate death, or a life of good works). Both were interested in the limitations of women's lives, and the options available to those who wanted to make something more of their existence than idling and chatting through the day; but their approach to the problem was of course widely different, and Yonge's deference to the religious upbringing of her childhood, and commitment to correct moral teaching through her fiction, inevitably narrows its readership, and reduces its long-term significance as literature.

Mary Ward, who grew up on Yonge's stories, and became one of her 'Goslings' (a group of young girls who exchanged competition questions and answers, organized by Yonge as their 'Mother Goose'), in her teens submitted a story, 'A Gay Life', to the *Monthly Packet*, which Yonge rejected because the love-interest was too prominent. Ward's writings subsequently became less like Yonge's family sagas and more like George Eliot's novels of spiritual and intellectual struggle. Like Linton, Ward had some personal knowledge of Eliot, having met her in 1870 at the Mark Pattisons' in Oxford, where Ward, as a young girl who had begun researching Spanish history and literature, listened deferentially to the novelist's account of her own travels in Spain. There seems to have been no real conversation or exchange of ideas: only, as Linton complained, the sage holding forth, and the bystanders expected to listen. Eliot's writing never seems to have excited Ward as much as one might have expected, given their shared interests. Indeed Ward was bored by *Adam Bede*: 'What a prig is Adam, & what a Sunday school tone much of it has,' she told George Smith in 1896.[18] In an article on Elizabeth Barrett Browning in 1888, she summed up the relative merits and shortcomings of the key women writers of the century, attributing to them what she considered to be their essential characteristics. While granting that George Eliot had 'greater general power and competence' than Jane Austen and Charlotte Brontë, she felt Eliot was also 'subject in comparison to more aggressive faults'.[19] Writing surprisingly little about Eliot, Ward never manages to summon up much passion, as she does in her analyses of Charlotte Brontë. But then Brontë was the woman novelist who most excited all the anti-feminist women novelists in this study, and caused them to think most profoundly, not only about women's role in a changing society, but also about the ways in which women novelists might write about it.

Beth Sutton-Ramspeck has recently argued, in an article in *Victorian Studies*, that Ward's writings on the Brontës are feminist in three different ways: first, in defending them against trivializing readings by powerful male critics such as Leslie Stephen and Matthew Arnold; secondly, in her unashamedly subjective, 'woman-centred' critical approach; and thirdly, 'both Ward's resistance to male literary authority and her own critical practice adumbrate contemporary feminist critical approaches'.[20] These are controversial claims to make for a woman whose name is practically synonymous with anti-feminism, but there is no doubt that Ward was strongly drawn to the Brontës and largely sympathetic to what they were trying to do. It seems all the more significant, as Sutton-Ramspeck has shown, that Ward's views on the Brontës developed out of discussions with Henry James, helping her to adopt a more consciously 'woman-centred' approach in the face of his masculine prejudices against the Brontës' limitations, and a critical preoccupation with their lives.

Ward's views on the Brontës are mostly to be found in the prefaces she wrote for the seven-volume Haworth edition of their works (1899–1900), though scattered comments turn up in her other reviews, and in her novel *David Grieve* (1892), both in a visit to Haworth made by David, and in her preface, where she talks more generally about the development of the novel in England. In 1917, Ward returned to the subject in 'Some Thoughts on Charlotte Brontë', written for a centenary memorial, edited by Butler Wood. Here she gave the highest praise to *Villette*, declaring confidently that it would outlast all the ephemeral journalism-novels (such as H.G. Wells's) of the late nineteenth and early twentieth centuries. 'Poetry, truth, feeling; and a passion which is of the heart, not of the senses – these are Charlotte Brontë's secrets,' Ward argued, summing up everything she particularly admired in her predecessor.[21]

Ward was aware that enjoyment of the Brontës' novels was often difficult to separate from a fascination with their lives. She herself had been given the Gaskell biography by her 'Aunt Fan' (Matthew Arnold's youngest sister) when she was seventeen, and had identified strongly with the three sisters. The sense of meeting a fresh and surprising personality was what she especially liked in the novels, unlike most readers preferring Lucy Snowe to Jane Eyre. The most important of these prefaces is indeed the one on *Villette*, which becomes, for Ward, the vehicle of a much broader statement on women's writing, and its dramatic development in the nineteenth century. Arguing that whereas women have long been strangers to the other arts, they are more at home with the art of speech, Ward emphasizes the foreignness of the symbolic order to women, who inevitably approach it as outsiders. Even in her own times she felt that women were still struggling with language: 'Mrs Browning, George Eliot, Emily Brontë, Marcelline Desbordes-Valmore – it is as though they had wrested something that did not belong to them, by a kind of splendid violence.'[22] Anticipating Virginia Woolf's comments in chapter 4 of *A Room of One's Own* on women writers grappling with the 'man's sentence', Ward's criticism seems strikingly modern, going to the heart of issues still discussed by feminist critics today. She also addresses a question that had been troubling Victorian critics such as G.H. Lewes and Harriet Martineau: the problem of women's limited subject-matter, and their preoccupation with love as the chief (perhaps the only) interest in women's lives. Ward boldly defended women's interest in love as a worthwhile subject, and saw it as a positive strength in their writing, again stressing the difference of view which women brought to the novel. It is, she argued, 'love as the woman understands it. And here again is their second strength. Their peculiar vision, their omissions quite as much as their assertions, make them welcome' (p. xxvi). In noticing what women omit as well as what they include, Ward is acutely aware of the limitations imposed on them by a sexually repressive culture, whose values they have partly internalized. Male-authored novels she saw as being far more damagingly limited – largely 'studies of manners, politics, adventure' (p. xxvii) – wondering whether the 'Hebraist and Puritan element in the English mind' (borrowing her uncle Matthew Arnold's terms) was responsible for their insular prudishness about passion, a subject treated much more openly in French literature. Ward felt that the modern mind craved equally for feeling and knowledge, elements she tried to bring together in her own novels.

Ward is also perceptive in being able to recognize Emily Brontë's genius, which critics were much slower to acknowledge. In fact, she thought Emily was greater than Charlotte, especially in her treatment of men. 'Emily knew less of men personally than Charlotte,' she wrote in her preface to *Shirley*. 'But she had no illusions about them, and Charlotte had many. . . . Charlotte is often parochial, womanish, and morbid in her imagination of men and their relation to women –' (p. xxiii). She also noted Charlotte's occasional temptations 'to scream and preach' – something that later annoyed Virginia Woolf – and felt the psychology of *Jane Eyre* was 'really childish'.[23] These criticisms apart, Ward was consistently enthusiastic about the Brontës, often using them as a yardstick to measure the failings of other writers whose interests seemed tame in comparison. Surveying, for instance, in 1884, 'Recent Fiction in England and France', Ward criticized the narrow concentration on romantic and idealist themes in the English novel, and called for more Brontës, 'as ready as the old to explore the furthest limits of sentiment and the strangest recesses of passion'. Realism, she felt, was the best medium for such an exploration, and she urged the next generation of novelists to embrace this means of discussing 'the great and passionate things of life as well as the interesting and the piquant things'.[24] Ward thus sounds a rallying cry against the parochial limitations of the English novel, and sees the Brontës (and potentially other women writers) as being in the vanguard of the new movement. Her criticism is important in stressing the way women could broaden the novel's range, and turn it away from the dry and narrow themes pursued by their male contemporaries. She therefore inverts the usual critical commonplaces, which see women as being 'narrow' and men as having the more universal approach. Like Virginia Woolf after her, Ward questioned whether male interests were necessarily more important than female ones, and paved the way for a more innovative approach by female writers.

Though less unequivocally enthusiastic than Ward, Margaret Oliphant also recognized the crucial importance of the Brontës in the broadening of the English novel, and the development of more daring attitudes to the portrayal of passion and sexual attraction. Charlotte Brontë was another of the more distinguished female contemporaries who preyed on Oliphant's mind, much as Eliot did, forcing her to make comparisons between her own life and theirs. Oliphant was honest enough to accept that her work was inferior to both Eliot's and Brontë's, but she could not help feeling her personality and self-sufficiency had the edge on theirs, and that she had certainly had more experience of life than Brontë. 'I have learned', she wrote in her *Autobiography*, 'to take perhaps more a man's view of mortal affairs, – to feel that the love between men and women, the marrying and giving in marriage, occupy in fact so small a portion of either existence or thought' (p. 67). In this she is exactly the opposite of Ward, who felt more needed to be said about love, and new literary approaches brought to the portrayal of it. She is also less comfortable about her role as a woman writer and critic appraising the work of other women, being so subjective in her approach that she is unable to separate another woman's achievement from her own, and see them as distinct entities. Oliphant constantly struggles against a conviction of her own superior sense and maturity (expressed, as here, as male-identification undermined by a dwindling reputation), which was already wearing thin towards the end of her life.

Oliphant was quick in her response to Charlotte Brontë's achievement, appraising the totality of her work in 1855, the year of her death. In her *Blackwood's* article, 'Modern Novelists – Great and Small', she draws on the militaristic language of the Crimean War to describe Jane Eyre's battle for recognition, and berates the novel's first critics for concentrating on its supposed grossness instead of acknowledging its more subversive meaning. 'No one would understand that this furious love-making was but a wild declaration of the "Rights of Woman" in a new aspect,' she complained, adding, equally wildly: 'Here is your true revolution. France is but one of the Western Powers; woman is the half of the world.' Of Charlotte Brontë herself Oliphant concludes: 'Perhaps no other writer of her time has impressed her mark so clearly on contemporary literature –'.[25]

At this stage of her career, Mrs Oliphant was still in her twenties, and liable to be more enthusiastic about individual novelists than she became in her more cautious middle age. Her response to Brontë can be used to chart the progress of her growing unease about the direction taken by the modern novel, which she felt was unduly preoccupied with what she called the 'sex-problem'. Returning to Brontë in 1887, after writing a series of major articles on the 'sensation' novel in the 1860s, Oliphant was inclined to rate Brontë lower than George Eliot, whose early works she admired. Brontë's novels, she thought, were 'reflections of an individual being, extremely vivid and forcible, but in no way, we think, to be compared with the far stronger, higher and broader work which we have just discussed'.[26] Emily she considered inferior to Charlotte, again taking the opposite view to Mary Ward's.

Ten years later, Oliphant wrote her longest appraisal of the Brontës for her *Women Novelists of Queen Victoria's Reign*, in which Linton's discussion of George Eliot also appeared. By this stage of her career, Oliphant distrusted Brontë's ability to sweep the reader along, against her critical judgement. The hold the novels had over her seemed unprofessional, and she set out to anatomize them more coolly. Taking the Brontës together as a group, she declared: 'Their philosophy of life is that of a schoolgirl, their knowledge of the world almost *nil*, their conclusions confused by the haste and passion of a mind self-centred and working in the narrowest orbit' (p. 5). Whereas Ward admired the portrayal of Caroline Helstone in *Shirley*, Oliphant disliked her obsession with Robert Moore, and her longing for love, although she accepted that it was 'the most virtuous thing in the world' for a *man* to want a wife and family. Even at the end of the nineteenth century, Mrs Oliphant baulked at the idea of *women* openly declaring their need to be loved: 'Personally I am disposed to stand for the superstition, and dislike all transgression of it' (p. 24). It was 'somehow against the instinct of primitive humanity, which has decided that the woman should be no more than responsive, maintaining a reserve in respect of her feelings, subduing the expression, unless in the "once, and only once, and the One only" of the poet' (p. 23). Far from comparing Charlotte Brontë with later novelists such as Hardy, who wrote freely about sexual relations, Oliphant thought the quiet governess-figure who had written *Jane Eyre* would have been deeply shocked at the new school of romance she had founded. She herself recoiled from any treatment of women as sex-objects, and felt that openness on the subject had gone too far. Her essay therefore reconstructs Charlotte Brontë as a naïve and innocent governess wishing to be married in the most conventional way, without any overtly sexual feeling. 'Those who took their first inspiration from this cry of hers, have quite forgotten what it was she wanted, which was not emancipation but an extended duty,' Oliphant reminded her readers (p. 49). Her rhetoric in this passage, and for much of the essay, also reconstructs love and marriage as serious responsibilities (as they had been for her), rather than self-indulgent adventures, as she feared they were becoming at the hands of Nineties novelists.

Whereas Linton and Yonge had little to say about Charlotte Brontë (Yonge preferred *Villette* to *Jane Eyre*, which she thought had been coarsened by Branwell's influence on his sister's mind[27]), Oliphant was a prolific reviewer of contemporary fiction, constantly reappraising individual authors and genres until she had reached a satisfactory summary of their position. Her comments on Brontë should be examined in the light of her response to the sensation novel, especially the works of Mary Elizabeth Braddon, whose achievement she discussed in a *Blackwood's* article of 1867. In many of her articles on women's rights and the portrayal of women in novels, Oliphant doubted whether violent deeds or emotions really existed in the minds of ordinary girls, and deplored the exaggeration of feeling that fuelled any such impression. What particularly disturbed her about Braddon was her assumption that women had strong sexual feelings, and worse still, enjoyed reading about them: 'this intense appreciation of flesh and blood, this eagerness of physical sensation, is represented as the natural sentiment of English girls, and is offered to them not only as the portrait of their own state of mind, but as their amusement and mental food'. Becoming increasingly disaffected with women writers, Oliphant turned for relief to her favourite men: Charles Reade and Trollope. 'It is not he who makes us ashamed of our girls,' she declared of the latter: in her view he was one of few writers 'who realises the position of a sensible and right minded woman among the ordinary affairs of the world'.[28]

In their response to their more distinguished predecessors, the anti-feminist women writers adopted an *ad feminam* approach that concentrated on the personality of the author and the portrayal of her women characters. Each rewrote or reconstructed the author in terms of her critic's preoccupations: thus, for Charlotte Yonge, George Eliot fails because she has lost her religious faith, and for Margaret Oliphant, Charlotte Brontë has opened the floodgates to immodest declarations of passion from young girls. Reader-response theory is helpful here in showing how women read other women, bringing to texts such as *Jane Eyre* and *Middlemarch* the distorting consciousness of a different, but related, female subculture. Ward and Oliphant, especially, wrote with a sense of superiority, based on their fuller experience of 'life', which seemed to entitle them to adopt an attitude dismissive of naïveté or narrowness in their predecessors. Linton, British Museum-educated as she was, gleefully picked on George Eliot's reputation for knowledge and wisdom. In fighting what may seem like an unwinnable rearguard action against three women writers whose reputations were likely to outlast their own, these four critics may seem at best simple-minded, at worst jealous and embittered; but in their criticism of Austen, Eliot and Brontë they were particularly concerned with women's issues, and the long-term standing of women in literature. Their observations combined care for the reputations of women as a group with an underlying sympathy for their subjects as individuals struggling against adverse circumstances.

Jonathan Culler, in his essay on 'Reading as a Woman', has commented that 'women's experience, many feminist critics claim, will lead them to value works differently from their male counterparts, who may regard the problems women characteristically encounter as of limited interest'. Nevertheless, argues Culler, 'reading as a woman is not necessarily what occurs when a woman reads: women can read, and have read, as men'.[29] This was especially true of Margaret Oliphant, who usually took a male persona in her anonymous articles for *Blackwood's*, and as has been shown, in measuring herself against other women in her *Autobiography*, sometimes took 'a man's view' of their relative positions. Oliphant's interests as a woman, however, usually poke through her thin disguise as a man: she returns, emotionally, to those aspects of her subjects' lives and novels that most concern the options available to women. In Culler's terms, the anti-feminist women read very much *as* women, and less as men, stressing the importance and validity of women's experiences.

While there is insufficient room here to summarize the responses of leading male critics of Austen, Eliot and Brontë, or, indeed, of other women critics (such as Elizabeth Rigby on *Jane Eyre*), it would be true to say that the anti-feminist women critics bring to their readings a fresh, 'woman-centred' approach, which often responds to earlier, more conventional criticism, and formulates a new standpoint, a more personal involvement with their subject. Beth Sutton-Ramspeck sees this as prefiguring the 'dialogic quality' of modern feminist readings (for example, Adrienne Rich's essay 'Vesuvius at Home: The Power of Emily Dickinson', 1975), where the woman critic talks to her predecessor and enters into her world.[30] This occurs when Mary Ward, in *David Grieve*, sends her hero to Haworth to absorb the Brontë atmosphere, but it also occurs in Eliza Lynn Linton's recollections of George Eliot at different stages of her life, and Margaret Oliphant's reconstruction of Charlotte Brontë as the prim, lovesick governess, shocked at the evolution of Jane and Rochester into the sex-obsessed heroines and heroes of Hardy and the 'New Woman' novelists. The literary-critical establishment has long since dismissed this kind of approach as emotional and lacking objective rigour, but it has some followers in feminist criticism, and emphasizes the critics' consciousness of a continuing female tradition of which they themselves were part.

Judith Fetterley has argued that a woman reader should be a 'resisting reader', refusing to assent to the male viewpoint which is assumed to be the norm, and by this refusal, 'to begin the process of exorcizing the male mind that has been implanted in us'.[31] This is a programme too extreme for the Victorian anti-feminist women, who always retain a modicum of 'male mind' in the construction of their self-identity (Yonge is a notable exception to this); but their criticism does resist a blanket application of cultural, gender-based expectations to women writers and their female characters. What they deplored most in the heroines of Austen, Eliot and Brontë was the self-destructive, narrowing conditions of their lives and aspirations. They focus repeatedly on the emotional damage suffered by women with nothing to think about except courtship, love and marriage, and on the ignorance of young girls whose daily lives revolve round trivial domestic rituals. By the time they themselves came to write, they felt that women's lives had broadened, and needed a more complex analysis in fiction. If their 'foremothers' had aroused in them conflicting feelings of antagonism and admiration, they also left them with what they perceived to be an imperfect model of the modern heroine. One by one, they set out to adjust the model to suit their own, apparently more adventurous, purposes.

3

'Ardour and Submission': Heroines

By 1855, Margaret Oliphant was finding heroines in fiction 'a sadly featureless class of well intentioned young women'. Apart from Charles Reade she felt few male authors were any more successful in creating strong heroines than women were in delineating convincing heroes, but the shortage of great and admirable women was acute. 'We have a strong impression that, except for the highest and most commanding genius, a woman of a high ideal, and yet of a distinct individual character, is almost an impossible achievement.'[1] She and the other anti-feminist women novelists created their heroines in the second half of the nineteenth century, when Charlotte Brontë was already dead, and George Eliot introducing a less radical type of heroine than Jane Eyre, though one who found herself, in Virginia Woolf's terms, not a natural inheritor of her civilization, but 'alien and critical'.[2] The anti-feminist women novelists inherited from their own female predecessors in fiction a combined tradition of ardent protest and struggling submission: a tradition that was both challenged and reinforced by the 'sensation' novelists of the 1860s. Heroines in the novels of Wilkie Collins and Mary Elizabeth Braddon (whose works Margaret Oliphant reviewed for *Blackwood's*) divide into those who suffer passively, and those who resist every turn of fate, and go on the offensive against society in general, and their male oppressors in particular. After the 'sensation decade', heroines were neither 'featureless' nor 'well-intentioned': Lady Audley and Magdalen Vanstone adopt disguises and lure wealthy men into marriage, though Laura Fairlie and Norah Vanstone win their ideal husband by simply sitting still and letting things happen to them. The endings of Collins's novels *The Woman in White* (1860) and *No Name* (1862), and Braddon's *Lady Audley's Secret* (1862), restore the sense of social order in that both good and bad get their just deserts; yet, as many critics have observed, the endings are also ambiguous, and leave several questions unsatisfactorily answered. Was Magdalen Vanstone right or wrong to challenge the legal disinheritance of her sister and herself because their parents were unmarried when their children were born? The fact that Collins rewards her with a heroic sea-captain husband after the death of her miserly and neurotic first husband, Noel Vanstone, suggests that he did not entirely disapprove. By contrast, Marian Halcombe, the active heroine of *The Woman in White*, is left as permanent domestic companion to her half-sister Laura and her second husband, Walter Hartright, with no further opportunities of employing her talents of leadership and initiative, that even the villain, Count Fosco, admired. It is difficult to accept that Marian does not deserve more, much as Lady Audley's fate – death in a lunatic asylum – troubles the reader convinced that she was not so much mad as impatient with the limitations of her existence as an apparently deserted wife.

Jane Eyre was perhaps the last major woman's novel where the heroine worked hard for her happiness, and was rewarded with the man of her choice, albeit a little the worse for wear. After that, the woman's fate was death (in Maggie Tulliver's case), indefinite loneliness (in Lucy Snowe's), or the kind of marriage that comes after much suffering and many errors of judgement (Mary Barton, Dorothea Brooke, Caroline Helstone and Shirley Keeldar). After 1850, the female novelist's heroine finds happiness less easy to achieve, for reasons that are both social and personal. The conditions of marriage were continuously under attack by reformers pressing for women's property rights; the 1851 census revealed a superfluity of single women who would never find husbands, simply because women outnumbered men; the precariousness of a woman's economic survival was highlighted by the concern about governesses' poverty, and the inadequate educational standard of girls' schools; revelations of sexual behaviour, and the assumed differences between male and female desire and capacity were being aired in textbooks and journals; and individual cases, such as Caroline Norton's, George Eliot's, Margaret Oliphant's and Charlotte Brontë's showed that marriage was either difficult to achieve in the first place, or problematic when it did occur. Far distant seemed the world of Jane Austen, whose heroines suffered social embarrassments, poverty, and misunderstanding, but who were safely assured of happiness and security with their sober and dependable hero.

The period covered by the anti-feminist women novelists extends to the age of the 'New Woman', who was well-educated, critical of marriage, anxious for sexual and economic freedom, but also neurotic and self-destructive.[3] For this kind of woman, too, a happily-ever-after kind of marriage was impossible, as Hardy shows with Sue Bridehead in *Jude the Obscure* (1895) or Grant Allen with Hermione Barton in *The Woman Who Did* (1895). As high-principled and outspoken as Jane Eyre, the 'New Woman' heroines lacked her success in finally obtaining what they wanted: they were usually felled by illness, hysteria or suicide, prompting a backlash of public opinion in favour of happy marriage and contented motherhood. Reactionaries feared the breakdown of borderlines between many areas they wished to keep distinct: sanity and insanity, male and female, heterosexual and homosexual. 'Either there must be a distinction between the sexes, or there must be none,' insisted a contributor to *All the Year Round* in 1894. 'It would almost appear as if Great Britain were becoming more emasculate year by year. Is that because these hybrid females, who are struggling to rule over us, are associated with emasculated men?'[4] In fiction there had been signs of this as early as 1862, in Magdalen's dominance over the nervous Noel Vanstone. Emasculated men are common in Wilkie Collins's novels; as common as powerful, manoeuvring women who refuse to accept society's designation of their role. From Collins to Hardy, heroines query the automatic glide towards matrimony (at least the kind considered appropriate by their families); but repeatedly they find little to put in its place.

Fictional heroines after 1850 no longer wait indoors to be married. Dorothea Brooke designs cottages, and discusses ways of relieving the local poor; she has no intention of being married to the eligible landowner Sir James Chettam, and marries Casaubon only because she expects his teaching to enlarge her mind. Maggie Tulliver and Mary Garth both contemplate a future of teaching or governessing; Lady Audley becomes a governess under an assumed name, and upgrades her husband; Tess of the d'Urbervilles works as a dairymaid and as a fieldwoman; even the aristocratic Marcella Boyce, in Mrs Humphry Ward's novel, works for a time as a district nurse in London, and Eliza Lynn Linton's Perdita Winstanley, in *The Rebel of the Family*, passes the Post Office Savings Bank exam, and becomes an office clerk. Those without jobs busy themselves in the local community, and no longer profess to be thinking of marriage to the exclusion of all else.

Nevertheless, marriage is usually their destiny, and the female *bildungsroman*, unlike the male, offers few alternative goals. Work and success in a professional field could hardly be seen as a likely outcome when so few professional openings were yet available to women: though it is odd, perhaps, that women novelists do not choose to show their heroines succeeding as novelists, the one area where spectacular achievement was a possibility. Whereas Dickens describes David Copperfield courting Dora, working in Mr Spenlow's office, and beginning his career as a writer, women novelists still sketch in the working life as something vague and temporary, to be set aside when life improves, and a lover appears on the scene. As Rachel Brownstein puts it, 'the fiction of the heroine encourages aspiration and imposes limits'.[5] Her quest for a coherent, integrated self, and her exploration of society's expectations of women, leave her, if anything, with a stronger sense of her own imprisonment: an apparently paradoxical and frustrating situation that the anti-feminist women novelists frequently examine. 'What can we do, we girls?' asks Cicely St John in Mrs Oliphant's *The Curate in Charge* (1876) – 'say out some of the things that choke us, that make our hearts bitter within us, and then be sorry for it afterwards? That is all we are good for. We cannot go and do things like you men, and we feel all the sharper, all the keener because we cannot *do*.'[6] Rachel Curtis, in Charlotte Yonge's *The Clever Woman of the Family* (1865), feels a similar impatience with female passivity. Discussing the popular conceptions of heroism with a military hero, Alick Keith, who subsequently becomes her husband, Rachel complains:

> 'No words have been more basely misused than hero and heroine. The one is the mere fighting animal whose strength or fortune have borne him through some more than ordinary danger, the other is only the subject of an adventure, perfectly irrespective of her conduct in it.'

Rachel rejects what she considers to be stale, outworn definitions of male and female heroism, and thinks the term should be applied only to those 'who in any department have passed the limits to which the necessity of their position constrained them, and done acts of self-devotion for the good of others'.[7] All the anti-feminist women novelists wanted their heroines to be more active than the usual role in a novel allowed, but they also recognized the dangers lying in so much unregulated energy. Yonge's definition succeeded only in redeploying the selflessness of the heroine. Instead of waiting for adventures to happen to her, she should exceed the calls of duty – provided she acted only for the good of others. Such satisfaction as she obtained from her own exertions should be no more than an irrelevant by-product.

Yonge was the novelist most middle-class women (and many men) read in childhood and adolescence from the middle of the nineteenth century onwards. She was therefore the formative influence, if subsequently overtaken by Brontë and Eliot, on the later anti-feminist women writers, especially Margaret Oliphant and Mary Ward. William S. Peterson thinks Yonge 'shaped Mary Arnold's literary tastes at a very deep level', which explains why her heroines, like Yonge's, were repeatedly humiliated and forced to submit.[8] Both writers believed that submission, however painful at the time, ultimately brought peace, though Ward's heroines operate on a much broader canvas than Yonge's, and face a much fuller exposure to the outside world. Margaret Oliphant also read Yonge, but was much more grudging about her. She doubted whether *The Heir of Redclyffe* and *Heartsease*, though worthy enough in their limited way, deserved all the praise they were given, and in *Phoebe Junior* (1876) has her own May family mock the Mays of *The Daisy Chain* (1856): 'We are not a set of prigs like those people.'[9]

This chapter will consider whether the anti-feminist women novelists attempted to redefine the concept of female heroism, and broaden the heroine's role in the nineteenth-century novel. They wrote at a time of considerable upheaval in the tradition of domestic realism, when sensationalism was invading the bourgeois home, and the patriarchal order, to which society continued paying lipservice, was under challenge from a series of subversive techniques from within the novel of middle-class family life. As Collins and Braddon had already shown, it was possible to attack respectability by exposing the strategies of hypocrisy and deception regularly practised by philanthropists, landowners, doctors, and a host of other such pillars of society. Heroines were far more openly expressing views on what was to become of them, and explicitly defying or ignoring their parents' advice. Critics noted trends in types of heroine, and attributed the spate of 'plain girls with plenty of soul', as the *Saturday Review* put it, to the influence of Jane Eyre.[10] Above all else, the women's heroine of the second half of the nineteenth century had powerful feelings, an inner life that at times threatened to engulf the narrative voice. It was common for male as well as female authors to identify strongly with their heroines, as Hardy did with Tess, and see them as pitted against the social injustices of their world. The heroine has frequently operated as an unconscious, disruptive force, questioning traditional attitudes, and taking her own way of alleviating suffering. In Dickens's *Bleak House* (1853), for example, Esther Summerson, whose illegitimacy places her outside the establishment, carries out private acts of charity and rehabilitation which stand in stark contrast to the bossy officiousness of organized welfare schemes, or the complete failure of the Chancery courts to do anything at all. Women's formal exclusion from the symbolic order at least freed them to act independently of institutions, establishing an alternative way of dealing with social ills.

The relationship between charitable actions like Esther's, a heroine's self-development, and her eventual marriage or death, forms the central interest of the novel, though it may be interwoven with other issues having a wider application to society. What is notable about the anti-feminist women novelists is their common commitment to placing women at the centre of their works, and foregrounding their importance in many of their titles. Whereas Esther's story formed only part of *Bleak House*, and neither Maggie Tulliver nor Dorothea Brooke gave her name to the title of the novel in which she appeared, Mrs Oliphant and the other anti-feminist writers came increasingly to emphasize the heroine's centrality. Titles such as Yonge's *The Clever Woman of the Family* and Linton's *The Rebel of the Family* draw attention to the heroine's disruptive effect within the domestic unit; while Oliphant's *Miss Marjoribanks* and *Phoebe Junior* hint at her status as single woman or daughter in an acutely hierarchical society. Mary Ward, who began with male titles, in the George Eliot tradition (*Robert Elsmere*, *David Grieve*), switched, as George Eliot never did, to female ones (*Marcella*, *Daphne*, *Lady Rose's Daughter*, *Delia Blanchflower*), acknowledging that the woman's struggle for self-definition was her main interest in the novel. All four novelists in this study take as their main theme the key years of self-development in a woman's life, beginning around the age of fifteen or sixteen, and finishing in her early twenties. Their method is one of dense realism, based on the notion that for a woman, apparently trivial domestic incidents are the equivalent of the man's heroic battles with external contingencies.

Between Yonge and Ward, however, the woman's battles become more challenging. They deal with broader issues, and have a wider significance beyond the family household. They involve author and heroine in political debate and re-examination of the woman's role in social reform. In the face of these challenges, the authors become more torn between opposing points of view, and their novels more fissured by unresolved tensions in their heroines' experiences. By Ward's time, too, it was no longer possible to ignore a woman's sexual needs, which were further disruptive of the social equilibrium. Even Charlotte Yonge recognizes their potential to overturn years of family loyalty and religious training; and though both she and Margaret Oliphant felt the 'sex question' was overstressed in the modern novel, they were forced to find some way of dealing with it. For all four women the heroine's life becomes a locus for debate, and a source of continuing self-division, as the woman's relationship to patriarchal society is scrutinized and reclaimed.

CHARLOTTE YONGE'S CLEVER WOMEN

Charlotte Yonge's first story, about the Melville sisters, written for her French master, followed a series of daydreams or mental stories, 'when "there were perpetual dreams of romance going on, and somebody was always being wounded in the Peninsular War and coming back with his arm in a sling"'. From the start, there was a connection between love, heroism and physical suffering: male and female invalids occur about equally in Yonge's novels, frequently halting the advance of a sexual relationship, and saving the woman from bearing as many children as the saintly Mrs May in *The Daisy Chain*. When she came to write about the Melvilles, Yonge told her cousin: 'my poor little girls meet with all sorts of dangers'. As an example, she explained: 'All their uncles, aunts, and cousins are staying with them, and in the midst of all poor Rosalie's horse threw her, and she had a strain which is keeping her on the sofa.'[11] At the heart of perhaps her two most successful novels (at least the two which have been reprinted by Virago), *The Daisy Chain* (1856) and *The Clever Woman of the Family* (1865), recline two female invalids, Margaret May, whose spine was injured in a carriage accident at the start of the novel, and Ermine Williams, who was accidentally burnt when her sister Alison carelessly threw down a match on their brother's collection of chemicals. Both women, whose loyal lovers court them on their sofas, were thus inadvertently injured by members of their own families, symbolizing the dangers inherent in the densely overcrowded, emotionally inflammable world of the Victorian household. Contrasting with the invalids are several other kinds of woman: the complacent domestic manager, who is worldly and vain (Flora May), the woman who is attractive to men (Bessie Keith, Meta Rivers, Fanny Temple), and the intellectual aspirant (Ethel May and Rachel Curtis) – all of whom revolve around the invalid's couch, like so many satellites round a sun. Both novels are essentially concerned with women's roles, and the difficulties faced by the heroines in coming to terms with their limited choices. The female invalid thus exposes not only the woman's sexual anxieties, but more widely her paralysed condition in society. Whereas Fanny Temple is tied by her six sons and her baby daughter, and Bessie Keith (like Fanny, married to a man old enough to be her father – even her grandfather) dies after tripping over a croquet hoop, which brings on the premature birth of her baby, Rachel faces the opposite challenge of female life: filling in a lifetime of emptiness. Yonge is at her best in emphasizing the daily trivialities of the Victorian household, and its ability to involve all its women in the attention to fine details.

The Daisy Chain, the earlier of the two novels, is a family chronicle, 'a domestic record of home events, large and small, during those years of early life when the character is chiefly formed', and 'an endeavour to trace the effects of those aspirations which are a part of every youthful nature'.[12] The novel's subtitle is, in fact, 'Aspirations': not just Ethel May's, but also her elder brother Norman's, and those of all the other brothers and sisters who launch themselves into careers or marriage. But Ethel was the favourite heroine, introduced on the first page as 'a thin, lank, angular, sallow girl, just fifteen, trembling from head to foot with restrained eagerness, as she tried to curb her tone into the requisite civility' (p. 1). From the start, therefore, Ethel is hemmed in by images of self-constraint, as she forces herself to comply with external standards of behaviour. An exaggerated version of her impulsive father, she competes with her brother Norman in his classical studies, but with the secrecy observed earlier in the century by women novelists at their writing. 'Ethel would not, for the world, that any one should guess at her classical studies – she scarcely liked to believe that even her father knew of them, and to mention them before Mr Ernescliffe would have been dreadful' (p. 7). Whereas the boys' progress at public school (one brother, Tom, goes to Eton) forms a subtheme of the novel, the girls endure dull daily lessons at home with a neurotic governess, and are excluded from the world of male professionalism, which comes to include medicine, missionary work, and high academic achievement at Oxford. For Ethel, the male world of intellectual competition is adjacent but out of reach, though Norman praises her work, and she is never seen to suffer, as he does, from overwrought nerves, or strained emotions. Uncharacteristically for a Yonge heroine, Ethel is strong, sinewy and energetic. She walks miles in the heat without fainting (unlike her plump sister Mary), teaches the poor children at Cocksmoor, and writes Latin verses: until her invalid sister Margaret warns her to stop. '"You see," said Margaret kindly, "we all know that men have more power than women, and I suppose the time has come for Norman to pass beyond you. He would not be cleverer than any one, if he could not do more than a girl at home"' (p. 163). Margaret considers intense study a waste of time because Ethel cannot 'take a first-class' (the Universities were still closed to women in 1856), and because she risks giving up 'being a useful, steady daughter and sister at home? The sort of woman that dear mamma wished to make you, and a comfort to papa'. Ethel's attempt to get out of her governess-lessons, and make time for her Greek is gently squashed by Margaret, and the rest of the novel shows her struggling to accept her narrowed horizons.

Yonge never makes Ethel's sacrifices look easy. Both she and her friend, the little 'humming-bird', Meta Rivers, at times resent their own femininity. 'I was just going to say I hated being a woman, and having these tiresome little trifles – my duty – instead of learning, which is yours, Norman,' Ethel complains to her brother (p. 164); while Meta wishes to be a boy, that she might be a missionary (p. 252). Ethel's impatience with her home life increases after she has been to Oxford to hear Norman recite his Newdigate Prize-winning poem in the Sheldonian: 'Ethel fought hard with her own petulance and sense of tedium at home' (p. 402); even her compensatory close companionship with her father is temporarily suspended by the arrival of a brother doctor. This is the first stage of Ethel's gradual realization that single life will not reward her with the close family relationships she seeks in place of marriage:

Her dear father might, indeed, claim her full-hearted devotion, but, to him, she was only one of many. Norman was no longer solely hers; and she had begun to understand that the unmarried woman must not seek undivided return of affection, and must not set her love, with exclusive eagerness, on aught below, but must be ready to cease in turn to be first with any. Ethel was truly a mother to the younger ones; but she faced the probability that they would find others to whom she would have the second place. (p. 593)

Yonge offers a stark picture of the single woman's life: sustained, of course, by religious faith, but with no real sense of the necessity of Ethel's self-sacrifice. Her cousin, Norman Ogilvie, was clearly attracted to her when they met in Oxford, and she to him, but Ethel decides she must devote herself to her father. Perhaps, subliminally, she associates sexuality with the guilt and suffering she sees in her father, Margaret, Flora, and even memories of her mother, but this is something that has to be inferred from the text, which does not spell it out. Although Yonge was originally more interested in Margaret than Ethel, the latter, as Christabel Coleridge noted, 'made girls want to do parish work, and to do it from its highest motives' (p. 184). Ethel becomes a new kind of girls' heroine: battling against her innate dislike of household organization, and the worldly temptations of intellectual pride and sexual attraction, she sublimates her energies into the creation of a school and church for the poor families of Cocksmoor: a form of heroism Yonge finds acceptable, unlike Flora's intervention in her husband's election campaign only days after the birth of her baby (the baby dies as a punishment) – not least, perhaps, because school and church reinforce the traditional patriarchal values of which Yonge approved.

Yonge never hesitates to frighten her errant daughters into submission, largely by showing how their egotism endangers their families. Alison Williams burns her sister Ermine; Ethel, too carried away by visions of her new school and church, carelessly allows her younger brother Aubrey to set fire to himself; and Rachel Curtis, 'the Clever Woman of the Family', is largely responsible for a poor girl's death from diphtheria. Her later novel poses more serious challenges to the heroine, who is, in any case, more arrogant than Ethel, and, at twenty-five when the novel begins, old enough for her mistakes to have more dangerous consequences. Determined to save the local children from the slavery of lace-making, she establishes a small school for them to learn wood-engraving, under the superintendence of a Mr Mauleverer, who turns out to be a fraud and a swindler. It is left to Lady Temple, young and diminutive widow and mother of seven, to sweep in and effect a rescue of the three children who have been forced to continue lace-making. Yonge attributes Fanny's unquestioning bravery to her training as Sir

Stephen Temple's wife in the British colonies: 'timid and tender as she might be, it was not for nothing that Fanny Temple had been a vice-queen, so much accustomed to be welcomed wherever she penetrated, that the notion of a rebuff never suggested itself'.[13] Fanny's training as a mother also helps her see that the children are being ill-treated, evidence that Rachel had missed. Indeed Yonge humiliates Rachel both on practical and intellectual grounds. Deceived by Mauleverer, naïve in her court appearance, pretentious in her attempts at journalism, Rachel is fit for nothing but to be a good wife and mother, and to recover her lost religious faith – a further example of the danger in which she has placed herself. 'I am not fit to be anything but an ordinary married woman, with an Alick to take care of me,' she humbly confesses towards the end of the novel (p. 345), when Yonge insists: 'She was certainly of far more positive use in the world at the present moment than ever she had been in her most assuming maiden days.'

Rachel defies the limitations of a middle-class woman's life far more dramatically than does her predecessor Ethel. The novel opens with a cry of protest against the wreath of white roses prepared for her twenty-fifth birthday, which seems to her symbolic of the trivialization and infantilization of grown women by their families. There is also a suggestion of marriage, which Rachel finds objectionable. What she wants instead is a worthwhile purpose in life, and not the dilettante pottering among cottages thought appropriate for the dutiful young lady. In a rather creaky soliloquy, Rachel rails against her own uselessness:

> 'And here am I, able and willing, only longing to task myself to the uttermost, yet tethered down to the merest mockery of usefulness by conventionalities. I am a young lady forsooth! – I must not be out late; I must not put forth my views; I must not choose my acquaintance; I must be a mere helpless, useless being, growing old in a ridiculous fiction of prolonged childhood, affecting those graces of so-called sweet seventeen that I never had – because, because why? Is it for any better reason than because no mother can bear to believe her daughter no longer on the lists for matrimony?' (p. 3)

Written six years before the publication of *Middlemarch*, these objections against the pointlessness of a middle-class woman's life anticipate Dorothea Brooke's frustrations, not only with the conditions imposed on her, but also with her duller, but more sensible sister. This is also the language of Florence Nightingale's unpublished essay 'Cassandra' (written 1852): an outburst against the passivity and emptiness of young women's lives. 'Passion, intellect, moral activity – these three have never been satisfied in a woman. In this cold and oppressive conventional atmosphere, they cannot be satisfied.'[14] Rachel's protest against her infantilization is also significant, coming from Yonge, who remained in a state of childlike dependence on her parents' approval until they both died. Only the somewhat stagey, unnatural form of Rachel's outburst undermines its effect, and warns the reader that she will eventually discover her mistake – though not before she plans to write a series of articles 'exposing the fallacies of a woman's life as at present conducted; and out of these I mean to point the way to more consistent, more independent, better combined exertion. If I can make myself useful with my pen, it will compensate for the being debarred from so many more obvious outlets.' (pp. 51–2).

Yonge adopts several tactics for cutting Rachel down to size. Apart from the humiliating turns of the plot, which expose her gullibility, Rachel's arrogant language and behaviour contrast with the more natural kindliness and good sense of Fanny Temple (previously assumed by the Curtises to be silly and vulnerable), and even more with the wheelchair wisdom of Ermine Williams. Yonge, as narrator, misses no opportunity to taunt her with the label 'Clever Woman of the Family', when her actions have shown her to be anything but 'clever' – as when she appears in the court case against Mauleverer: 'Here was she, the Clever Woman of the family, shown in open court to have been so egregious a dupe that the deceiver could not even be punished, but must go scot-free, leaving all her wrongs unredressed!' (p. 253). Having reduced her to a state of abject shame, compounded by illness and religious doubts, Yonge rehabilitates her by means of love, Bessie Keith's orphaned baby, and, most important of all, male company. Rachel gives in gradually, with one last protest against the demeaning consequences of marriage. 'I used to think it so poor and weak to be in love, or to want any one to take care of one,' she tells Ermine Williams. 'I thought marriage such ordinary drudgery, and ordinary opinions so contemptible, and had such schemes for myself' (p. 283). In Yonge's novels, marriage may mature and feminize women, but singleness remains the higher option, nobler because it avoids active sexuality.

What exactly is Rachel's main fault? Ethel May was permitted to stay single and do good works: indeed Yonge engineers the plot so that Ethel, apparently with her author's approval, sidesteps her relationship with Norman Ogilvie, and disappears before anything can happen, even though, as the novel makes clear, her services are not really essential to the family. Ethel Romanes suggests that *The Clever Woman* is not an 'attack on clever women or writing women, or women who do anything at all worth doing, but on presumption, overmuch talk, and silly contempt for authority. The story is not at all an attempt to prove that women were never to venture out of the beaten tracks.'[15] More recently, Catherine Sandbach-Dahlström argues that lack of religious faith is the main thing wrong with Rachel, though the novel also offers an ambiguous view of marriage (Fanny is much healthier when she is widowed and her incessant childbearing comes to an end), and shows up 'aspects of women's lives that cannot be accommodated adequately within the ideology the book upholds'.[16] Marriage is always viewed ambivalently by Yonge, who was well aware of its risks to women's health, while also conveying the pleasures of life – for the children – in a large family. But within the scheme of the novel, women are shown to need men, both emotionally, and if they wish to effect any practical purpose. Something similar happens in *The Daisy Chain*, when Dr Spencer squashes (or charms) the recalcitrant Ladies' Committee, which has been the bane of Ethel's life, and within a few days arranges to buy land for the extension of the Cocksmoor school project. Ethel herself does not need a husband, because, unlike Rachel, she has a father and several brothers. Rachel is finally rescued, not just by her husband Alick, but more by Alick's uncle, the blind clergyman, Mr Clare. 'And after all,' says Yonge reasonably, towards the end of the novel, 'unwilling as she would have been to own it, a woman's tone of thought is commonly moulded by the masculine intellect, which, under one form or another, becomes the master of her soul' (p. 337). Rachel herself agrees, on the last page: 'I should have been much better if I had had either father or brother to keep me in order' (p. 367). Thus although the novel inveighs against two kinds of mistaken cleverness – Rachel's arrogant but dull intellectuality and Bessie's flirtatious femininity – its real purpose seems to be to make women listen to men and recognize their superior wisdom. Even Fanny Temple, the valiant deliverer of abused children, acts under the guidance of Major Keith, her husband's military secretary, and the novel overall endorses the values of military heroism.

As a gloss to her comments on clever women, Yonge described the life of Ellen Watson, a Girton scholarship-winner, who turned down a place at Cambridge 'because she thought her mother needed her at home'. Becoming interested in science, she abandoned religion as incapable of proof, took a BSc at London University, and died (presumably of mental exhaustion) at the age of twenty-four, having regained her belief in God. 'What led her on', comments 'Arachne' in the dialogue about George Eliot in the *Monthly Packet*, to which this story is appended, 'was the feeling that our life here needed a further development into perfection.' From this she wonders what would have happened if George Eliot had struggled with her gloom and depression and worked on alone: 'Surely much greater experiences might have been the consequence.'[17] Yonge's response to each of these cases, mentioned one after the other, further complicates her treatment of the clever woman. On the one hand, she seems to understand Ellen Watson's desire to do something more with her life than be a household drudge; on the other, she feels George Eliot would have written better novels if she had kept her religion and never met Lewes. A good deal depended, of course, on the kind of man a woman took as her adviser; but her comments on Ellen Watson, George Eliot, Ethel May and Rachel Curtis – two real women and two fictitious ones – show that Yonge sympathized with intellectual aspirations, personal struggle, and a woman's wish to be different from other women. Her novels often imply that there is something slightly degrading about marriage, and that only the weaker women, such as Fanny Temple and Flora May, succumb to it. However strongly she argues for domestic happiness, her novels leave her readers with a sense of diminution at the end. Wings have been clipped, humiliations endured, and her clever women face the rest of their lives inevitably more subdued than they were at the beginning.

ELIZA LINTON'S REBEL

Eliza Lynn Linton's Perdita Winstanley, the Rebel of the Family, belongs to a more vigorous and aggressive world than any of Charlotte Yonge's recalcitrant heroines. At the age of twenty-one, she has 'the presumption to talk about Bismarck and Gambetta, the Nihilists and the trades-unions, as if she understood what she was saying –'.[18] Apart from discussing politics, her main crime against conventionality is her wish to work for money, whereas the rest of her family – her widowed mother and two sisters – concentrate on landing wealthy husbands for the daughters. Like Ethel and Meta, she wishes she had been born a man, and is impatient with the limitations of womanhood: 'If only there was a civil war and I might disguise myself as a man and enlist on the side of the people!' she says, sounding like Louisa May Alcott's Jo March. The narrative voice sympathizes with her – as it must, given the hypocrisy and calculating complacency of Perdita's family – but regrets 'this same impatience with her womanhood, of which she had not yet learned the noblest use nor the best development' (vol. I, p. 31). This is precisely Linton's point: Perdita has *not yet* learned the use of her womanhood, therefore she is still redeemable, and the heroine's story in this novel is structured round the discovery of her proper role. This is a very different task from that confronting the typical hero of the nineteenth-century novel, who may be searching for a fulfilling vocation, but who does not need to accustom himself to his gender-role. Linton shows that for a woman, this may not be easy.

Not that Perdita is ever, in Linton's own terminology, a Girl of the Period. This notorious figure, who first appeared in the *Saturday Review* in 1868,

> is a creature who dyes her hair and paints her face, as the first articles of her personal religion – a creature whose sole idea of life is fun; whose sole aim is unbounded luxury; and whose dress is the chief object of such thought and intellect as she possesses.[19]

The 'G.O.P.' as she became known, threatened the borderline between respectable society and the 'demi-monde', which Linton, ever mindful of the need for clearly-marked boundaries between the sexes, different nationalities, and distinct classes, deplored at length. Moreover, the G.O.P., as ultimately unpleasing to men, and dismissive of both marriage and motherhood, was likely to remain unassimilated by society, but floating on top, as an unfortunate emblem of British life. By emphatically *not* making Perdita a Girl of the Period, Linton indicates that her faults are only skin-deep; that she is, as her name suggests, lost, but not for ever. At the same time, she blurs the issue at the centre of the novel, and leaves the reader feeling uncertain about her response to the most important character.

At the heart of the problem is Perdita's desire to work, which seems laudable in her straitened circumstances. 'I long for nothing so much as to be able to earn money and be independent,' she soon announces (vol. I, p. 67), eager to break the taboo on 'ladies' working for pay. Disowned by her family, who are embarrassed by her views and her awkward social manner, Perdita succeeds in finding herself work as an office clerk, but quickly falls into a pattern of inadequate feeding, and is overcome by faintness outside a chemist's shop. The chemist, Leslie Crawford, is the man she subsequently marries, after undergoing further adventures in her growth to womanhood. From this point in the novel, she is alternately belaboured by traditionalists and rebels, the first represented by Leslie's mother, who believes 'all nice girls like babies' (vol. II, p. 10), and the second by the lesbian women's rights woman Bell Blount, who laughs at love, and slums it among biscuit crumbs and bottles of beer, soda-water and brandy. The clash of values is crude enough, though Perdita gets into trouble with her family for knowing both sides of the debate, and by volume III, is banished to lodgings: not least for opposing her sisters' mercenary marriages, and intercepting her younger sister Eva, on her way to elope with her unprincipled French lover. Perdita's role in the novel switches from scapegoat to champion of sound views and unshakeable morality, thus blurring still further her status as rebel against the family and society. What rescues her finally is her love for Leslie Crawford, whom she marries at the end of the novel: but Perdita has always admired men, and felt that love was a woman's highest calling. 'She had the natural woman's instinctive admiration for masculine strength – the loving woman's instinctive glory in acknowledging her own comparative inferiority – and she had the modest maiden's vague desire to love and be beloved' (vol. I, p. 299). Perdita never doubts that going to work is only a substitute for being married and having children: all she wants is the single woman's right to earn a salary, until or unless she fulfils her destiny as a woman and finds a husband.

Bell Blount's pro-feminist arguments, by contrast, are exaggerated, and undermined by the squalor of her neglected household (Linton herself was an exceptionally fastidious housekeeper, whose marriage with W.J. Linton foundered partly on his disorderly habits). Women, generally, emerge from the novel as being evasive, weak, mercenary and hypocritical: everything for which Linton had upbraided them, both in *The Girl of the Period*, and in related collections of essays, such as *Ourselves* (1869),[20] which attacks the notion of women's quasi-sacredness in the eyes of men, and berates women for their unstable temperaments and habits of deception and concealment. Here, and in *The Girl of the Period*, Linton reluctantly concedes that some unfortunate women may need to work, if there is absolutely no other source of family income, but she fails to address the social changes that Harriet Martineau and others had been tackling since the 1851 Census revealed that a substantial number of women needed paid employment in order simply to survive. Until the end of the century, Linton went on arguing that all true women wanted a loving marriage and children; but the *Saturday Review* was confused about *The Rebel's* message, and what the reader should make of it: 'for at one moment he will think that Mrs Linton is disposed to applaud, at another to condemn, the unattractive, if conscientious ways of the Rebel of the Family'; he might even doubt 'whether there is not a considerable touch of sarcasm in the author's eloquent approval of her heroine's marriage with a chemist and druggist, whom she exalts into a hero because he has pulled her back from the brink of the pond in Kensington'.[21] Moreover, Leslie Crawford has a mad first wife, in the true Rochester tradition, though safely stowed away in an asylum. As so often in the anti-feminist woman's novel (and in many other novels written in the mid-nineteenth century), the convenient marital dénouement seems disappointing; yet Linton had proved, in her own life, that it was perfectly possible for a woman to make a living for herself as a professional writer. As Carolyn Heilbrun has argued, 'with remarkably few exceptions, women writers do not imagine women characters with even the autonomy they themselves have achieved'.[22] Marriage is seen as the only truly acceptable solution to a woman's problems, even though George Eliot had shown that it was also the instigator of many more, and the heroine's crusade against society's injustices to women is, in Lee R. Edwards's words, 'bought off with inappropriate rewards'.[23] Linton tries to show that the reward here is not 'inappropriate', because Perdita has always longed for love, but with Margaret Oliphant's heroines, the marital dénouement is even less convincing – or even necessary.

MARGARET OLIPHANT'S GENIUSES

'Independent! What woman can ever be independent? That is your pride; it is just what I expected. An independent woman, Cicely, is an anomaly; men detest the very name of it.' So declares a complacent male character in *The Curate in Charge* (p. 194), a brief but mature novel, in which Mrs Oliphant fully vents her frustrations with the traditional marriage plot, and comes near to avoiding it; but she realizes that even a courageous and impoverished heroine such as Cicely is at the mercy of her male friends. 'If Cicely had been a lad of nineteen instead of a girl,' Oliphant admits, 'something might have been possible, but nothing was possible now' (p. 192). The two St John sisters suffer not only from being women, but also from being 'ladies', who would lose caste, as a curate's daughters, by taking paid work. The one man who could have married her, Mr Mildmay, the new rector, does not at first think of it: a point Oliphant underlines by arguing that the sudden 'good marriage' 'comes dreadfully in the way of heroic story' (p. 193), and Cicely's brave plans to survive on her own, and make money for her two little half-brothers, 'would be the highest and best, the most heroical and epical development of story' (p. 193). Oliphant here explicitly challenges the widespread traditional conceptions of the heroine's role in a rarely outspoken, but self-conscious essay, which sits awkwardly in the novel. ('Pardon the parenthesis, gentle reader,' comments Oliphant, recognizing this herself.) The ending is suitably ambiguous, as Cicely does indeed work as parish schoolmistress, but Mr Mildmay also proposes marriage to her. Her response is confused, in that she does not love him, and says so, but she loves no one else. She is reluctant to burden him with all her responsibilities, but appears to give in, 'her colour wavering, her eyes filling, her lips quivering' (p. 207). Her sister Mab, meanwhile, tries for a career as a book illustrator, and is one of a series of artistic sister-figures in anti-feminist women's novels who attempts a professional career. The violinist Rose Leyburn, in *Robert Elsmere*, is the strongest example, but Oliphant's Rose Lake, in *Miss Marjoribanks*, is the more frustrated by the difficulty of establishing herself as an artist. Responsibility for the younger children in her family is the main obstacle, expressed with sympathetic vehemence.

Although a relatively minor novel, *The Curate in Charge* is significant in Mrs Oliphant's oeuvre for its extended discussion of female heroism among ordinary women in commonplace domestic situations. Like many other Oliphant heroines, Cicely and Mab are stuck with small children to look after – the consequence of a middle-aged father's second attempt at romance (Rose Lake, in *Miss Marjoribanks*, feels a similar impatience with younger children, as does Ursula May in *Phoebe Junior* – showing that young girls are often burdened with childcare, even before they marry, whereas their brothers are never expected to help). Although the novel's title draws attention to the male career role, the heroic characters are the women, in their hidden domestic activities. Each woman character is introduced in heroic terms: first the girls' mother, Hester Maydew, who marries the curate, and becomes a great household economist:

> She was a woman of genius in her way – not poetical or literary genius – but that which is as good, perhaps better. She managed to live upon her two hundred a year as few of us can do upon three or four times the sum. Waste was impossible to her; and want appeared as impossible. She guided her house as well, as only genius can – without any pitiful economies, without any undue sparing, making a kind, warm, beneficent, living house of it, and yet keeping within her income. I don't pretend to know how she did it, any more than I can tell you how Shakespeare wrote *Hamlet*. (p. 10)

Dying when her elder daughter is twelve, Hester's place is taken by the girls' governess, Miss Brown, who also works conscientiously to keep the household running efficiently. 'She was a heroic woman,' Oliphant comments (p. 31); but she sees Mr St John's second marriage as unromantic, founded on pity for his former employee who has nowhere better to go than the Governesses' Benevolent Institution. Both men and women drift into marriage, in Oliphant's novels, because society offers them no viable alternative. Men need wives because they are incapable of looking after themselves, whereas women need husbands because they lose caste by working. Oliphant regrets both necessities and pours scorn on those who abide by them, while also accepting that they have little real choice.

Charles Reade seemed to her the one writer who had created truly independent heroines, and whose ideal woman was genuinely heroic. 'He has sent her forth not as a passive, but an active being, able to do almost anything she puts her hand to, and encumbered by no miserable timidity or self-consciousness, though white and splendid with natural modesty,' she enthused in an article on Reade in 1869.[24] Oliphant's own heroines are rarely such goddesses: Q.D. Leavis sees Lucilla Marjoribanks as 'a Victorian anti-heroine, large, strong, unsentimental, insubordinate to men and with a hearty appetite';[25] while Ursula May and Phoebe Junior are pleasant, ordinary girls, hemmed in by society's snobbishness about religion and trade. Contrary to the common view that Oliphant is mainly interested in motherhood, and has little knowledge of other emotions,[26] her novels declare an absence of mothers, and a scepticism about the happiness of family life. The most outspoken of Victorian writers, Oliphant treats even the death of Lucilla's feeble, ineffectual mother with tart irony: finding herself neglected for the last ten years of her life, she takes to her sofa: the consequence being, 'that when she disappeared from her sofa – except for the mere physical fact that she was no longer there – no one, except her maid, whose occupation was gone, could have found out much difference'[27] – a marked contrast to the centrality of the invalid's couch in Yonge's novels. There is sufficient contrast with the deaths of Mrs Gaskell's Mrs Barton at the beginning of *Mary Barton*, and Milly Barton in the first of George Eliot's *Scenes of Clerical Life*. Mrs Marjoribanks is more like Jane Austen's inert Lady Bertram in *Mansfield Park*, though the latter has the hardihood to survive until the end of the novel.

Oliphant's women are rarely burdensome drones (men are more likely to play this role); they are usually obsessional neurotics, who are impulsive and hysterical (such as Gerald's wife Louisa, in *The Perpetual Curate*), or professional organizers (such as Lucilla and Phoebe Junior). There are other types as well – the strong-minded middle-aged woman, and the plump, insensitive flirt, for example – but on the whole, Oliphant keeps to a familiar pattern of recurring female types, who are both heroic and ludicrous in the earnest attention they give to trivial domestic campaigns. Lucilla comes home from boarding school to 'be a comfort to poor papa', as Ethel May wishes to do for her father, but apart from that there is no similarity in the treatment of the two cases. An unashamed egotist, Lucilla sets out to become a leader of Carlingford society, by holding exclusive 'Thursday evenings' and good dinners, ostensibly to cheer her widowed father, but largely for her own satisfaction. Oliphant brings to these social happenings the language of government, sovereignty and the military campaign, thereby both heightening and trivializing their importance, as Pope does with Belinda's social activities in *The Rape of the Lock*. Oliphant refers to Lucilla as 'the young sovereign' (p. 49), though after her father's death she becomes a replica Queen Victoria: 'As long as she remained in Grange Lane, even though retired and in crape, the constitutional monarch was still present among her subjects' (p. 421). Having hoped for freedom, her female 'subjects', or 'revolutionaries', as Oliphant calls them, hold back, and feel unable to usurp her place: 'Such an idea would have gone direct in the face of the British Constitution, and the sense of the community would have been dead against it' (p. 421). By the end of the novel, Lucilla is fully reinstated in her 'empire of hospitality and kindness and talk and wit' (p. 427), directing her weak husband Tom in the government of a new colony, the estate of Marshbank, of which he will be titular head, while her 'more original genius' suggests how to govern (p. 487). Oliphant's linkage of the household with the empire is really no more than an extension of the 'separate spheres' philosophy, and Ruskin's notion of 'Queens' Gardens', but it complicates her portrayal of the heroine's role. Is Lucilla ridiculous to take her entertaining so seriously? Has she any notion of her own self-importance? Does Oliphant admire her, or find her preposterous? No clear answers emerge from the novel.

Lucilla can be seen as a rebel against small-minded middle-class society, or as its arch-exponent, perpetuating its tendencies to gossip and touchiness. She is perhaps best viewed as a woman who uses society for her own ends, working from within accepted practices, and subtly forcing people to act as she wishes. She even arranges her own chaperone, telling her father, who thinks it unnecessary in his house, 'I don't say it is not quite absurd; but then, at first, I always make it a point to give in to the prejudices of society. That is how I have always been so successful' (p. 72). In the second half of the novel, she goes into politics, exploiting her feminine ignorance so as to ensure that Carlingford elects the right man for the district, irrespective of political party. With supreme complacency Lucilla declares: 'I am sure I wish I had a vote ... but I have no vote, and what can a girl do? I am so sorry I don't understand politics. If we were going in for that sort of thing, I don't know what there would be left for the gentlemen to do' (p. 373).

Lucilla remains emotionally detached from her own life, busying herself in the public and private affairs of her neighbours, matchmaking and electioneering, until she tires of her trivial social round, and longs for something more satisfying to occupy her time. Here Mrs Oliphant seems to be protesting against the emptiness of existence for a woman of Lucilla's managerial skills and self-sufficiency. At the age of thirty, she cares about Mr Ashburton's election, 'for she had come to an age at which she might have gone into Parliament herself had there been no disqualification of sex' (p. 394) – a moot point in 1866, shortly before the Second Reform Act (1867), which broadened male suffrage, and J.S. Mill's unsuccessful petition in favour of women's enfranchisement. She avoids ladies' committees (these are also treated with scorn by Charlotte Yonge, as bringing out the worst in self-importance and squabbling), nor does she have a husband and nursery to fill her days: instead, she has reached 'that condition of mind' when, having nothing important to do, 'the ripe female intelligence ... turns inwards, and begins to "make a protest" against the existing order of society, and to call the world to account for giving it no due occupation' (p. 395). Her only possibilities seem to be through marriage – either to the Member for Carlingford, or to a poor man, to give her managerial skills the ultimate test. Her father comments that if she had been a boy, she might have been a doctor and carried on his practice (p. 396).

Lucilla's situation worsens when her father dies, leaving her with nothing but £200 a year. At this stage she is trapped, as Cicely St John is, by considerations of class as well as gender: a lady can only wed her way out of a tight financial corner, instead of setting up a business, as her servant Thomas plans to do. She even envies her maid, Betsy, who is going to marry Thomas and help him run his public house. 'It was life the housemaid was about to enter on', Lucilla feels, '– an active life of her own, with an object and meaning – clogged by Thomas, no doubt, who did not appear to Lucilla as the bright spot in the picture – but still an independent life; whereas her mistress knew of nothing particularly interesting in her own uncertain future' (p. 426). Typically, for Mrs Oliphant, the dull husband is the main drawback to the plan: but ultimately Lucilla's situation turns out to be very similar, as she marries her weak cousin Tom, who rushes home from India with no job. Unlike *Middlemarch* (which was as yet unwritten), *Miss Marjoribanks* ends with the prospect of cottages to be repaired, and Marshbank village to be superintended: Lucilla's work is before her, and as a married woman, she will be as active and busy as she was before. The novel is more like *Middlemarch*, however, in conveying a sense of disappointment and diminution over the heroine's marriage. Having expected her, if she married at all, to accept Mr Cavendish or Mr Ashburton, her neighbours are stunned: 'But then the people in Grange Lane were not capable of discrimination on such a delicate subject, and had never, as was to be expected, had the smallest insight into Lucilla's heart' (p. 489). Again, the irony of Mrs Oliphant's comment leaves the reader uncertain whether the people of Grange Lane were right or wrong: a doubt repeated in the last sentence of the novel, where there is comfort in Lucilla's future usefulness for 'the few remaining malcontents, whom not even his own excellent qualities, and Lucilla's happiness, can reconcile to the fact that after all it was Tom' (p. 499). What further comforts Lucilla herself is the knowledge that she will neither be changing her name, nor moving far from home: a comfort shared by Mrs Oliphant, who clearly relishes Lucilla's assertion of her own identity, even in marriage.

Lee Edwards has asked whether the structure of marriage can be changed in fiction, 'in order to suggest the possibility of and necessity for a corresponding change in life?' (p. 27). In a sense, all the anti-feminist women writers discussed here disposed of their heroines in unconventional marriages: Perdita to a chemist, the bookish Rachel to a military hero; and now the strong Lucilla to a cousin with no job; but whereas Yonge and Linton found their heroines a husband who would guide and re-educate them, Oliphant subverts the whole institution of marriage by marrying Lucilla to a man in every way her inferior. Nor is this a quirk of one individual novel. In *Pheobe Junior*, the eponymous heroine accepts Clarence Copperhead, the buffoonish son of a wealthy industrialist, but she has no illusions about him: 'He was a blockhead, but he was a man, and could stand up for his love, and for his own rights as a man, independent of the world.'[28] Phoebe seems to admire him for the most basic reasons – he is man enough to stand up to his father; but a more serious underlying explanation for her willingness to marry him is that he represents a challenge to her ingenuity. 'He was but a poor creature, but Phoebe knew she could make something of him, and she had no distaste to the task' (pp. 267–8). There is not even any necessity for her to marry Clarence, since the more eligible Reginald May is also in love with her, and she, in return, finds him attractive. Oliphant suggests that apart from anything else, human beings are 'paradoxical': hence Phoebe's relief sometimes when Clarence is absent, and she can devote herself to Reginald. As she watches her lover and her grandfather eat breakfast, towards the end of the novel, when her engagement is coming to a head, Phoebe wonders languidly, 'as girls will wonder sometimes, if all men were like these, braggards and believers in brag, worshippers of money and price' (p. 316). By this point in Oliphant's career, there is a tired, wry acceptance of men's fundamental inferiority to women, but a grim determination to keep up the cycle of courtships and marriages among the young characters of her novels. Clarence Copperhead, as his name suggests, is pure caricature, while

Phoebe's complex inner life, her social embarrassments and cool planning of her future, are treated with sympathetic, if ironic, understanding. Like Lucilla, Phoebe chooses her husband because he is the next best thing to a career of her own: 'Yes; she could put him into parliament, and keep him there. She could thrust him forward (she believed) to the front of affairs. He would be as good as a profession, a position, a great work to Phoebe' (p. 234). Lucilla and Phoebe both reject far more eligible men in favour of their intellectual inferiors: if Oliphant appears cynical about this way of arranging marriages (especially in her treatment of romantic love, which her heroines either fail to experience at all, or else consciously reject in favour of a largely practical arrangement), she at least seems to be suggesting that her heroines will have plenty to do after marriage. Phoebe pushing her husband into parliament, or Lucilla renovating the Marshbank cottages, will at least be spared the nullity of a woman's life in a round of minor social calls and evenings of embroidery.

Oliphant tries to see marriage not just as an end to a search, but as giving fresh purpose to her heroines' lives. Jane Austen's Emma is in a similar situation, as a woman needing something to do, and attempting to control her neighbours' lives: but whereas Emma is finally rewarded with a sensible man, in Mr Knightley, Mrs Oliphant repeatedly provides only a foolish husband incapable of running his own career. If the man were sensible, there would presumably be nothing for the woman to do, and Mrs Oliphant seems anxious to save her heroines from the stultifying life of childcare which was the usual lot of the Victorian woman. Unlike Dickens, she never feels the need to complete her couples' happiness with the promise of rosy-cheeked progeny: to be married, for Oliphant, is to have a vicarious career, overlooking any disappointment in the choice of partner. It occurs in her heroines' lives just at the point where they are running out of things to do, or, as in Ursula May's case, where the care of a household full of children has become unbearable. Phoebe and Ursula are contrasting heroines: not only in the different coloured dresses they wear at the ball (one black, one white), but also in their social status (Phoebe from a wealthy dissenting family, a grocer's granddaughter; Ursula, daughter of a poor but respectable clergyman, a 'gentleman', unlike Phoebe's grandfather, old Tozer). Ursula is largely passive, and taken in hand by other people, whereas Phoebe is another of Oliphant's active managers, who is rewarded, unlike Ursula, with what seems like a ludicrous marriage. It is as if Oliphant is unable to imagine a man who could be Phoebe's equal.

Her heroines experience only the dimmest inklings of sexual attraction, and sensuous feelings are scarcely acknowledged. Oliphant is far more likely to attribute attraction to a sense of convenience on both sides, though a common theme in her novels is the indefinite delay of marriage by emotionally inhibited middle-aged couples, or the equally protracted process of flirtation. In the older generation, widowers frequently remarry merely because a weak and grateful woman (for example, their daughters' governess) is to hand, and glad of a roof over her head. Oliphant's ironic detachment from human feeling is particularly strong when she considers the attitude of husbands to wives. Limited sexual feeling (usually little more than a hopeless 'crush') occurs in her younger men, and coy flirtatiousness in her women, but her older couples largely just put up with each other. As for Clarence Copperhead's father, he remarries mainly 'to have something belonging to him which he could always jeer at, and in this way the match was highly successful' (p. 10).

MRS HUMPHRY WARD'S HARROWING DOLLS

To enter one of Mrs Humphry Ward's novels after Mrs Oliphant's is to exchange a world of minute particulars examined with polished cynicism for one of tumultuous passion and rebellion, set against a background of violent social change, political earnestness and spiritual crisis. Whereas Yonge's, Linton's and Oliphant's novels have only a fairly general reference to the times in which they were written, Ward's tremble with a consciousness of socialism, religious scepticism, changing relations between landlords and tenants, and most of all, between men and women. Anne M. Bindslev sees her as 'the classic example of the *female* Victorian psyche at war with itself', though in many ways Ward's writing combines the instincts, though not the poetry, of Charlotte Brontë and D.H. Lawrence.[29] Françoise Rives goes further in pinning Ward's internal divisions to the name-endings of her heroines: most end in 'y', 'ie', or 'a' – as in her own names, Mary Augusta. What Rives calls the 'a/y opposition', which represents two types of heroine, the passionate and the cultivated, becomes, for her, 'the unconscious expression of the inner tensions of self' in Ward's writing. Her heroines stand half way between the conventional Victorian woman who wants to be loved, and the late-Victorian 'New Woman', who scorns both marriage and motherhood, and wants to be free. As Rives argues, 'her Marcellas, Lauras, Dianas reflect that state of equipoise between the traditional subjection of women and their total liberation – from men and from moral restrictions'.[30] Ward's novels offer the fullest analysis of the middle-class woman's position in a rapidly changing society, and yet still return an answer that is confused and ambiguous. This is partly because of Ward's own fundamental fascination with men's lives, and the world to which men belonged: school, clubs, the House of Commons, committee-rooms, working men's institutes. This world is exciting in a way that the domestic setting, for Ward, never is: nevertheless, she tries to insist that women are too unstable to belong in the public sphere, or to survive on their own, without a strong man to guide them. In this respect, she harks back to the pattern established by Charlotte Yonge in *The Clever Woman of the Family*, though she is far more sophisticated than Yonge in exploring her heroines' frustrations.

Marcella (1894) seems to be modelled on a combination of Jane Eyre (1847) and Maggie Tulliver (1860). She is depicted at school as a rule-breaker, 'cursed with an abundance of curly unmanageable hair', which makes her seem like a madwoman.[31] Like her Victorian predecessors, she never sustains unbroken bursts of revolt, but is frequently restrained by an 'aching, inmost sense of childish loneliness and helplessness' (p. 6). 'Childish' is a word applied as often by Ward to adult women as 'genius' was by Oliphant to her girl-managers, who are never 'childish', or even, for long, emotionally vulnerable like Ward's. Everything about Marcella's life is split and inconsistent: she lives like an orphan, and yet has parents; she is half English and half Italian; half rebel and half conformist; half socialist and half proud of being 'Miss Boyce of Mellor', with deferential labourers turning out to admire her (p. 40). This split is further represented by the traditional device (also in *Jane Eyre* and *The Mill on the Floss*) of contrasting lovers: the correct, upright, English Aldous Raeburn, whom she finally marries, and the morally insecure, socialist Harry Wharton, whose mother, significantly, had taken to speaking in public, dragging Wharton to campaigning platforms with her (p. 250). (Improperly political mothers therefore produce sons who are not only on the wrong side ideologically – a similar situation arises in *The Coryston Family*, 1913, between the domineering mother and her eldest son – but who also have no sound moral principles to guide them in their relations with women.) Marcella gradually learns to distrust Wharton's passion, and to accept Raeburn's traditional authoritarianism, but not without a colossal struggle.

Much of the novel is concerned with Marcella's search for a worthwhile purpose in life. Like Ethel May and Rachel Curtis, she initiates a project to help the poor (in this case, straw-plaiting for the women cottagers), but this is dismissed by Aldous Raeburn as economically unsound. She is herself largely an outsider in her own class, and approaches most social events as a stranger, drawn to the glamour of country house life, while also feeling oppressed by its grandeur and the formal behaviour expected of its women. To Aldous she declares: 'I shall *never* be a meek, dependent wife. A woman, to my mind, is bound to cherish her own individuality sacredly, married or not married' (p. 121). Yet there are early signs that Marcella will never manage to sort out the complexities of her life and the tenants' on her own. Concerned, like most women in Victorian novels, for individual cases of hardship, rather than for general theories of economic growth or the rights and wrongs of the game laws, she longs to help, and either makes drastic mistakes like Yonge's Rachel Curtis, or collapses into emotional helplessness. 'She felt ready to cry,' Ward comments, when Marcella is upset about one of the tenants, Jim Hurd; 'and nothing could have been more womanish than her tone' (p. 108). Ward shows that Marcella will never be any use politically, because she is incapable of logical, dispassionate argument, without reference to individuals. While Aldous Raeburn and Harry Wharton are absorbed in their public political lives, Marcella, like a century of Victorian heroines before her, lives in the world of her own feelings. A recurrent motif in Ward's novels is the heroine's involvement with a working-class couple or family whose problems she attempts to solve on a personal rather than a political basis. Pleading for Jim Hurd, who has murdered the bullying gamekeeper, Westall, Marcella turns the event into a 'tragic poem' (p. 284), but fails to save him from the gallows; similarly, Marcia Coryston takes up the case of Mrs Betts, a divorced woman, who is forbidden by her staunchly High Anglican landlord to live with the man she has married since her divorce, but she fails to stop the Betts from committing suicide. In each case, the heroine's defence of a dependent couple disturbs her relationship with her authoritarian lover. Ward thus associates the woman's cause with the worker's, implicitly seeing both as powerless subordinates in the social and political system. Such attempts as either makes to defeat the system are doomed to failure.

Nevertheless, Ward allows her heroines considerably more freedom than George Eliot's, and even than Charlotte Brontë's. Marcella moves to London, and works as a district nurse: an experience that both fulfils her need to be helping the poor, and also humbles and humanizes her. It teaches her to value the work of rural landlords in housing the poor, while in the city, with no one to care about them, the slum-dwellers struggle with far worse conditions. Overall, the London experience re-educates and trains Marcella, so that she comes to realize the emptiness of her previous life, and undergoes a kind of agnostic spiritual reawakening. Like Yonge, Ward believed that character, what a person *is*, is far more important (especially in a woman) than cleverness. 'And character – soul –', Marcella realizes, 'can only be got by self-surrender; and self-surrender comes not of knowledge but of love' (p. 386). Love of other human beings, and then of Aldous Raeburn, leads to her dismissal of socialism as unworkable (she sees it as being just another mechanical system), and a longing for someone to love and live for. Her dying socialist friend, Edward Hallin (modelled on Arnold Toynbee), tells her: 'There is one clue, one only – *goodness* – the *surrendered will*. Everything is there – all faith – all religion – all hope for rich and poor' (pp. 511–12).

The surrendered will is clearly not something specific to women, but Ward sees it as being especially needful for a proud and confused aristocrat like Marcella. She learns the real worth of social good, and loses the posturing self-consciousness she displayed at the beginning of the novel. Unlike Dorothea Brooke, for example, she has been exposed to a full experience of both rural and urban hardship, and professionally trained to deal with it; but Ward wants her trained to be a better landowner's wife and leader of society, not to choose a lifelong career as an independent woman working among the London slums. She learns that institutions, whether of property, law, or religious custom, are 'necessarily, in some degree, divine and sacred', but they can be modified and altered (p. 555). The last of these institutions offered to Marcella for study is marriage. 'Would marriage fetter her?' she wonders (p. 555). Deciding that it will not, she asks for Aldous's forgiveness, and makes him hear her confession, treating him as a secular priest, a kind of god, in a strange formal tableau scene (p. 557); yet her doubts about what she calls 'Marriage in the abstract, with a big *M*' (p. 559) are not entirely assuaged, and the final stages of the tableau are ambiguous. The proud Marcella is tamed and humbled; the longing for forgiveness places her in her future husband's hands, and gives him god-like powers over her, while she is infantilized by shame. 'Piteously, childishly, with seeking eyes, she held out her hand to him, as though mutely asking him for the answer to her outpouring – the last word of it all' (p. 560). Marcella, at Aldous Raeburn's feet, asking for forgiveness, reasserts the traditional balance of power between man and woman, and ensures that their marriage is founded on a basis of romantic deference as well as sexual attraction.

Summarizing Marcella's career two years later in *Sir George Tressady* (1896), Ward was clear that her heroine had been at first selfish and dishonest about her feelings for Raeburn (Lord Maxwell), whom she had agreed to marry so that she might use his wealth and position to further her philanthropic aims. 'But in the end,' explains Ward, 'Maxwell tamed her; Maxwell recovered her.'[32] The marriage elevated her ideas, and 'spread with transforming beauty over the whole nature, till at last the girl who had once looked upon him as the mere tool of her own moral ambitions threw herself upon Maxwell's heart with a self-abandoning passion and penitence, which her developed powers and her adorable beauty made a veritable intoxication' (p. 120). From this point, however, Marcella loses much of her reality as a character, and becomes instead a goddess-like symbol of power and beauty, whose slim white hand and sweeping skirts are never far away when a crisis occurs. Not that Marcella is entirely tamed, even by marriage to Lord Maxwell, and much of *Sir George Tressady* is concerned with the problems caused by her impulsive gestures of friendship towards the hero, a new MP unhappily married, and by her attempts to win the support of East End sweated workers for her husband's Factory Bill. Ward remains dubious about political wives, though she understands their enthusiasm for the plotting and campaigning involved in parliamentary debates; but if Marcella brings passion and beauty to assist her husband's cause, she lacks his steadiness and powers of argument. In a scene anticipating a similar incident in her later novel, *Delia Blanchflower*, Marcella is hit with a stone thrown at her after she has spoken to a meeting of irate workpeople, and she has to be rescued – white and bleeding – by Sir George and a car.[33] Nevertheless, Ward is less severe on her political wife than Yonge is on Flora May in *The Daisy Chain*: she becomes so engrossed in her husband's campaigns that she neglects her baby, who dies of opium dependency, the consequence of Godfrey's Cordial too liberally administered by an ignorant nurse.

If marriage partially tames Marcella, it also develops and matures Aldous Raeburn, though he remains dry and reserved in comparison with his wife. Ward's heroines frequently pit themselves against authoritarian forms of religion upheld by their lovers (Catherine Elsmere is a notable exception to this trend). Marcella, for example, boils over with rage against the conventional Christian prayers offered up for Jim Hurd on the eve of his execution, 'her whole being one passionate protest against a faith which could thus heap all the crimes and responsibilities of this too real earth on the shadowy head of one far-off Redeemer' (p. 296). Ward's most extensive exploration of this theme occurs in *Helbeck of Bannisdale* (1898), in the struggle between the freethinking heroine, Laura Fountain, and her Catholic lover, Alan Helbeck. Introduced as an 'alien and a mocking spirit', into Alan's austere, religious home, Laura originally planned to take up a profession, go to Cambridge, or live an independent life in London.[34] In Ward's terms she represents everything that is new and perplexing to the modern woman: essentially split and vacillating, she longs both for love and freedom. She is 'clever' and yet badly educated, leading the haphazard, unplanned life common to Ward's heroines, while her heroes are busy training for a profession, or carrying out their public duties and responsibilities. Ward narrates: 'Her education was a thing of shreds and patches, managed by herself throughout, and expressing her own strong will or caprice from the beginning. She put herself to school – a day school only; and took herself away as soon as she was tired of it' (p. 31). This early experience establishes a pattern of impulsive stops and starts in her adult life, though Ward presents her, even at the age of twenty-one, as something half way between a child and a woman, not unlike Charlotte Brontë's Paulina Home in *Villette*.

Laura's 'childishness' (Ward's favourite term for the emotional susceptibility of women) is emphasized by her small build, and the considerable age-difference between herself and Alan. Sexual attraction is nearly always represented by Ward as a quivering awareness, on the man's part, of a woman's fragility ('she had never seemed to him so small, so childish, or so lovely', p. 158); while the woman often feels frustration, even a foot-stamping shame, at the physical and emotional differences between them. Laura is more than once described as a 'personality' rather than a 'character'. The latter is the end-product of psychological development, which Laura is yet undergoing, so that at the beginning of the novel she is still 'a bundle of loves and hates; a force, not an organism' (p. 34). She is also the product of her upbringing by her freethinking father: 'She represented forces of intelligence, of analysis, of criticism, of which in themselves she knew little or nothing, except so far as they affected all her modes of feeling' (p. 317); guilty, perhaps, of having too much personal dignity, which Ward believed was a modern substitute for the 'humiliations of faith' (p. 319). Laura is at first treated as a child by Helbeck, who waits up for her when she is out with her uncouth cousin Hubert, and reprimands her as a worried father might his daughter. Ward's favourite way of writing about the relationship between men and women was to see it in terms of an adult–child balance of concern, affection and disapproval. When Alan Helbeck begins to symbolize the safety of home, as contrasted with the dangers of sexual appropriation by a man of a lower social class, Laura at last responds, and allows herself to be helped indoors.

For Ward, the contest between man and woman is usually won by the man as the stronger physical force, though the woman has the power to hurt him by rejection or humiliation. The battle between Alan and Laura is both religious and sexual, a theme that will be explored further in Chapter 6; both elements of her characters' lives involve a struggle for mastery over the weaker being. Laura's masochism urges her to return repeatedly to the fight with Alan, in a battle of wills that finally exhausts her. If the ending of *Marcella* suggested, paradoxically, that a woman can develop character or 'soul' only by self-surrender gained through love rather than knowledge, the outcome of Laura's battle with Alan indicates that refusal to submit leads to death. What is unclear at the end is whether Ward blames Catholicism for being too peremptory in its demands on human emotion, or Laura for being too irrational and uninformed about the basis of freethought to fight her ground; or both Alan and Laura for letting their religious differences stand in the way of a grand passion. Theirs is a conflict of instincts, too ingrained for serious reappraisal; and perhaps Ward herself was uncertain of her intentions, as a letter of 1898 implies:

> Of course you have seen the point of *Helbeck*, which so many people have missed. Life cannot be lived safely without guiding ideas, – and education, in any lesser sense is nought without

them. That, on the side of thought, was what Laura meant to me. But I confess the story took so much hold upon me as a love-story, that I never was less concerned to point a moral or uphold an 'ism. There *is* a moral – but I think & hope it grew as it does in life, out of situation and character.[35]

Anne Bindslev has suggested that the novel's religious theme is inextricably interwoven with that of women's education (if Laura had been better educated, she would have been able to put up a stronger fight against Alan); but she also feels it is 'about "the weakening effect of passion on the will" and the final victory of the will, of conscience, over passion'.[36]

This is a struggle enacted in most of Ward's novels, as it was in the Brontës', with the author, in each case, making a strong plea for the urgency of passion, while acknowledging that self-restraint must prevail if society is to survive in its hierarchical and gendered condition. Both Ward and Brontë ultimately position themselves with the status quo, however deeply they feel the woman's entitlement to emotional fulfilment, and recognition of her needs as a passionate being. For Ward, as for Brontë, a woman's battle of wills with a man can lead only to marriage or to death, with religious and educational issues fuelling the fight. The uneducated woman, who is often anti-religious as well, seems for Ward to represent the combined forces of the modern age, fighting a losing battle against history and established tradition, as represented by the man.

What appeals about Ward's stance in novels such as *Marcella* and *Helbeck*, is her apparent sympathy for the rebel woman in the face of her lover's stiff-necked, humourless opposition. A strong personality herself, she admires characters, especially women, who stand up for themselves. 'Is it not something to be *somebody* with a will & a character at all? And may not almost anything be hoped, except from the nonentities?' she asked Mandell Creighton in 1893.[37] The problem for Ward is that strong personalities in her women impede both their chances of maintaining successful relationships with men, and their hopes of finding a fulfilling career in the wider world. Neither the career, nor the grand passion, by itself, seems to satisfy their sense of self-worth and purpose in the confusing modern age into which they are born.

Writing in 1908, Arnold Bennett felt impatient with Ward's 'English maids. That skittishness! That impulsiveness! That noxious winsomeness!' Inventing a destiny for 'those harrowing dolls', as he called them, he imagined Ward's heroines abandoned with unloaded revolvers in the siege of a great city by a foreign army.[38] The implication is that he would not be sorry to see them all raped: a sign of his frustration with their hypersensitive, vacillating ways, their acute awareness of all the issues, political and personal, that a woman must take into account before committing herself to marriage. If, as many critics have agreed, the woman's *bildungsroman* quashes aspiration in its women characters, and rewards their efforts with death or marriage, Ward's heroines, and those of the other anti-feminist women writers, at least debate long and hard within themselves about the advantages and disadvantages of marriage. It is no longer the simple answer to the problems of a woman's destiny, and indeed opens up more complex issues for discussion by the author, as well as her heroine. Annis Pratt has suggested that novels of marriage illustrate the 'conflict between conformity to and rebellion against gender norms',[39] a conflict enacted at length in the novels discussed. All the heroines reviewed in this chapter rebel in some way against gender norms, though only Ethel May and Laura Fountain permanently evade marriage: the former by a vow of spinsterhood and eternal devotion to her father and the rest of the family, the latter by death. The shadowy image of Mrs Oliphant's Mabel St John, the would-be professional illustrator, is never more than a distant mirage of what an ambitious woman might become. The others, mostly stronger and healthier than the men in their relationships, and certainly capable of teaching, nursing, and working as government clerks, are given only a brief exposure to the outside world before being convinced that marriage and family life are their true destiny as middle-class women.

All the novels discussed in this chapter to a greater or lesser extent scrutinize the middle-class woman's position in the family and society, often by making the heroine an oddity or an outsider: a 'clever woman' like Rachel, Ethel or Perdita; an outsider in her own class, like Marcella; an orphan (Laura), a motherless daughter (Cicely, Mabel, Lucilla, Ethel), or a woman who is in some way at odds with those around her. This technique heightens the heroine's perceptions of what is wrong with society, and increases its feeling of 'foreignness'; she is the 'other', outside the norms, but not necessarily a monster. In this respect, the anti-feminist women writers have invented a new kind of heroine, based on those of George Eliot and Charlotte Brontë, but with her criticisms of traditional feminine behaviour far more sharply focused and articulated. Tamed and captured though they are in the end, these heroines have also forced their male counterparts to think, review their prejudices, and, in some cases, modify their expectations – as Jane Eyre reformed Rochester, and Caroline Helstone Robert Moore. The battle between hero and heroine becomes more evenly balanced; in Oliphant's case, the man's power is no more than a charade to satisfy public opinion, and female heroism becomes a form of ingenious manoeuvring based on cunning intellectual skills.

All these novels end with a sense of power and excitement curtailed; their heroines chastened, disappointed, often humiliated by their mistakes. This trend is more in line with the pattern of George Eliot's novels than with Charlotte Brontë's, where the men are defeated and the women generally triumphant. The heroines of the anti-feminist women novelists, on the other hand, are far more active than George Eliot's, and, for the most part, less naïve. They fight their families, insist on entering the public sphere, and are initially contemptuous of the conventional marriage. In Oliphant's novels, they remain contemptuous, even of the men they decide to marry. Yet their authors do not suggest that they are hardened man-haters of the modern age: their heroines attract the reader's sympathy, because of their energy, honesty, incorruptibility, and impatience with the trivial nothings of a woman's social life. For women of this strength of character, love comes as an additional battle to be fought. 'Woman's most persistent problem', according to Carolyn Heilbrun, 'has been to discover for herself an identity not limited by custom or defined by attachment to some man': a problem not experienced, in her view, by male writers such as Thackeray, Lawrence, Forster and Hardy, who have created women characters with a strong sense of their own selfhood.[40] Ward's, Oliphant's and Linton's women characters, in particular, have a stronger sense of selfhood than most of George Eliot's, though all but Oliphant's are continuously torn by divided affinities: chiefly based on the psychological (or 'feminine') instinct for submission, versus the self-protective instinct for rebellion.

Critics of the heroine tradition, especially Carolyn Heilbrun, Annis Pratt and Lee Edwards, are right to see the debate about love and marriage as being at the centre of a heroine's struggle for selfhood, and to argue that the covert desire for emotional and sexual fulfilment rarely wrecks a hero's ambitions to the same degree. What the anti-feminist women novelists particularly stress, however, is the cost involved in a woman's experience of love and pressure to marry. Rachel Curtis, Laura Fountain and Marcella Boyce feel humiliated and angry at the realization that their happiness is no longer under their own control; while Oliphant's heroines marry largely to escape the drudgery of looking after younger siblings, and begin a more stimulating career of directing their husbands' future activities (one assumes they will avoid having too many children themselves). New concepts of female heroism, tentatively sketched by the antifeminist writers, allow the woman a more active role while recognizing her tendency to self-important exaggeration of the role she already fulfils.

There remains a sense, however, in all these writers, that men are the true fighters, and that their tactics are more open and honest. The ideal solution to the battle between the sexes becomes a 'marriage of true minds', where husband and wife co-operate in work, and not just in producing babies. Dorothea Brooke's marriage with Will Ladislaw points this way in *Middlemarch*; but Oliphant and Ward take it further. The sequel to *Marcella*, *Sir George Tressady*, shows Marcella, now the mother of a son, continuing her work among the London poor, and even living in rented digs in the Mile End Road to help her husband investigate sweated workshop and housing conditions for his Factory Bill. For Marcella, this constitutes a five-month escape from high society, with all the fun and excitement of pretending to be an ordinary woman, meeting Aldous 'at the train in the evening like any small clerk's wife, to help him carry the books and papers with which he was generally laden along the hot and dingy street' (p. 129). Motherhood alone is not enough for Marcella, any more than it was for Ward herself; yet in Ward's ideal ending, the natural feminine sympathy with suffering is harnessed to the political energies of wealth and position, showing, as in most of the other novels discussed in this chapter, that the concept of female heroism is usually inseparable from courtship and marriage. At the courtship stage, however, female heroism becomes temporarily associated with social reform and potential, even actual, revolt against men and patriarchal tradition. The split is never fully resolved, and the anarchic underside of each of these novels retains its suggestion of female ridicule or protest. Much depends on the reader's decision, as in the Victorian sensation novel, to interpret the text radically or conservatively. Both possibilities exist, as does the sense that in many of these novels the heroine's self-sacrifice was futile or out of proportion to what she has achieved.

4

'Goody Men and Brutes': Heroes

'A woman cannot do a man truthfully from within, any more than one nationality can represent another from within,' wrote Charlotte M. Yonge in 1892, towards the end of her career as a novelist.[1] Her choice of phrase suggests that to her, men were indeed like foreigners, truly the 'Other', whom it would be virtually impossible for a woman to depict without sacrificing her own womanliness, and she was astute enough to recognize that many women's heroes were consequently 'prigs'. 'Manly dash', as she called it, seemed to her beyond a normal woman's reach, and women writers must simply learn to live with their handicaps and make their heroes less priggish by endowing them with the odd lovable weakness.

The debate about women's heroes had been in full flow since Jane Austen's time, and was often conducted alongside disputes about men's heroines. Where was the handicap of ignorance greater? Because the heroine dominated the Victorian novel, and men had created women such as Becky Sharp, Marian Halcombe, Tess Durbeyfield and Isabel Archer – women who were complex and psychologically convincing – critics began to feel that men laboured under fewer difficulties in this respect than women. After all, men also inhabited drawing-rooms, and had frequent access to women's conversation, besides knowing something of their troubles with childbearing, running a household, and falling in love. Women, on the other hand, were less likely to understand the nature of men's work and what they did when they left the house in the morning. The most well-known of women's heroes, men such as Rochester and Heathcliff, are conspicuously men whose work is involved with home and land ownership, and whose experiences abroad are quickly glossed over. George Eliot is unusual in showing her male characters earning their living in a range of professions – though these again are careers such as medicine, the church, and estate management, of which a woman could be expected to have some knowledge from the men in her own family. But as Jane Miller has demonstrated, men in women's novels are seen from an outsider's vision of a culture, and function chiefly as lovers.[2] Lovers' professional lives are important only in so far as they affect the ability to support a wife, and few women writers before George Eliot write in much detail about this mysterious 'other life' of their heroes.

Margaret Oliphant was critical even of George Eliot's men, and fully acknowledged women's shortcomings as creators of heroes:

> The men of a woman's writing are always shadowy individuals, and it is only members of our own sex that we can fully bring out, bad and good. Even George Eliot is feeble in her men, and I recognize the disadvantage under which we all work in this respect. Sometimes we don't know sufficiently to make the outline sharp and clear; sometimes we know well enough, but dare not betray our knowledge one way or other: the result is that the men in a woman's book are always washed in, in secondary colours. The same want of anatomical knowledge and precision must, I imagine, preclude a woman from ever being a great painter; and if one does make the necessary study, one loses more than one gains.[3]

Her final point is similar to Charlotte Yonge's: a woman cannot study her subject too closely, or blunt her sense of propriety in assuming his language and attitudes. For both, the issue of a woman's disadvantages in depicting male characters was a clear open and shut case, the limitations of which appeared to be accepted without demur. But Oliphant subtly discriminated between the kind of hero who appealed to male readers and writers, and the kind who was more attractive to women. She began formulating these ideas when she was planning an article for *Blackwood's* on Samuel Richardson as a representative novelist of George II's reign, and confessed to her publisher 'that as a matter of taste I actually prefer Lovelace to Tom Jones – I suppose that is one of the differences between men and women which our Ladies Colleges will not set to rights'.[4] Enlarging on what she meant by this in the article itself, she argued that women would prefer Lovelace's vivacious and intellectual form of vice to Tom Jones's 'frank animalism' and sensuality: Lovelace's wickedness 'which sets all the powers to work – which is full of plot and contrivance, of insatiable love of approbation and necessity for conquest, of emotion and mental excitement, and remorse and passion – is something which they can understand and realise'.[5] In other words, women, according to Oliphant, have little sympathy with men's purely physical urges, but can identify with their emotional and psychological experiences: significantly the 'insatiable love of approbation' and 'emotion and mental excitement', which were traditionally seen as female rather than male responses.

Elaine Showalter has argued that women's heroes are not so much ideal lovers as extensions of their own egos: fantasies about how they would act and feel if they were men. They are thus, as Oliphant suggested, more devious than men's heroes, because they rarely resort to stand-up fights and arguments, preferring instead to work their results by trickery and plotting. Showalter stresses the importance of power and authority as the main attraction, for a woman, in being a man, and shows how Victorian women's heroes divide into brute projections of physical and social vigour, such as Rochester, and didactic illustrations of moral influence properly exerted, as in the many clergymen heroes who flourished around the middle of the century.[6] Eliza Lynn Linton also split them into recurring types, and thought a convincing woman's man was more rarely encountered than a convincing man's woman:

> They are all either prigs, ruffians, or curled darlings; each of whom a man longs to kick. They are goody men of such exalted morality that Sir Galahad himself might take a lesson from them. Or they are brutes with the well-worn square jaw and beetling brow, who translate into the milder action of modern life the savage's method of wooing a woman by first knocking her senseless and then carrying her off. Or they are impossible light-weights, with small hands and artistic tendencies...

Much as Margaret Oliphant had felt many male writers were unable to create high-minded female characters, Linton believed women failed to understand the 'loftier side of a man's nature', especially where it concerned itself with anything except love-making. A woman, she insisted, 'knows nothing, subjectively, of the political aims, the love for abstract truth, the desire for human progress, which take him out of the narrow domestic sphere, and make him comparatively indifferent to the life of sense and emotion altogether'.[7]

In fact, the four anti-feminist women writers reviewed in this study were less ignorant of men's interests and experiences than were many of their contemporaries. Charlotte Yonge studied with her military father and with John Keble; she also had a brother, who lived nearby for most of his life. Eliza Linton worked in the men's world of journalism and newspaper-editing, besides being the devoted disciple of Walter Savage Landor, and marrying William James Linton. Margaret Oliphant was the sole prop of numerous male dependants: her two sons, Cyril and 'Cecco', her unsuccessful brothers, and her nephew Frank; and Mary Ward, the niece of Matthew Arnold, and frequenter of intellectual parties in Oxford, produced a son (almost as unsuccessful as Margaret Oliphant's) whose military and political careers she did her best to superintend. Yonge led a sheltered life, but the rest were unusually active in what were normally regarded as male spheres – Oliphant with some misgivings about her position. 'I am sometimes doubtful whether in your most manly and masculine of Magazines a womanish storyteller like myself may not become wearisome,' she confessed to John Blackwood in 1855.[8]

The fact that Oliphant could see a magazine as being 'manly and masculine' raises another issue which is of crucial importance in a discussion of women's heroes, and that is the contemporary construction of masculinity, both in fiction and in lived experience. Anti-feminist women might be expected to have a peculiarly complex relationship with so-called 'masculine values', however these were defined in the age in which they lived. Opposing the advancement of their own sex, anti-feminist women presumably think that men are already doing a good job in those areas where women are seeking access: particularly politics, religion, medicine, higher education, and the professions generally. Or they assume that whatever the imperfections in the present system, men are still the rightful holders of authority and will eventually improve upon it, as it is their business to do so, while women safeguard the traditional values of home and family. Although these four representative anti-feminist women held varying views on men's ability to run the key areas of public life, they generally accepted that this was the rightful order of things, and that men were the natural leaders of society. What was less clear during their lifetimes was the nature of the masculine ideal, subject to continuous alteration as the Victorians redefined their notion of the 'great man' and the values his admirers should adopt.

Thomas Carlyle believed that by 1840, when he gave his series of lectures 'On Heroes', hero-worship had gone out of fashion, and the age itself denied the existence of great men.[9] He himself notoriously admired the great commanders and military leaders, who were the true heroes of bygone ages, and whose spirit he did his best to revive. As it happened, 'manliness', an important characteristic of heroism, was re-entering the Victorian vocabulary with a new resonance, and a wider meaning than mere physical strength. Michael Roper and John Tosh have recently defined the meaning of 'manliness' between 1840 and 1930 as encompassing 'moral courage, sexual purity, athleticism and stoicism', the emphasis changing in tune with the movement from 'the moral earnestness of the Evangelicals and Dr Arnold to the respect for muscle and might so prevalent at the close of the Victorian era'. They also make the point, essential for fictional heroes, that 'masculinity is never fully possessed, but must perpetually be achieved, asserted, and renegotiated'; because of its relationship with power, it is often experienced as tenuous.[10] Masculinity thus generates its own culture of anxiety, like femininity, as men feel the need to prove and test themselves against accepted ideals. Women, by contrast, experience anxiety for different reasons. Their femininity is founded on notions of passivity: by simply 'being', a woman is fulfilling her role, whereas a man must be actively addressing challenges, pitting himself against the outside world, and protecting those entrusted to him. While women were expected to 'endure', or 'suffer and be still', men, in Roper's and Tosh's terms, were given the more heroic quality of 'stoicism', with all its suggestions of Roman soldiers on the battlefield. Similarly, sexual purity, which was assumed to be the norm for women, was actively professed by men, who at least had a choice. So far as athleticism was concerned, women had no choice at all, beyond the constitutional walk recommended for everyone.

The concept of masculinity as involving anxiety is a helpful one in the background to understanding women's heroes, and is especially relevant to any discussion of the relationship between masculinity and domesticity. The 'separate spheres' philosophy of the Victorians overstates the case for men's ignorance of the family household, as John Tosh has argued in his study of Edward White Benson, the first headmaster of Wellington College, and subsequently Archbishop of Canterbury. Tosh suggests that many mid-Victorian middle-class men felt the need to be masters in their own homes, and to superintend areas such as domestic expenditure, their children's education, family prayers, and the overall discipline of the household. A man's anxieties about his own manliness, his ability to control his wife and children and impose his will on the household thus gained no respite when he came home, but continued to trouble him at the very heart of the domestic sanctuary, the family hearth.[11] Writers such as John Stuart Mill, Harriet Martineau and Samuel Smiles were already stressing the importance of the family as a school of moral training, involving parents as well as children;[12] it was a short step for the novelists to include a whole family, as Charlotte Yonge did, in the experience of a spiritual crisis or other practical or philosophical problems, contrasting the different responses of family members. The father or eldest brother were the natural leaders, but not always the most reliable moral guides; and there might be an unseemly jockeying for power within a large household. Male heroism in the home was of a subtly different kind from the female version, being more concerned with leadership and discipline than with the 'cleverness' and skilled manoeuvring characteristic of Mrs Oliphant's 'genius' heroines, or the patient endurance of spiritual and psychological hardship of Charlotte Yonge's. Moreover, it was considered human enough for a woman to fail; less excusable for a man. The home might then become a place of protracted shame and humiliation, as it is for Charlotte Yonge's Philip Morville in *The Heir of Redclyffe* (1853), or for Mr May (who has forged another man's signature) in Mrs Oliphant's *Phoebe Junior* (1876).

With the steady decline in classically heroic male characters in the novel, noted by Mario Praz,[13] and the tendency, in novelists such as George Eliot, to find the ordinary, or anti-heroic, more interesting than the heroic, the possibilities for strong male characters had notably diminished by the second half of the nineteenth century. It was more common for a hero to be seen gradually losing his high aspirations and arrogance, as Lydgate does in *Middlemarch*, or realizing that his ambitions are unrealistic. Few heroes of major novels finish with their pride undented, their body in pristine condition, or their ego intact. Rochester is burnt, maimed and blinded, Robert Moore, in *Shirley*, suffers serious illness, M. Paul, in *Villette*, is presumed drowned, and even the glamorous Dr John Graham Bretton loses a baby; in George Eliot's novels, Tom Tulliver drowns, Adam Bede is deceived in his first love, Hetty, the Reverend Amos Barton loses his wife, Milly, Lydgate dies of diphtheria in his fifties, disappointed both in his career and in his marriage; while among Mrs Gaskell's heroes, various forms of lying and deception are more common than in her heroines (Mr Benson and Mr Bellingham in *Ruth*, Philip in *Sylvia's Lovers*, Harry Carson in *Mary Barton*, Osborne

Hamley in *Wives and Daughters* – many of whom pay with death or humiliation). Nor is the tally much more encouraging in novels written by men. The heroes of Trollope's *Barchester Towers* are too patently blustering, pompous or comic to be looked up to; *Vanity Fair* declares itself to be 'a novel without a hero', and many of Dickens's heroes, as Praz and others have recognized, are too conventional and puppet-like to be viewed in classically heroic terms as achieving their goals by bravery, energy, or what Yonge called 'manly dash'. Hardy's heroes, particularly Angel Clare, Michael Henchard, Jude Fawley and Clym Yeobright, follow the George Eliot tradition in being steadily disabused of their own self-confidence or high aspirations, finding life to be a series of disappointments or missed opportunities.

The reasons for this decline of the fictional hero are many and complex. In some respects the phenomenon seems odd, given the meteoric rise of successful businessmen and manufacturers in the nineteenth century, and the widely-publicized optimistic philosophy of men like Samuel Smiles. It seemed as if any man, so long as he worked hard and was determined, might fight his way to the top; or he might practise the Arnoldian code of gentlemanliness and win distinction by more subtle means. But in some ways the domestic cult of the Victorians worked against the survival of a more swashbuckling kind of heroism, stressing as it did such virtues as self-control, self-restraint, piety, quietness, and consideration for others. As early as the late 1830s and early 1840s, Sarah Ellis's advice to the Wives, Daughters and Mothers of England was hinting at the moodiness of men, whose foibles of temper and behaviour needed tactful management by their womenfolk. Ellis believed that women could be more easily brought under the influence of Christian principles than men, and were less likely to go seriously astray, not least because the range of possible temptations was far smaller. She advised women to direct their conversational skills at distracting men from their own preoccupations, and urged sisters to correct their brother's moral faults, but, by doing some extra service for him, demonstrate that 'though she can see a fault in him, she still esteems herself his inferior, and though she is cruel enough to point it out, her love is yet so deep and pure as to sweeten every service she can render him'.[14] Much of Ellis's philosophy is geared to convincing men that they are still in charge, while advising women to humour their peculiarities and provide unobtrusive moral leadership. With the growing revelations of men's brutality in marriage, and recourse to prostitutes, it was less easy, as the century wore on, to preserve an untarnished, idealistic notion of men's virtues, while the domestic setting of the novel between 1850 and 1870 brought the daily failings of husbands and lovers more closely under the microscope. Domesticity both threatened men, by making their shortcomings more visible to the family than if they had occurred at work, and gave them a new arena for a different concept of heroism, which fostered self-discipline and spirituality rather than feats of physical daring. The measurement of heroism becomes a more elusive and complex task, both for critic and author, after the middle of the nineteenth century.

The anti-feminist women novelists created heroes at a point where the whole concept of fictional heroism was in disarray, alternately undermined by the tarnished image of man in society, and boosted by the spread of 'muscular Christianity', athleticism, the growth of empire, and the increasing opportunities for men to distinguish themselves in action abroad. The writing of Yonge, Linton, Oliphant and Ward spans the years of most dramatic change in the options available to middle-class men, when it was also legitimate for them to think carefully about their relationships with God and the family. The Victorian ideal of manliness was constantly repositioning itself in relation to the role of women, the status of the church and religion, the cult of family life, and the attractions of military service. While the majority of women novelists were downgrading masculinity and exposing its serious moral shortcomings, the anti-feminist women were faced with a more awkward dilemma. Were they to reinforce their notions of female inferiority by exalting male leadership and integrity, or were they to acknowledge men's well-publicized tendency to serious moral failure, which was often the indirect cause of their heroines' 'genius' and distinction? More fundamentally, what kind of man did the anti-feminist woman novelist admire? And did she do anything to change the pattern of thwarted ambition and humiliation in the Victorian hero's moral progress?

CHARLOTTE YONGE'S WOUNDED HEROES

The Heir of Redclyffe opens with a scene familiar to all Yonge readers: a drawing-room containing a young lady, 'and a youth, lying on a couch near the fire, surrounded with books and newspapers, and a pair of crutches near him'.[15] The youth is Charles Edmonstone, not in fact the novel's hero, but a sardonic counsellor whose moral judgement is vindicated by subsequent events. He is one of three male invalids in a novel which allows most of its women reasonable health, but prostrates the personable Guy Morville and his cousin Philip with a fever caught on Guy's honeymoon in Switzerland. Philip, the solider, suffers more acutely, but recovers, while Guy, whose constitution is weaker, and who lacks the drive to fight disease, dies with a beautiful expression on his face, having forgiven Philip for trying to prevent his marriage, and for spreading false rumours about him.

The novel is Yonge's most extensive examination of heroes and heroism, in which she distinguishes between a priggish and self-satisfied kind of goodness, and a more human and vulnerable kind – though as Guy nears death, he becomes too other-worldly and idealized to sustain the role he performed at the beginning. Charles's scepticism initially sets the scene in a mood inimical to hero-worship, and Guy himself has nothing but contempt for Sir Charles Grandison: 'How could any one have any sympathy with such a piece of self-satisfaction?' (p. 23). Philip is dangerously Grandison-like in his complacency, but Guy admires him for his powers of self-sacrifice, which prompted him to forgo a university education and go into the army, so as to save his sisters from having to marry for money (in the event one does so anyway, and the other dies, making Philip's sacrifice unnecessary). Guy himself is emotional, sensitive, guilty and badly-educated: in many respects more like a woman than a man, especially when he puts himself under Mrs Edmonstone's special tutelage and embarks on a long and difficult course of restraining his feelings. In Switzerland he avoids identifying himself with 'Byron's brooding and lowering heroes' (p. 311) and is instead painted as Sir Galahad (his real name, Sir Guy Morville, is only slightly less in the traditionally heroic mould). His role in the novel oscillates between the feminine and the masculine, so that he is at one point leading the rescue party of a shipwreck near his house, and later, despite his 'slight frame, and excitable temperament' (p. 339), gently nursing Philip, 'showing himself an invaluable nurse, with his tender hand, modulated voice, quick eye, and quiet authority' (p. 322). He is always most at home in a room full of family, either tending Charles or discussing his problems with Mrs Edmonstone, and least comfortable in the solitary, masculine world of Redclyffe, a place of probation where he develops spiritually before being rewarded with re-entry into the happy world of Hollywell where the Edmonstones live. Guy emerges as a new kind of hero in some respects – he is thoroughly likeable, though initially hot-tempered – but in others he conforms to the pattern of the typical woman's hero. Elaine Showalter thinks he behaves like a woman 'who was encouraged to seek influence through martyrdom';[16] and he is certainly reduced to the state of invalidism and weakness characteristic of the woman's hero – as is the handsome military hero, Philip, who lies on a sofa 'suffering from languor, pain in the head, want of sleep and appetite' (p. 398). The difference between the two is that Guy has done nothing to deserve it: though Yonge sees his peaceful death as a reward for his goodness, rather than as a punishment for his failings. Like Mrs Gaskell's Ruth, he dies after nursing the man who has ruined his life, but he is unlike Ruth in having committed no actual sin.

His morbid sense of guilt seems to arise from consciousness of enmity towards Philip, following the family tradition of a feud between the two main branches of the Morvilles. In Freudian terms, he can be said to be suffering from the frustration of his erotic needs (he is kept from seeing his future wife, Amabel Edmonstone, because he is suspected of gambling), which in turn calls up aggressiveness against the person (Philip) who has caused the frustration, and the aggressiveness, in turn, makes him feel guilty. Both his parents died at the time when he was born, and he dies shortly after Amabel has conceived their child, suggesting a subliminal association, in Yonge's mind, between sex, death and guilt. The ancient feud between the Morvilles ends when Amabel's child turns out to be a girl, and the Redclyffe estate goes to Philip. His own erotic dangerousness has long been destroyed by recurring attacks of illness, and when he finally comes to an understanding with Laura, she quickly settles him on the sofa to recover: 'her only care was to make him comfortable with cushions, and he was too entirely worn out to say anything he had intended, capable only of giving himself up to the repose of knowing her entirely his own, and of having her to take care of him' (p. 418). In that last phrase Yonge quietly crushes any notion of a vigorous manliness which would make Philip Laura's protector, and instead establishes Laura as a substitute mother, who will sit by his sofa as Mrs Edmonstone has by Charles's.

The patterns introduced in *The Heir of Redclyffe* – of guilt, anxiety, male sickness, and a connection between sexuality and death are continued in *The Daisy Chain* and *The Clever Woman of the Family*. In the earlier novel, Dr May, who has just fathered his eleventh child, kills his wife by reckless carriage-driving, and injures his eldest daughter, who dies seven years later without recovering full use of her limbs. Yonge heightens the doctor's sense of guilt by connecting a dream he had when he was 'courting' with its sequel shortly after the fatal accident. In the first dream, he was the victor of a medieval tournament, and his future wife gave him her token, a daisy chain. In the second dream, the daisy chain saves him from being trampled to death:

> 'Last night came the tournament again, but it was the mêlée, a sense of being crushed down, suffocated by the throng of armed knights and horses – pain and wounds – and I looked in vain through the opposing overwhelming host for my – my Maggie. Well, I got the worst of it, my sword arm was broken – I fell, was stifled – crushed – in misery – all I could do was to grasp my token – my Daisy Chain,' and he pressed Margaret's hand as he said so. 'And, behold, the tumult and despair were passed. I lay on the grass in the cloisters, and the Daisy Chain hung from the sky, and was drawing me upwards.' (p. 56)

Margaret interprets the dream as suggesting that in their younger days people care for victory, but as they grow older they care less. A deeper explanation might be that Dr May is being punished for killing his wife (and perhaps for his sexuality), and all that can save him is devotion to his children (his 'Daisy Chain') and to God, who draws him heavenwards.

Guilt about achievement is like a thread running through *The Daisy Chain*, accompanied, at a less explicit level, by a thread of guilt about sexuality. Once again, the most potent male, Alan Ernescliffe, is immobilized by disease before and after his engagement to the other invalid, Margaret, and finally dies, as Margaret does, before they can marry. The latent sexuality of the other great swashbuckling hero of the novel, Dr May's lion-like son Harry, is defused by his romantic devotion to his sister Mary. But the novel also introduces another kind of hero in Norman May, the sensitive and nervous scholar of the family, who is too squeamish either to be a doctor or to face his father after the accident. Like Guy Morville, he suffers from an emotional sensitivity that makes him more like a woman than a man, and he and Ethel, the other great scholar of the family, are in a sense two halves of the same person. Ethel, as the woman, is not allowed to marry, but stays at home to tend her father (as a desexualized, intellectual version of her mother), while Norman is engaged to the innocent 'humming-bird' Meta Rivers, and goes out to New Zealand as a missionary. The only one of the May children to indulge her eroticism openly, the second daughter, Flora, is punished with the loss of her first baby, and a long period of exhaustion and despair before the birth of her second. Her husband, George Rivers, is the kind of amiable, brainless oaf usually married by Oliphant's heroines.

A similar pattern emerges again in *The Clever Woman of the Family*: two elderly fathers, Sir Stephen Temple, and Lord Keith, die soon after their young wives have conceived; and the two military heroes, Colin and Alick Keith, are both anxious about their health; the former engaging himself to the invalid Ermine Williams, and the latter eventually marrying the Clever Woman, Rachel Curtis, after she has recovered from diphtheria. Alick is Yonge's most extensive treatment of the invalid hero in this novel. Like many of her heroes, he has already performed his feats of bravery before the novel opens, and is resting in the state of nervous exhaustion and anticlimax that is the common condition of her male characters. His hand is mutilated, and he has won the Victoria Cross; yet he has a laziness, and even an air of vacuousness, which lead Rachel to dismiss him at the outset as a lightweight. Yonge implies that heroism is a more elusive quality than women in particular are able to recognize, expecting a great military man to look aggressive and muscular. Alick, by contrast, turns out to be a good nurse (like Guy), when Rachel is recovering from illness and despondency: 'It was not for nothing that he had spent a year upon the sofa in the irritably sensitive state of nerves that Bessie had described' (p. 276). By gradually winning her confidence, Alick becomes the soothing brother/father-figure Rachel never had, breaking off the honeymoon at Rachel's request to spend a quiet time of recuperation and re-education at his uncle, Mr Clare's. Yet even the blind clergyman, Mr Clare, has lost his wife and baby daughter, becoming yet another muted symbol of arrested male sexuality, safely defused into a gentle father-figure steering his charges, his grown-up children, towards the religious faith which Yonge believed was the only guarantee of salvation.

Yonge's portrayal of men is always influenced by her commitment to unremarkable demonstrations of steady goodness as a preferable alternative to worldly success and ambition (Dr May's disappointing eldest son, Richard, who is too dull to be a success, nevertheless provides his family with reliable moral guidance not always available from his more impulsive and emotional father). Because her novels are set in a family context, her heroes are fully domesticated, with their bravery behind them or transmuted into nursing skills; their world, which was once the army or navy, strangely emasculated, and their sexuality limited by languor. Like women they experience the curtailment of their energies and ambitions; marriage becomes their goal in place of distinction in their careers; and they end their professional lives in the drawing-room, either sofa-ridden themselves or tending on others who are. As Norman Vance has shown, the relationship between manliness and Christianity is itself problematic, however cheerfully men like Kingsley seemed to embody the two: 'The entertaining and healthy activism of the manly hero, whether in fact or fiction, was bound to jar with the less vivid religious imperatives: patience and heroic martyrdom, self-abnegation and the discipline of the will.'[17] This is certainly the case with Guy and Alick, though Mary Ward later came closer to reconciling the two impulses in Robert Elsmere. As for Yonge, whether her treatment of heroes was punitive in the Rochester tradition, or simply a way of keeping her male characters in a familiar and feminized setting, purified of any gross physicality, the effect is a levelling of the distinctions between men and women in her novels. R.H. Hutton indeed was quick to guess that *Heartsease* and *The Heir* were written by a woman, and not only because 'the sacerdotal element is so very feebly and so unquarrelsomely presented'. All the male characters 'ably as they are delineated – are drawn in the aspects in which they present themselves to women'.[18]

The only advantage left to men is their wider experience of life outside the home. Both Amabel and Rachel are re-educated by their invalid husbands, in accordance with Yonge's view that every woman needed the kind of steady male guidance that she had received from her father and John Keble; yet Amabel stands out as the image of serene resignation to fate, happy for ever with her baby daughter and invalid brother – two sublimated relationships free of the taint of male sexuality.

ELIZA LYNN LINTON'S GUILTY HUSBANDS

If Charlotte Yonge surrounded sexuality and marriage with a deathly atmosphere of invalidism and languor, Eliza Linton more sensationally hinted at bigamy and mystery in the lives of her heroes. In *Grasp Your Nettle* (1865), a novel published, like *The Clever Woman of the Family* (which also contains melodramatic incidents in the Mauleverer subplot) in the 'sensation decade', when Wilkie Collins and Mary Elizabeth Braddon were at the height of their powers, the heroine, Aura Escott, marries the mysterious Jasper Trelawney, who has just moved into their isolated country district of Clive Vale. George Somes Layard has rightly commented that Jasper is 'nothing more nor less than an adumbration of Rochester':[19] indeed, he even proposes beneath a large horse-chestnut tree, appearing to Aura in a new guise from the usual haughtiness familiar to the village community. 'Who would have recognized the cold Master of Croft in that wild lover, with all the force of manhood and the exaltation of youth in his love?'[20] All that is known about him at the time of their marriage is that he has been married before, and has two young daughters; also that he is a 'man of strong will, intense pride, and almost passionate haughtiness, yet sensitive as a woman in certain matters touching his honour; and above all, he was a man of silence and reserve' (vol. I, p. 46). Most of the novel's plot is concerned with unravelling the supposed mystery behind Jasper and his previous marriage to Lavinia Field, a Bertha Mason type, who tricked him into marriage, and who turns out to be not mad, but a professional thief and forger working with her father and brother. 'I had married into a family of known and convicted swindlers, notorious throughout Paris,' Jasper tells Aura in a long confessional scene, when she, like Jane Eyre, reconsiders her status in her husband's life and wonders whether to leave him (vol. II, p. 199). Jasper behaves like Rochester, in wanting the relationship to continue, despite allegations that his previous wife is still living; Linton punishes him with the statutory attack of brain fever, but nothing worse, since Lavinia has been safely dead in Madeira, buried under a false name, for the last seven years, and her brother Gregory, who is continuing to blackmail Jasper, conveniently shoots himself when the police confront him. The plot is a melodramatic version of an already melodramatic *Jane Eyre*, interspersed with passages of George Eliot-like village gossip and matchmaking. What seems significant for Linton's development as a novelist is the atmosphere of guilt she establishes around her hero, and by extension, the woman who has married him.

Her biographer, Nancy Fix Anderson, has argued that throughout her life Linton felt both guilty and angry about her mother's death: feelings that were later compounded when she married William James Linton after the death of his previous (and second) wife. In her novels, she repeatedly gives her husbands and lovers a mysterious history which threatens to involve the women destined to marry them, as if, for her, marriage was inextricably associated with ideas of encroachment, duplicity, sexual transgression, and danger to the wife. Strongly as she upheld the ideal of the traditional marriage when she wrote about it in her journal articles, male sexuality, in her novels, is seen as tainted and threatening. This may be because the man is middle-aged and wealthy, seeking a young wife against her will, as with Mr Brocklebank, the successful industrialist in *The Rebel of the Family*, or Launcelot Brabazon, the grotesquely-named fifty-year-old fastidious bachelor of *The One Too Many* (1894), whom Moira's mother insists she marry. Linton has no sympathy with this sort of mercenary, self-seeking marriage; but she also taints even her young men, such as Leslie Crawford, the heroic chemist of *The Rebel*. Leslie rescues Perdita once from drowning herself, and once when she feels faint outside his shop. He is a conventional hero in looks – 'tall, handsome, brown-haired' – and in manner: 'His voice was gentle but firm; his manner protecting but commanding' (vol. I, p. 262). But even he has an unfathomable mystery, a previous wife who lost her reason two years ago (the Rochester influence again), complicating Perdita's feelings for him and his child, and making her the innocent encroacher on another woman's territory. By then Linton had become her husband's third wife and failed in the attempt: they spent the rest of their lives in a state of amicable separation, with the Atlantic between them, and the knowledge that succeeding other wives had not been the glorious vocation Linton had hoped. Her father had also remarried – confirming the pattern, in Linton's mind, that women were innocent, but men had a previous history.

But her strangest hero is Christopher Kirkland, herself disguised as a man, in the transvestite autobiography she published in 1885, with all the key roles switched to the opposite gender. Born into an identical family to Linton's own, her hero becomes a journalist–novelist, lives in Paris, meets the famous people of the day, and marries Esther Lambert, the William Linton equivalent, who shares his disorganized lifestyle, and whose husband had died of consumption, like Linton's wife. Christopher mentions that he is married more from a sense of duty than from personal taste, stipulating that Esther should give up her public work as a women's rights campaigner; like the real W.J. Linton, Esther soon resents the restrictions of home life and the attention to clean tablecloths and the accurate adding-up of butchers' bills – details on which Eliza Linton had insisted when she was married. But although Esther purports to be a picture of W.J. Linton, she also seems to embody some of Eliza's guilt about being an active professional woman, who at no stage of her adult life accepted care of a house, husband and children as her only work. Esther's criticisms of Christopher are another way of blaming herself for what went wrong, so that under cover of fictitious autobiography, Linton was able to chastise herself for all the blameworthy aspects of her life both as a wife and as a professional woman.

The cross-dressing of the *Autobiography* also enabled Linton to declare her passionate love for other women (such as the characters of Mrs Dalrymple, whom Christopher adores in his youth, and Claudia, an eighteen-year-old left in his charge by her father, Christopher's brother-in-law). Later he falls ill and is nursed by Felicia Barry, 'type of the Ideal Woman ... strong, hopeful and unselfish', but none of Christopher's relationships is successful, any more than Linton's were.[21] By this stage of her life, Linton had taken on a series of adoptive mother–daughter relationships with younger women, such as Beatrice Sichel (the original of Claudia) and Beatrice Harradan (who went off to California for several years): all went well until they deserted her – Beatrice Sichel to be married twice – and Linton was left feeling miserable and lonely. Having, in the *Autobiography*, indulged her passion for this series of deserters (who were mostly women, both in real life and in the novel), she ended it by insisting on a philosophy of self-annihilation and altruistic duty as 'the absolute law of moral life' (vol. III, p. 320). Old and alone, Christopher Kirkland concludes: 'Life has shown me that this personal happiness comes to us in fullest quantity when we give most and ask least; and that in the pain of renunciation itself is the consolation which is born of strength' (vol. III, p. 313). In the emphasis on renunciation it is easy to recognize the tradition of the Victorian woman agnostic writing in the style of George Eliot: all the more since Christopher was originally ambitious to distinguish himself academically or in public life. The self-contradictory views he expresses in his *Autobiography* allow Linton both to voice her own burning ambitions, and to punish herself for them. The *Autobiography* finally becomes an exercise in public self-humiliation – but under cover: Christopher Kirkland, no less than Jasper Trelawney and Leslie Crawford, turns out to be a man who is not quite what he seems, living under a false identity.

Much critical attention has recently been given to the history of cross-dressing, especially by Marjorie Garber, who in *Vested Interests* (1992) argues that the 'current popularity of cross-dressing as a theme in art and criticism represents an undertheorized recognition of the necessary critique of binary thinking'.[22] In other words, it forces people to think less rigidly in terms of the opposition between men and women and all that stems from it in the power structures of society. If this is true of Linton, the implications of her cross-dressing in *Christopher Kirkland* are in direct conflict with her usual efforts to preserve sexual boundaries at all costs. Inveighing against womanish men and mannish women is normally in Linton's line, as if desperate to keep the two sexes and their rightful territories firmly demarcated from each other, and fearing an unholy commingling, long before this became a more widely acknowledged fear in the *fin de siècle*. At its simplest, the cross-dressing of *Christopher Kirkland* clearly allowed Linton to express controversial views more openly than she could have done in a female autobiography, and to have more outrageous adventures (though ironically most of them are modelled on her actual experiences). It also allowed her to explore the experience of belonging to the other sex (though again Christopher had to fight as hard as she did for permission to leave home and go to London), and to see women from a man's point of view, as she seemed to do anyway for much of her career. If it also broke down barriers, and questioned the binary structures of gendered society, the cross-gendering of the autobiographical novel perhaps betrayed Linton's unconscious desire for a less rigidly arranged allocation of spheres, which might have made her own struggle for independence and acceptance in society less isolating in personal terms. In *Christopher Kirkland* few characters seem to be at home in the social role allocated to them.

MRS OLIPHANT'S POOR CREATURES

Margaret Oliphant spent most of her adult life looking after men and trying to believe in them. Her sons were handsome and clever schoolboys: of Cyril she told her niece, Madge Valentine, after his death, 'I used to say he was like Chaucer's squire. . . . I do not feel as if he could ever change from that perfection of being.'[23] But her experience of men was largely coloured by disappointment. Cyril and Cecco failed to distinguish themselves at Oxford, and then died in their thirties after several false starts in their careers, following the tradition of her own mysteriously idle brothers. When she wrote her *Autobiography* she could hardly believe what had happened to them, and to her nephew Frank who died in India. She was still unsure of how Cyril had gone wrong. 'My dearest, bright, delightful boy missed somehow his footing, how can I tell how? I often think that I had to do with it, as well as what people call inherited tendencies, and, alas! the perversity of youth, which he never outgrew' (p. 147). Oliphant's displaced sense of guilt reappears in her novels in the form of querulous, interfering women – mothers and aunts – who paralyse her young men in their progress towards a successful career or marriage.

Concurrently, Oliphant had become interested in the shape of male biography, as if anxious to trace how men's professional lives normally developed, and what might go wrong with them. Apart from reviewing biographies and autobiographies for *Blackwood's*, she wrote biographical articles on a wide range of notable Victorian men, including the Prince Consort, Dickens, John Wilson, Tennyson, Laurence Oliphant, Dean Stanley and John Gibson Lockhart. She extended her interest in famous men to European writers, such as the Count de Montalembert, whom she met in 1865, and analysed years later in her *Autobiography*, finding him 'keen and sharp as a sword, and yet open to every belief and to every superstition, far more than I ever could have been, who looked at him and up to him with a sort of admiring wonder and yet sympathy, not without a smile in it' (p. 99). She was also afraid of him, adding yet another emotion to her already complex series of responses. Her description builds him up as a great and formidable figure, while also indicating that she could see through him: very much the kind of dual focus that she applies to her fictional characters.

Oliphant was equally fascinated by the charismatic preacher Edward Irving, of whom she wrote a biography (1862) after exploring his career in a *Blackwood's* article of 1858. Seeing him as a tragic figure, 'a dethroned king', 'an apostle and prophet errant to the world – a mailed knight consecrate and sworn to war and to conquest', she identified a moment of error when he expressed opinions on the nature of Jesus which alienated him from his followers, and he was eventually rejected by his own congregation. Oliphant was appalled that a man of such distinction should have been at the disposal of his ignorant followers. 'Edward Irving formed his sect to obey it – to submit his honour to it – to give up his leadership for a servant's office – to bow his heroic soul to the unspeakable presumption of some dozen nameless men.'[24] Irving's story throws some light on what happens to Arthur Vincent in *Salem Chapel*, though Oliphant complicates the story by making Arthur snobbish, arrogant, and dragged down by women. What the two men have in common, however, is the power of oratory, not altogether matched by common sense.

Lucy Poate Stebbins has suggested that Oliphant learnt mixed love and contempt for men from her own mother and her feelings for *her* sons; at any rate, 'Mrs Oliphant could never believe in a hero. Her charming young men are, after all, poor creatures. She treats them leniently and either spares them the demanding situations with which they are unfit to cope, or extricates them by a flick of coincidence.'[25] R.C. Terry goes further, and argues that the theme of her novels is the 'woman's sacrifices to the Victorian male ego'.[26] This is undoubtedly true, yet Oliphant frequently suggests that her male characters are as trapped and helpless as her women, and stand little chance of survival unless taken in hand by an energizing wife.

Oliphant's literary reviews for *Blackwood's* show that she felt Victorian novelists were living in an unheroic age with few certainties, and that, on the whole, men were doing less well than women in the struggle for supremacy. She also felt, unusually, that men were less dangerous than women, and could do less damage, as she argued in an article on Mary Braddon in 1867: 'there can be no possible doubt that the wickedness of man is less ruinous, less disastrous to the world in general, than the wickedness of woman'.[27] Writing the year before on women's suffrage, and John Stuart Mill, she declared that she did not envy men, and found that 'most of them, in reality, instead of being the free, bright, brave creatures we had dreamed, required a vast deal of propping up and stimulating, to keep them with their front to the world'.[28] Doubting the allegations of domestic violence against women, which were adduced as reasons for altering the marriage laws in women's favour, Oliphant came to see men less as household tyrants than as 'poor creatures' to be humoured and safeguarded. In this she was partly influenced by the rise of the 'New Woman', both in fiction and in real life, and a younger generation of women who seemed to feel that they were entitled to whatever satisfaction they could obtain. Disturbed by *Jude the Obscure*, Oliphant worried about the novelists' assault on marriage as an institution, objected to the prominence given to sex rather than love, and by 1896 was convinced that man, not woman, was 'the suffering member; and he is generally a good and contented creature, satisfied with very little, almost too kind and compliant with the endless requirements of the woman who is never content whatever happens'.[29]

Her sympathy with men had increased since she had read the novels of Sarah Grand, but her most extensive studies of male characters were written in the 'sensation' decade of the 1860s, when she repeatedly portrayed innocent, naïve men struggling to defend their reputations from association with women of dubious backgrounds. In *The Perpetual Curate* (1864), the respectable clergyman Frank Wentworth is assumed to be involved with Rosa Elsworthy, a shopkeeper's niece; while in *Salem Chapel* (1863) the Dissenting hero, Arthur Vincent, has to defend his name from false linkage with several women: the grocer's daughter, Phoebe Tozer, Lady Western (whom he admires from a distance), and the mysterious Mrs Hilyard, who describes herself as 'an equivocal female figure'.[30] In fact, men in these novels of Mrs Oliphant's most successful period function very much as women, needing society's approval for their wellbeing, being trapped and powerless economically, either as Dissenting ministers, or as poor relations with wealthy aunts, and needing, as clergymen, to preserve their reputations in a state of immaculate order. Oliphant, as narrator, makes this last point herself in *The Perpetual Curate*, when she says that 'Mr Wentworth was quite well aware that the character of a clergyman was almost as susceptible as that of a woman, and that the vague stigma might haunt and overshadow him all his life.'[31]

Salem Chapel and *The Perpetual Curate* are remarkably similar novels, in that both are concerned with the intractable professional and family situations of two young single ministers with romantic aspirations that are continually being thwarted by the sordid realities of their lives. While they are trying to make a success of their careers in the gossipy community of Carlingford, both are distracted by crises in their families. Arthur Vincent's sister Susan appears to have run away with a seducer, while Frank Wentworth's brother Jack has become involved in fraudulent money deals with Tom Wodehouse, brother of Lucy, with whom Frank has long been in love. Oliphant's point seems to be the impossibility of shaking off undesirable family ties. Whatever Arthur and Frank do to forward their professional and romantic lives is likely to be undone by the clumsy and thoughtless behaviour of their families. Symbolically, the point is emphasized by the repetitive speech-patterns of the family and community elders who have such a hold over them. Mr Tozer is always telling Arthur, 'it ain't the thing to do'; Mrs Tufton, wife of his predecessor, repeatedly says: 'The minister often says to me that he is a precious young man, is Mr Vincent, and that a little good advice and attention to those that know better is all he wants to make him a shining light' (p. 435); and in *The Perpetual Curate* Frank's Aunt Dora harps on 'how nice it would be when he was old enough to take the Rectory, and marry Julia Trench –' (p. 61), ambitions that have never been Frank's in the first place. Oliphant's own style is itself dense and repetitive, reinforcing her characters' sense of entrapment. Unlike Lucilla Marjoribanks, who can always come up with another idea to further her plans for Carlingford, Frank and Arthur, both men of integrity and sensitivity, find themselves hemmed in by the claustrophobic busybodying of the Carlingford community, as ready to take umbrage at a declined tea invitation as at the discovery of an improper relationship.

Moreover, Oliphant's clergymen, like Trollope's, are often specifically at the mercy of women. In the opening chapters of *Salem Chapel*, Arthur Vincent is successively disturbed and unsettled by a series of female parishioners, who obtrude their views on his notice: Phoebe Tozer, Mrs Hilyard, Adelaide Tufton and Lady Western. Frank Wentworth, meanwhile, can do nothing without the approbation of his aunts, and makes no progress in his courtship of Lucy Wodehouse. Self-absorbed, proud and overlooked, both men have to give way to the more urgent needs of their siblings; their own dull, monotonous routine of parish work invaded by the subterranean 'sensation' world which exists uneasily, in Mrs Oliphant's novels, alongside her densely documented world of domestic realism. The 'sensation' subplots may be only a response to popular taste at the time when Oliphant was writing, or she may have a more serious point to make by allowing the two worlds to abut on to each other. The overall effect is to imply that below the surface of even the most mundane community like Carlingford are seething human emotions, an uncontrolled, collective id, liable to break out and disturb the false calm of bourgeois society. This was, of course, what made the 'sensation' novel so exciting: the suggestion that violent emotions and crimes existed, not in Gothic castles, but in Victorian homes. Oliphant's novels in general distrust passionate outbursts, though they can be useful to clear up misunderstandings and promote relationships. On the whole, however, she prefers to reserve her heroes' passions for their sermons, as happens two-thirds of the way through *Salem Chapel*, when Arthur Vincent writes a sermon which sounds more like a sensation novel:

> He set forth the dark secrets of life with exaggerated touches of his own passion and anguish. He painted out of his own aching fancy a soul innocent, yet stained with the heaviest of mortal crimes: he turned his wild light aside and poured it upon another, foul to the core, yet unassailable by man. Saving souls! – which was the criminal? which was the innocent? A wild confusion of sin and sorrow, of dreadful human complications, misconceptions, of all incomprehensible, intolerable thoughts, surged round and round him as he wrote. (p. 305)

Oliphant had already written on sermons for *Blackwood's*, rejecting the cold, abstract approach, and arguing that the preacher should keep his congregation persuaded of the human reality and truth of the invisible.[32] In his sermon, however, Arthur Vincent voices his sense of the chaos in bourgeois morality, the breakdown of simple barriers between good and bad, which Oliphant could do far more effectively using Arthur as her mouthpiece than in her own person. He also appears to speak for his sister Susan, who is silenced by her ordeal, and remains a statuesque figure, magnificent in her grief and fever, 'a solemn speechless creature, abstracted already out of this world and its influences' (p. 403).

Heroic as Arthur's behaviour is, and Frank's too, Oliphant always implies that men acting alone are liable to go wrong. She allows them to express a woman's frustration with the limitations of society, but, like women, they are ultimately unfit to stand alone. Although Arthur's mother is portrayed ambiguously, as obsessional and over-anxious, she senses that her son is losing control of his congregation and endangering his career, while she is helpless to act. 'Many a time before this, the widow had been compelled to submit to that female tribulation – to be shut up apart, and leave the great events outside to be transacted by those incautious masculine hands, in which, at the bottom of her heart, a woman seldom has perfect confidence when her own supervising influence is withdrawn' (p. 339). She tries to intervene by warning Mr Tozer that Arthur might resign his ministry if he is harassed any further: a decision he finally makes. Like many of the other heroes discussed in this chapter, Arthur ends chastened and disappointed, overcome by the sense of circumstances being too strong for him. 'I find my old theories inadequate to the position in which I find myself,' he tells his congregation, 'and all I can do is to give up the post where they have left me in the lurch' (p. 453).

Mrs Oliphant rarely allows her heroes a triumphant ending. Most of the men in *Miss Marjoribanks* are exposed as vain philanderers or weak fools, and Tom Marjoribanks succeeds only because Lucilla takes him in hand. Frank Wentworth in *The Perpetual Curate*, unusually, wins everything he wanted – the rectorship, and marriage to Lucy Wodehouse – but the feeling at the end is less than joyful. Lucy feels disappointed of her desire for self-sacrifice, and Mrs Morgan, wife of the previous rector, has learnt to be disillusioned about marriage, for which she had waited so long. 'She had found out the wonderful difference between anticipation and reality; and that life, even to a happy woman married after long patience to the man of her choice, was not the smooth road it looked, but a rough path enough cut into dangerous ruts, through which generations of men and women followed each other without ever being able to mend the way' (pp. 538–9). Men in Mrs Oliphant's novels tend to be more optimistic about marriage than women are, perhaps because for them it means an increase in home comforts and companionship without the effort of maintaining them. Oliphant's men rarely show much knowledge of how houses are run, but merely return home at the end of the day to be fed and entertained. On the other hand, she has little sympathy with women who pull men down by constant harping on trifles, though she does at least see this as an outlet for their nervous energies. Her romantic young couples are increasingly surrounded by a chorus of disappointed elders who have learnt that marriage is not all they used to imagine in their youthful days of courtship.

By the 1870s, Oliphant's men have grown still feebler. In *The Curate in Charge*, the resourceful young heroines deal with a succession of fastidious and emasculated men, such as the aptly-named bachelor aesthete from Oxford, Mr Mildmay (a gentle forerunner of Mr Langham, in Mary Ward's *Robert Elsmere*). Mildmay is too devoted to his china to have much emotion left for a wife, yet he longs for 'life'. As Oliphant herself recognizes, his is very much a woman's dilemma: 'Such a man in such a self-discussion is as many women are. If he works, what is the good of it? It is to occupy, to please himself, not because the work is necessary to others' (pp. 74–5). At the end of the novel he is 'still wondering where life was'

(p. 199), with Cicely St John his only hope of a more fulfilling future. As his parishioner Mr Ascott puts it, 'If a girl like Cicely chooses to tell him to marry her, he'd do it' (p. 195). This is virtually the situation with Lucilla Marjoribanks and Phoebe Junior, who both marry men much feebler than themselves. In Phoebe's case, the man, Clarence Copperhead, is even portrayed in an entirely different style – Dickensian caricature, as opposed to the comic domestic realism of the other characters – reinforcing the point that Phoebe is throwing herself away on a fool. The other men in the novel gradually lose their better principles and succumb to different forms of temptation. The clergyman Mr May convinces himself that there is nothing wrong in forging Mr Tozer's handwriting to extend a period of loan; later he becomes Phoebe's 'charge, her burden, as helpless in her hands as a child' (p. 304); while his son Reginald reluctantly accepts a sinecure (a wardenship, like Mr Harding's in Trollope's *The Warden* and *Barchester Towers*) and fails to win Phoebe, though he is clearly a better man than Clarence Copperhead. Another hero of the novel, the Dissenting clergyman Northcote, resigns, like Arthur Vincent, from his position, but not having something to fight for 'was a drawback to him, and cramped his mental development' (p. 340). Few Oliphant heroes make triumphant career moves or achieve unalloyed success by the end of the novel: what they do normally achieve is marriage to a much cleverer woman than themselves, which Oliphant sees as being the best hope for them. She shows their professional lives (usually as clergymen or doctors) as being inseparable from the social life of Carlingford, with each case history involving a succession of social embarrassments and the occasional melodramatic incident dragging them into a murky underworld of forbidden passion. Ultimately, her men are as powerless as women, trapped in a gluey medium of gossip, touchiness and domestic trifling, which either drives them out, or settles them in marriage in the midst of it.

MRS HUMPHRY WARD'S SENSITIVE ENGLISHMEN

'How little room there is for the heroic in this trivial everyday life of ours!' Mrs Humphry Ward comments as narrator in *Robert Elsmere*.[33] Yet all her novels prove that in her terms, at least, there are still heroic opportunities for her men and women, as they fight poverty and suffering in rural communities or the East End of London, while also battling more momentously with their own consciences. The sheer strenuousness of her characters can become mentally exhausting, and places them in an entirely different category from the other heroes in this chapter. Yonge's troubled doubters are never seen wrestling in much detail with their theological problems (presumably because this might endanger the souls of her younger readers); nor does Oliphant provide much insight into her clergymen's theological experiences. But Ward's are at the cutting edge of Victorian thought, and she herself had far more direct experience of men (Arnoldian men at that) than any of the other anti-feminist women writers. Attending Oxford and London dinner-parties, arguing with Gladstone, visiting Mark Pattison, talking literature with Henry James, studying Ernest Renan, and trying to understand her father's conversions and deconversions back and forth between Protestantism and Roman Catholicism, gave her a much fuller understanding, albeit a rather rarefied one, of the male intellect and emotions. Ward's world is vigorous and masculine, where the others' are purely domestic; her heroes are seen in the House of Commons, at political rallies, at philosophical debates, in Oxford rooms, in all-male communities – discussing everything from sweated labour to the Book of Daniel. Yet, as Anne Bindslev has pointed out, her contemporaries criticized her portrayal of men, and thought they were less convincing than her women.[34] One of these, William Lyon Phelps, in 1910, identified two types of hero in her novels: the dusty, bookish, dissertational type, and the 'Byronic, clever, romantic, sentimental, insincere man – who always degenerates or dies in a manner that exalts the dull and superior virtues of his antagonist'.[35] Tiring of this dichotomy, Phelps decided that she was better at creating old men.

Ward's favourite kind of man is in fact the upper-class Englishman who is reserved, Oxford-educated but with some exposure to practicalities, athletic perhaps, and certainly sensitive, though he is not always able to express his feelings as fluently as the woman he loves. He also has an old-fashioned regard for traditional femininity, and likes women most when they are vulnerable and, to use Ward's favourite word, 'childish'. Such a man is Aldous Raeburn in *Marcella*, or Mark Winnington in *Delia Blanchflower* (1915), 'a countryman, an English provincial, with English public school and university traditions of the best kind behind him, a mind steeped in history, and a natural taste for all that was ancient and deep-rooted.'[36]

His tough, virile Englishness must, however, be modified by a sensitive inner life, as it is with Jacob Delafield in *Lady Rose's Daughter* (1903):

> On the one side he was a robust, healthy Etonian, who could ride, shoot and golf like the rest of his kind, who used the tense, slangy ways of speech of the ordinary Englishman, who loved the land and its creatures, and had a natural hatred of a poacher; and on another he was a man haunted by dreams and spiritual voices.... He read much poetry; and the New Testament spoke to him imperatively, though in no orthodox or accustomed way.[37]

Ward's men are abreast of their times, responding to all the philosophical and religious currents, as well as the trend towards a more outwardly virile kind of masculinity which was characteristic of the 1870s and 1880s and beyond. Her men generally resist the other tendencies of the *fin de siècle*: namely homosexuality and decadence, though she never undervalues the importance of strong male friendships formed at university or public school, which are often hostile to women.

Ward began her writing career with a children's book, *Milly and Olly* (1881), and the tale of an actress, *Miss Bretherton* (1884); but it was her first novel about a man's life, *Robert Elsmere* (1888), that turned her into a best-selling novelist. Robert himself is a charismatic, 'modern "Man of Feeling"', as Ward calls him (p. 204), who resigns the rectorship of Murewell when he has irresolvable doubts about the truth of the Christian miracles. He then devotes himself to the working men of the East End, until he dies of exhaustion and tuberculosis, leaving a wife who has never swerved from an austere, puritanical religious faith, inculcated in her by her father. In future, Ward would normally reverse the gender roles, and make the man representative of a religious tradition, and the woman a rebel critic or freethinker: a situation more in keeping with the notion of women as outside the symbolic order and ready to assail it, with the widening of opportunity at the end of the nineteenth century. At this point in her career, however, Catherine Elsmere, raised in an isolated Lake District community, belongs to a dead theological past, while Robert, eager and adventurous, conducts private historical research, while also finding time to interest the local boys in natural history. Yet even Robert is described ambiguously in gender terms. He was raised by his mother, and first appears on the scene in the role most favoured by women writers for their heroes, as an invalid being nursed back to health by a motherly friend. His face has 'the pink and white complexion of a girl', and 'Robert Elsmere's hand was the hand of a woman' (p. 25). 'Eagerness' seems to Catherine 'the note of the whole man' (p. 38), while he finds in her, 'austerity, strength, individuality' (p. 39). 'The man, quick, sensitive, sympathetic, felt in the woman the presence of a strength, a self-sufficingness which was not all attractive' (p. 41). Indeed, Ward would take considerable pains to alter this in her later novels; but for the time being, Elsmere's undoubted masculinity (the Charles Kingsley variety, which combined a love of fishing with a confident sexuality) is modified by his naively romantic temperament and womanish state of invalidism, with which the novel begins and ends.

Like Oliphant's heroes, Robert Elsmere is also the victim of circumstance, though at a more elevated level than the clergymen of Carlingford. Happening to make friends with Roger Wendover, the local squire, who normally dislikes parsons, and intends to dislike Elsmere, too, Robert strays into Biblical criticism, and reads the Squire's book, *The Idols of the Market-place*. 'Over the young idealist soul there swept a dry destroying whirlwind of thought' (p. 275). Ward seems to admire Robert Elsmere's idealism and find him an attractive personality, while also acknowledging his naïveté: though for her, he is largely a representative of the age, tossed to and fro by its tumultuous intellectual currents. As a clergyman he is, like Oliphant's characters, a social subordinate who can be easily humiliated by neglect from his betters: he is also dependent on the Squire for books to further his researches (another sign of his kinship with the woman writer, and with Ward herself, a Bodleian reader at a time when few women held admission tickets). She defends him from the charge of mere weakness in not resisting the squire's influence, even when he realized what it was doing to him. If half the world would condemn him, Ward argues, 'might not the other half plead that in every generation there is a minority of these mobile, impressionable, defenceless natures, who are ultimately at the mercy (shall we say?) of truth; and that, in fact, it is from this minority that all human advance comes?' (p. 315). For Elsmere himself, however, these crisis weeks in his life are marked 'by a constantly increasing sense of oppression, of closing avenues and narrowing alternatives', a labyrinthine shrinking reminiscent of Mr Casaubon's world in *Middlemarch* (p. 315). Elsmere becomes a moral crusader, but ultimately a martyr who dies of physical exhaustion, survived by his strong wife. Symbolically, the traditional, conservative church has triumphed, but Elsmere represents a far more dynamic movement with wide social and educational repercussions. There is no doubt where Ward's own sympathies lie.

Many of her heroes after Elsmere occupy a position more like Catherine's: rigidly wedded to tradition and their own personal past, prepared even to sacrifice their own happiness for the sake of a larger ideal. The heroines, meanwhile, become more like Catherine's younger sister Rose, a talented violinist desperate to escape from the cramping conditions of home, emotional and turbulent as the age, and fatally attracted to a dry, donnish man, who partly returns her feelings, but is unable to show it. Ward repeatedly explores the ideological and emotional struggle between a man and a woman, who love and fight each other until the conclusion of the novel, when the battle is ended either by death or by exhausted reconciliation. In this she is both Victorian and modern, continuing the pattern established by George Eliot (for example in the struggles between Dorothea and Casaubon, or Tom and Maggie Tulliver), and anticipating that of Lawrence in his mature novels, though with less sexual openness. Nevertheless, Ward, more than Yonge, Linton or Oliphant, or indeed many of the other Victorian novelists, shows that straightforward sexual attraction is an important element in her characters' lives – in the form of a crucial look or an electrifying touch. Her moments of passion are usually brief, slightly shocking (especially to the woman) and exciting: her characters take a long time to confront them and accept their implications. In many cases, moreover, this attraction runs counter to their religious affiliations, and forces them to re-examine their whole way of life. Love, for Ward, is a revolutionizing experience, which marks a character's ability, or lack of it, to face a full panoply of human responsibilities: hence its inseparability from politics and religion, which always figure as a type of passion in Ward's novels. 'I am so made that I cannot picture a human being's development without wanting to know the whole, his religion as well as his business, his thoughts as well as his actions,' Ward admitted in her preface to *David Grieve*.[38]

In *Helbeck of Bannisdale*, the roles of Catherine and Robert Elsmere are reversed, in that all the stubbornness of tradition is given to the man, and the fiery rebellion to the woman, though Laura, like Catherine, is strongly influenced by her father (in this case, a freethinker), while Alan is surrounded by shadowy female figures, nuns and his sister Augustina. A considerable age-gap between the two also heightens the father–daughter feeling about the relationship, which may have been the result of Ward's relationship to her own father, a Catholic convert. Ward's couples have a habit of drifting in and out of engagements, their wedding plans off and on, as their emotions fluctuate – almost like her own father's off–on relationship with Catholicism, and another aspect of the general philosophical turbulence of her novels. Despite its title, *Helbeck of Bannisdale* is essentially the story of its heroine, Laura Fountain, and Alan remains more in the background as a man tortured by his attraction to an alien spirit, himself constitutionally monkish and devout, while his religion tries to undermine his understanding of women. Ward's novels, more than those of her anti-feminist predecessors, set the male world further apart from the female, and make the passage from one to the other a crucial struggle for both sexes.

In *Marcella*, Ward moved towards a more standardized kind of masculinity, to which she remained committed for the rest of her career as a novelist. In chapter 5, Aldous Raeburn looks over the central plain of England – 'symbolic, all of it, to an English eye' – and soaks up a deep sense of history. 'He had seldom stood on this high point, in such an evening calm, without the expansion in him of all that was most manly, most English, most strenuous' (p. 43). From now on, manliness, for Ward, is inseparable from Englishness, and her upper-class heroes quiver with the sense of responsibility and history transferred to them by land ownership: an area of England dependent for its future wellbeing, as Ward puts it, 'upon his one man's brain and conscience, the degree of his mental and moral capacity' (p. 44). Although a woman can share in this, she never feels it as her own special responsibility, and thus 'manliness' breathes a charm for Ward that 'womanliness' fails to echo. Whereas 'manliness', for her, implies steady and masterful control of an area of England and all the people who live in it, 'womanliness' tends to suggest spasms of feeling and sympathy – as when Marcella, in *Sir George Tressady*, swoops down on a child injured in a road accident and hurries her into hospital.

Conscious of conservatism's limitations, however, Ward ensures that Raeburn is exposed to socialism, through his college friend Edward Hallin, whose 'slight figure and fair head', his 'eager slightly parted mouth' and weak health make him a womanish contrast to the more conventionally manly Raeburn, 'a true son of his fathers'

(p. 45). Womanliness, as so often with Ward, is associated with passionate idealism of a self-destructive kind. Hallin ultimately burns himself out, as Elsmere does and Laura, though he is reborn, in name at least, as the son of Aldous and Marcella. Between them, Marcella and Hallin humanize Raeburn, who is otherwise inclined to be reserved and fastidious. She appeals to the strain of poetry and fidelity in him, yet in reality, as Ward notes, 'a man like Aldous Raeburn is born to be the judge and touchstone of natures like Marcella Boyce' (p. 49). In the first flowering of their relationship, the language of command and obedience reinforces this sense that Raeburn is essentially Marcella's master; and even when they reach a maturer understanding of their relationship, Raeburn remains in command, with a reliable judgement and superior knowledge of the world. When another man, Harry Wharton, appears on the scene, as a possible rival, Raeburn stands 'upright, with his back to the hearth, a strong, capable, frowning Englishman, very much on his dignity. Such a moment', quavers Ward admiringly, 'must surely have become him in the eyes of a girl that loved him' (p. 186). The fact that Marcella is for the time being unimpressed, proves that she is not yet ready to marry him.

Ward bolsters her heroes' masculinity by contrasting them with feebler, more mercurial examples of the species. Hallin has the sensitivity, but not the physique; while Harry Wharton (now unfortunately a name associated with Billy Bunter) is too gushing, relaxed and self-confident. Masculinity, for Ward, is always combined with a degree of reticence about feelings and shyness with women: to be too at home with the opposite sex seems to suggest that a man is himself lacking in true manly reserve, and those familiar with Ward's usual danger signals quickly sense that something is seriously wrong with Wharton, when he says, for example, 'I *must* have enough sugar in my tea!' (p. 143) or 'I *love* this dilapidation' when he is being shown the disused library at Mellor, the Boyces' country house (p. 161). His manner towards Marcella is too direct, too flattering and personal; he makes love to her when she is engaged to Raeburn, and kisses her in a moment of faintness, when she is too weak to resist. Symbolically, 'a piece of maidenhair' falls from her dress when the forbidden kiss is over (p. 225). Morally and emotionally unstable, Wharton likes to be on the winning side, and finally marries Lady Selina Farrell, a thirty-five-year-old heiress whose father is a Conservative; having by then sunk himself in gambling, and accepted a bribe to discourage, through his influence with a newspaper, the outbreak of a strike which, as a socialist, he should have supported. The point emphasized by Ward is that Wharton has already proved his untrustworthiness in his relationship with Marcella, and what happens with the *Clarion* is just the final proof of his unmanliness. The worst that can be said of Raeburn, by contrast, is that he is too reserved and unbending. Like Yonge's Philip Morville he partially redeems himself by acquiring a new and disturbing sense of what it means to be a landowner, realizing its impact with all the freshness of a newcomer from outside the system. When Aldous Raeburn again surveys his territory in Book IV, chapter iv, his mood has changed since the parallel scene near the beginning of the novel. 'What was in Aldous's mind, as he stood with drawn brows looking out over the view which showed him most of his domain, was a sort of hot impatience of being made day by day, in a hundred foolish ways, to play at greatness' (pp. 525–6). Embarrassed by his tenants' deference, and by all the 'small old-world pomps and feudalisms of his own existence', Aldous 'constantly felt himself absurd' (p. 526). Lest this feeling should go too far, however, Ward counterbalances it with a 'tyrannous sense of obligation, which kept him to his place and his work'.

In Ward's world, an honourable man like Aldous Raeburn has less to learn than a tempestuous woman like Marcella. His lesson is largely one of increased self-awareness, rather than any radical change of direction, and the continuing work on softening his manner is performed by Marcella after their marriage. In her later novels, Ward remains attached to her ideal of upper-class, upright English masculinity, and distrusts not so much emotional turbulence in a man, as the outward expression of it, much as her uncle, Matthew Arnold, distrusted emotional exhibitionism in literature. In *The Coryston Family* (1913), socialism is again associated with failed masculinity, in the figure of Lady Coryston's eldest son, Corry, who is volatile, unstable, and, like Wharton, dominated by a strong mother. Ward's anti-feminism repeatedly leads her to link socialism with strong-minded mothers and somewhat emasculated men, fair-haired and puckish; while her model men are usually dark, reserved, and influenced either by their grandfathers (as Guy Morville was) or by college friends who offer complementary qualities to counterbalance the hero's. Ward is more aware than the other novelists of the importance of male camaraderie, and able to trace the boyish evolution of friendships made at Oxford or Cambridge. In *The Coryston Family*, however, Ward allows her heroine to dismiss her aristocratic neighbour, Edward Newbury, as a husband, and marry the librarian, who is more flexible on social and political issues. Marcia herself is torn between the desire to be dominated (which Ward sees as being a key factor in the female psyche, though one that women themselves have enormous difficulty in accepting), and a determination not to be her husband's slave: a dilemma similar to Marcella's. Always conscious of her unsatisfactory schooling, Ward makes Marcia thrill to Edward's superior knowledge; masochistically, she is also attracted by his ability to refuse her what she wants – in this case, permission for a divorced woman, Mrs Betts, to live with her new husband on the Newbury estate. 'It brought home to her once more that touch of inaccessible strength, of mysterious command in Newbury, which from the beginning had both teased and won her.'[39]

Ward shows her heroines being alternately repelled and attracted by the most commanding form of masculinity: that of a man with position, wealth and political experience behind him, especially if the man is in some specific way placed in authority over the woman, as happens in *Delia Blanchflower* (1915). Before meeting Delia, the pro-suffragist heroine, whose guardian he becomes, Mark Winnington talks to a Swedish feminist, who raises his consciousness about women's issues, and leaves him torn between residual sympathy and an old-fashioned preference for vulnerable femininity. As a governess in his Tyrolese hotel comments, on his behaviour towards women: 'He treats them like princesses, and yet he makes them learn', a comment which 'very fairly expressed the mixture of something courtly with something masterful in the Englishman's manner' (p. 16). The rest of the novel is a series of struggles between Delia and Mark, as she continues fighting for the vote (encouraged by her activist chaperone, Gertrude Marvell), and coping with her new position as her father's heir, and owner of his large country house. Delia, like many other Ward protagonists, finds herself caught at the crossroads between Victorian tradition (landowning and responsibility to tenants) and the new challenges, especially for women, of the dawning twentieth century. Even Mark Winnington confesses to having an open mind on the suffrage question, though he is opposed to violence, and thinks too much importance is attached to the vote. When Mark's wrist is hurt by a flying fragment of bottle at a suffrage meeting, Delia uses her handkerchief as a bandage, and notices his wrist – 'brown and spare and powerful, like the rest of him' (p. 178). Their roles are reversed when she later slips on a step, and Mark saves her from falling (p. 205), and again, when her arm is injured, and Mark gets her away in a car. 'Was such a form made for sordid violence and strife?' Mark asks, with Delia leaning faintly against him (p. 348). Acknowledging that the new century has brought an 'imperious call to women' (p. 411), Ward suggests, through Mark, that they find valuable work in the community and in their own households, rather than through the vote: discrediting the suffrage campaign when Gertrude Marvell burns down a neighbouring country house, killing herself and a crippled child in the process. Ward is confident that however complex and challenging the new situation for women, the old attraction between a strong, protecting man and a 'childish' and beautiful woman will make all come right between them, and quietly diminish the woman's interest in political campaigning. Less densely argued than her earlier novels, especially *Robert Elsmere* and *Marcella*, *Delia Blanchflower* has more recourse to stirring rhetoric about the glories of England and the Empire, and women's work at home.

Before Ward's heroes arrived on the scene, the anti-feminist novelist's man was rarely strong, and more likely to experience a woman's disadvantages in pursuing his career, or winning his way towards a happy marriage: the man's main object in most of these novels, as much as the woman's. In *The Heir of Redclyffe*, the heroes seek women – first Mrs Edmonstone and then Amy – as their mentors, Guy's moral strength passing into his wife after his death; while his one dramatic act of boys' heroism – his rescue of the shipwrecked sailors – stands out as an isolated episode in the long series of domestic misunderstandings and self-communings which make up the main body of the novel. For Yonge, acts of 'manly dash' take place on the high seas or in the Antipodes; the more regular kind of heroism consists of continuous self-regulation and restraint, as it frequently does for Ward, and before her, for George Eliot. Although the Rochester model thrilled Ward and Oliphant, their heroes are more closely related to Adam Bede and Tertius Lydgate: men who experience disappointment, either in their relations with a small community, or in their plans to fall in love and marry. Like George Eliot, Ward and Oliphant, and to some extent Yonge and Linton, see their male characters as being trapped and frustrated in situations from which they can be rescued only by the love of a good woman.

Between Yonge and Ward, however, considerable ground was

covered. Whereas Yonge's heroes live in drawing-rooms, lie on sofas, suffer swingeing headaches, and go to church, their heroic life behind them, and their present existence very similar to a middle-class woman's, Ward's spend only a small part of their day with women, and devote most of their energies to social or political action. At the same time, she returns to a more old-fashioned pattern in the social settings of her novels, glorifying the male of the English upper classes for his breeding and self-restraint, his essential 'gentlemanliness', which was so important to Trollope, and contrasting him with the plausible, fast-talking activist whose antecedents are not quite as they should be. Linton's men add little to the development of the woman's hero, while Oliphant's are firmly mired in the petty squabbles of Carlingford, with only tangential involvement in the sensational subplot of passion and intrigue. Her men are as emotional and self-divided as her women, without the continuous support a woman can normally expect from her family. Even Ward suggests that apparently strong men can be demoralized by failure with women, or ossified into prigs or monks by too stern a commitment to unbending ideals.

Oliphant's letters show that she watched her sons growing up with a mixture of anxiety and incredulity. 'Cecco as a man continues to be a constant wonder and amusement to me,' she wrote of her youngest, who was then nineteen.[40] When both her sons were at Oxford, she moved house for a while to keep an eye on them, like Ruskin's mother. 'I fancy that women are stronger than men after they get over their danger,' she told Principal Tulloch.[41] All four writers in this study shared a sense of the peculiar anxieties of masculinity: in particular the conflict between a man's outward appearance of calm and control, and his inner sense of inadequacy and powerlessness – whether against blackmail, false rumours, or rivals in love. The involvement of men in sensational blackmail plots (as in *Grasp Your Nettle*) or the more prosaic scandal-mongering plots (as in *The Perpetual Curate*) exposes their basic vulnerability, and shows how difficult it is for them to prove their innocence. The fact that men are also driven to forgery and deception is a sign of their authors' disbelief in muscular heroism. Their men are more like women in their attempts to struggle free of cramping situations: Yonge's Philip Morville, for example, paying heavily for his failure to inform Laura's parents of their unofficial engagement, which he begs his fiancée to keep secret; while Oliphant's Mr May, in *Phoebe Junior*, feels overwhelmed by responsibility for his large family of children, and his growing debts.

For most of the women in this group the problem of male 'otherness' is tackled by turning men's difficulties into variations on women's, and containing the threat of male sexuality, either by sudden death, or through a rhetoric of idealized romanticism which focuses on the protecting role of masculinity. Their ideal heroes are men of feeling and conscience, with perhaps a single act of bravery safely behind them, or a lifetime of political leadership or estate management ahead, rooting them firmly in the power structure of English society. The notion of male superiority, in all except Oliphant, is based on faith in man's larger experience of life, natural qualities of leadership, and supposedly greater emotional stability, though the events of the novels often disprove many of these notional suppositions. Their attempt to uphold the dignity of masculinity is generally a failure, and the woman's personal or political views tend to be expressed with more passion and commitment.

What seems most inconsistent and surprising about the Victorian anti-feminist women novelists' portrayal of men is their failure to glorify them as the natural leaders of society and superior guides within the family. Yonge's heroes are often invalids, Oliphant's are weak and confused, Linton's are caricatures, and Ward's, though the strongest, are stiff and formal, needing the humanizing touch of a woman to prove her point that the sexes are made for one another and cannot survive successfully on their own. There may be several reasons for this failure of the positive male image, beginning with the absence of strong examples in their own families. Possibly, too, they believed that women were genuinely strengthened by family and domestic trials, while men tended to remain untested, except by untypical adventures in the external world. Their women characters tend to have purer and stronger motives for good behaviour, and are less confused by conflicting pulls of ambition and sexuality. Finally, the novelists seem to have found it difficult to move away from their main theme of courtship and marriage, their preoccupations with women's anxieties: this may have made their male characters turn out more like women, and suffer similar frustrations in their attempts to achieve emotional fulfilment. In any case, all four novelists were fully committed to ideals of self-restraint for men as well as women, and therefore to the domestic setting as a site for heroism: a factor that again merges together male and female experience. In their journalism, the situation was different. Less distracted by the details of daily living, they argued their case against women's advancement and in favour of male leadership more confidently, as the next chapter will show.

5
Work that Influences the World: Journalism

In chapter 3 of Charlotte Yonge's novel *The Clever Woman of the Family*, the heroine, Rachel Curtis, writes an article on 'Curatolatry' (curate worship), which she intends as 'the beginning of a series, exposing the fallacies of woman's life as at present conducted' (p. 51), thus anticipating by three years the launch of Eliza Lynn Linton's similar, and notorious, 'Girl of the Period' series in the *Saturday Review*. The difference is that Rachel means her articles to be pro-feminist, while attacking the emptiness and foolishness of many women's lives as they were forced to live them, without meaningful employment. She shows the article to her friend Ermine Williams, who is later revealed to be a very different kind of journalist, the mysterious 'Invalid' of the *Traveller's Magazine*. While the editor is away, he leaves the 'Invalid' in charge, though she keeps back some letters for him to answer because her own hand 'betrays womanhood' (p. 95). When Colonel Keith admires her important position, she tells him, in a significant sentence: 'If you had been in England all this time, you would see how easy the step is into the literary world.' Charlotte Yonge appears to have found it so. She was the editor of the *Monthly Packet* before she was quite thirty, and remained at the helm until 1890, when a change of approach was somewhat overdue. Margaret Oliphant was similarly a mainstay of *Blackwood's Edinburgh Magazine*, to which she contributed serial stories, book reviews and articles on major issues of the day; finally writing a two-volume history of the Blackwood dynasty and publishing house, which stresses the patriarchal and fraternal organization of a business enterprise which largely excluded women.[1] Whether they acknowledged it or not, Victorian women who wrote for the major periodicals were in a minority among the journalists of their day, and were uniquely positioned to speak out (if they wished) on the role of their sex.

Histories of the Victorian periodical press repeatedly emphasize its masculine nature and role in a male clubland of Oxford and

Cambridge colleges, politics, the church, and public life. John Gross's book title *The Rise and Fall of the Man of Letters: Aspects of English Literary Life since 1800* (1969) is no accident, since the key figures of his survey are G.H. Lewes, R.H. Hutton, Walter Bagehot and Leslie Stephen: Eliza Linton and Margaret Oliphant, certainly widely read and prolific journalists writing during the years covered by Gross's book, are missing from the index.[2] Oliphant herself, in her history of the Blackwoods, expands on the personalities of John Gibson Lockhart, John Wilson, James Hogg and William Maginn, from the Magazine's early days, and admits: 'I find few women's names among this large and changing group.'[3] As late as 1855, after the heyday of this notorious constellation, she referred to *Blackwood's* as 'your most manly and masculine of Magazines', making timid proposals to her editor whenever she wanted to write on something outside the usual 'feminine' range. Harriet Martineau, as leader-writer for the *Daily News* and a regular contributor to the *Edinburgh Review* in the 1850s and 1860s, was unusual in tackling heavy political subjects, such as the American Civil War, the Crimean War, and the anti-slavery campaign, at a time when women were more likely to write the lighter book reviews and frothy society articles. Even more unusual was Christian Isobel Johnstone (1781–1857), who was first sub-editor (1832–4) and then co-proprietor of *Tait's Edinburgh Magazine* (1834–46), besides being a regular contributor of review articles. But women like Mrs Johnstone were rare. Those who made it to the top earlier in the century either remained concealed by the widespread practice of anonymity, or were fêted as stars, as happened to Maria Jane Jewsbury (1800–33), elder sister of Geraldine (also a journalist) and a lead contributor to the *Athenaeum*. Either way, their careers were untypical of the pattern followed by their male contemporaries, who often formed a solid, clubbable phalanx around their London or Edinburgh offices. If not as reticent and domesticated as Yonge's 'Invalid', women were more likely to write from homes outside London (Harriet Martineau mailed her articles down from the Lake District, and Margaret Oliphant hers from Windsor; Elizabeth Gaskell wrote in Manchester for Dickens's *Household Words*), and to socialize less with groups of professionals, especially if they were married and tied to family responsibilities.

Many women writers, however, became involved in journalism at its high point in the century, which critics agree to be around 1850. According to John Gross, 'in the 1850s the whole tempo of journalism accelerated sharply', with the *Saturday Review* marking most decisively the new era (pp. 62–3). Founded in 1855, the *Saturday* planned to concern itself less with news than with comments and criticisms, and was addressed to 'the educated mind of the country, and to serious, thoughtful men of all schools, classes, and principles, not so much in the spirit of party as in the more philosophic attitude of mutual counsel and friendly conflict of opinions'.[4] In its review of 'Current Criticism' in October 1858, the *Saturday* argued that writers must lead a particular kind of life suited to their work; specifically, the critic 'should be in some sort of relation with the classes who govern, or assist in governing, the country'.[5] Far from being neutral, however, the critics of the *Saturday Review* soon gained a reputation for being 'Saturday Revilers', anti-feminist 'snarlers', 'scorpions' and 'scourgers'. According to Merle Bevington, who made a close study of the *Saturday*, it 'assumed as a fact that women were inferior to men', asserting that women had never reached the first rank in literature or the arts.[6] By the time she began her association with the *Saturday*, in 1866, Eliza Linton had already been writing anti-feminist articles in other journals, such as the *London Review*: she was therefore in sympathy with the overall tone of the *Saturday*, and the policy of its editor, John Douglas Cook, to increase the excitement by setting 'woman against woman, and to see who would make the best fight of it'.[7] Linton thus found her way into a prominent place as a journalist by co-operating with a specific anti-feminist programme: one, however, that she had already anticipated and begun to practise.

Charlotte Yonge's entry into journalism appeared to be at the opposite end of the spectrum, with women and girls targeted as a special constituency of readers who needed their own journal. When she launched the *Monthly Packet* in January 1851, Yonge stated in her editorial introduction that the magazine was meant to help girls who had left school and not yet married to form their characters, and make them steadfast daughters of the Church of England. The medium of instruction was mostly to be stories, scenes from history, exemplary conversations, and articles on missionary work. A series of dialogues between three girls all baptized on the same day, and now preparing for confirmation, explored the temptations of the flesh and the world in terms that were not too shocking, and to which the average middle-class girl could relate. Journalism of this kind was clearly uncontroversial, and women had been associated with the production of women's magazines, as Alison Adburgham has shown, since the eighteenth century.[8] What was far more problematic was the entry of women into mainstream literary and political journalism. As late as 1898, Arnold Bennett was advising aspiring women journalists against writing for the politico-literary weeklies, such as the *Saturday Review*, *Speaker* and *Spectator*. 'They are fastidious; they demand advanced technique, and moreover they touch subjects with which women are not often conversant.' He also warned women off the *Nineteenth Century*, *Fortnightly* and *Contemporary Reviews*, on the grounds that they require 'expert knowledge, scholarship, or high technique'. *Blackwood's*, *Macmillan's*, the *Cornhill* and *Longman's* he felt were more suitable, though he warned all women against treating journalism as a game, and sending in badly spelt slipshod articles. He felt that women journalists as a class were 'unreliable', because they were insufficiently businesslike and attentive to detail. Lack of restraint was another problem: he recommended would-be women journalists to practise on a manageable subject – for example, 'an exposure of the New Woman'.[9]

Arnold Bennett's advice notwithstanding, by 1898 there had been several distinguished women contributors to the journals and periodicals he advised them to avoid. Besides Harriet Martineau, a regular contributor to the *Edinburgh Review* and *Daily News* in the 1850s and 1860s, women journalists of the mid-nineteenth century included Marian Evans in the *Westminster Review*, Elizabeth Rigby, the future Lady Eastlake, in the *Quarterly*, Anne Mozley in *Blackwood's*, Anna Jameson in the *Edinburgh*, Frances Power Cobbe in the *Fortnightly*, Dinah Mulock in the *Contemporary Review* and *Macmillan's*, and Caroline Norton in the *Edinburgh*, *Macmillan's* and *New Monthly Magazines*. Certainly, most wrote on subjects considered appropriate for women, such as women's novels, society, art, travel, the lighter religious matters, and those concerning the changing position of women in public life. Here, women journalists lined up on either side of the debate, not necessarily assuming that because they had a voice in the forum, others should enjoy the same opportunities to express their opinions. The practice of anonymity clearly made it possible for women contributors to maintain a lofty distance, and regard themselves as participating in a wider debate. In theorizing the periodical, Margaret Beetham, who sees the Victorian journal as involved in a 'process of negotiation and struggle over meaning', argues that despite its open-endedness and heterogeneity, it is formally 'more likely to be conservative and repressive rather than disruptive and liberating'.[10] Women adapted themselves rapidly to the genre, and, being used to the private role of instructing the children and poor, took up the magisterial tones of the reviewer with little apparent difficulty. Writing even occasional articles for a national periodical was an opportunity for them to express an opinion that perhaps their own family circle might normally disregard. The 1881 Census recorded the existence of fifteen women 'reporters', besides 452 female 'Authors, Editors, and Writers',[11] evidence that women were also beginning to broach the less feminine, more physically active aspects of professional journalism. This chapter will focus on two of the most prolific, Linton and Oliphant.

ELIZA LYNN LINTON AND THE WILD WOMEN

The most extensive fictional examination of women's role in journalism in the mid-nineteenth century occurs in Eliza Lynn Linton's *Sowing the Wind* (1867), a thinly-disguised account of her own work for John Douglas Cook on the *Morning Chronicle*, but also, in the character of Jane Osborn, a brusque self-caricature. Early in the novel, Jane, the only daughter of a doctor's widow who is too ineffectual to provide for them, sends a 'crude but vigorous article' to the *Comet* newspaper, accompanied by an apologetic letter of explanation saying she 'must fight her way as if she was a man, and put aside all false shame'.[12] Anticipating Arnold Bennett's complaints about women journalists, Smith, the editor of the *Comet*, grumbles about taking women into the office: 'Their two worst faults are looseness and partiality; and their most annoying, the uncertainty of their work and their want of reliable power' (vol. I, p. 26). Jane, however, is so good at her job that she deputizes for the sub-editor when he goes on holiday, and unlike the working heroines of so many Victorian novels, is not rescued from her professional duties by marriage, though she only narrowly escapes having to adopt a baby. Relieved that her more feminine cousin Isola, the baby's aunt, is able to take him, Jane rushes off to 'do what your soft women cannot do', to write a leader for a daily newspaper:

> 'Ah, you may talk as you like, Isola! – babies, and love, and the graces and prettinesses are all very fine, I dare say, but give me the real solid pleasure of work – a man's work – work that influences the world – work that is power! To sit behind the scenes and pull the strings – to know that what one says as We in the "Comet" is taken among thinking men as a new gospel, when if

one had said it as I, Jane Osborn, it would have been sneered at as woman's babble – to feel that strange thrill of secret mental power – no, I would not give up that for all the happiness of your so called womanly women!' (vol. III, pp. 29–30)

As an unequivocal declaration of a woman's pleasure in active, influential work, Jane's outburst is heartfelt and powerful: all the more so in view of Isola's miserable marriage to a fastidious and jealous husband who tries to murder his own nephew. For all her commitment to the ideal of marriage (at least for other people), Eliza Lynn Linton frequently marries her patient and feminine heroines to selfish husbands who will scarcely let them breathe without criticism; whereas her women who work are happy, vigorous and healthy. Jane's pleasure in her work is both intellectual and a celebration of her power over public, specifically male, opinion. She recognizes that the name of the newspaper gives her the authority she would lack as a private woman.

Known in the office as 'Mr Jane' or 'Mr John', Linton's woman journalist has, however, one fatal weakness: not so much her inability to love (she is emotionally involved with Harvey Wyndham, the sub-editor), as her failure to *be* loved. Once Harvey marries someone else, Jane 'aged and hardened till all womanhood seemed rasped out of her' (vol. III, p. 285). She becomes a standing institution in the *Comet* offices, exciting 'no more sensation among the boys and men of that establishment than if she had been an office boy herself'. She ends her days writing virulent articles like Linton's own, content to 'make women generally understand that they were slaves and idiots' (pp. 285–6). Indeed, in the novel itself she functions largely on the level of caricature, muscling her way in and out of rooms, shattering her mother's nerves, telling Isola to bestir herself and do something useful, and vigorously rubbing her nose in a brisk, unfeminine gesture. Jane is both a joke and a heroine, without the redeeming gentleness of Perdita Winstanley in *The Rebel of the Family*, but she reveals Linton's self-division over her choice of career. Only by making Jane into a mannish hoyden entirely without the social graces can Linton admit that women may earn a living as professional journalists, offering herself, in the process, as an Aunt Sally for public amusement. Yet the only other female role-models in the novel are those of vapid heiress, dying hysterical pregnant woman, submissive wife, or foolish widow. Jane, at least, is the strongest, and the only woman able to survive on her own without resorting to marriage.

As a woman who enjoyed her work and had found marriage a failure, Linton was well placed to write a serious recommendation of the professional life for her own sex. She discovered that she could write as prolifically as any man, that her work was accepted in the top newspapers and journals, that she could establish herself as a novelist simply by going to London and studying in the British Museum, and that neither her health nor her reputation suffered as the result of her lifestyle. Why, then, was she so anxious to prevent other women from following her example, and why is her journalism so much more overtly anti-feminist than her fiction, which repeatedly offers ambiguous pictures of marriage and femininity? Why, too, did she go on maintaining an untenable position, stubbornly reiterating views that her own experience, and that of her closest friends, had shown to be unjustified or unfair? Linton's role in the evolution of the woman journalist remains crucial, if historically mystifying, and deserves careful scrutiny in the context of the Victorian anti-feminist debate.

Reviewing John Stuart Mill's *Subjection of Women* for *Blackwood's* in 1869, the year of its publication, Anne Mozley noted that many clever women were disparaging about their own sex. She attributed their attitude to 'an admission on their own part of a need of masculine support in their higher efforts'.[13] In other words, women's anti-feminism seemed to her rooted in insecurity and male dependency. Eliza Lynn Linton's anti-feminism is also partly attributable to similar tendencies, though there have been many other explanations of her virulent opposition to women's emergence from the home into a more public, active sphere. Nancy Fix Anderson sees the early death of Linton's mother as having a crucial psychological effect, making her feel let down and abandoned by her own sex;[14] a combination of male-identification and maternal/lesbian relationships with younger women building on this childhood sense of female betrayal. On this basis, her desire to keep mothers by their children's cradles may derive from a thwarted need to keep her own mother by her cradle; and her unsuccessful attempts to mother William J. Linton's motherless children may have reinforced her misgivings about the feasibility or even durability of motherhood: hence her determination to insist on its importance, in increasingly strident and emotional articles.

Motherhood was, in fact, probably the most emotive aspect of womanhood for Linton, as it was for Margaret Oliphant, except that they approached it from different angles. Whereas Oliphant had been a mother of a thriving family, and lost them all, Linton had no children of her own, and made several fleeting attempts to 'adopt' other people's. Similarly, whereas Oliphant had had a good and close relationship with her mother, Linton had lost hers as a baby. In *Sowing the Wind*, the two heroines, Isola and Jane, find themselves responsible for an orphaned baby boy, whom Jane dreads having to adopt. Isola, on the other hand, gladly takes him, despite her husband's opposition; the two heroines embodying contrasting sides of Linton's frustrated longing to be part of a mother and child relationship, and her relish of independent work and freedom. In *Grasp Your Nettle*, however, Aura Escott both acquires adopted daughters and has children of her own, devoting herself entirely to their welfare. Yet if adoption and biological motherhood are recurrent themes in Linton's novels, so is the character of the foolish middle-aged mother of grown-up daughters, such as Mrs Winstanley in *The Rebel*, Mrs Escott, and Mrs Osborn, Jane's mother in *Sowing the Wind*. Ironically, Linton implies that women who do devote themselves wholeheartedly to their children, especially daughters, and lose contact with the world of employment, degenerate into embarrassing simpletons, concerned only that their daughters make socially advantageous marriages. Nevertheless, Linton concludes in one of her later periodical writings, '"The Wild Women" as Politicians', 'be it pleasant or unpleasant', it is 'an absolute truth – the *raison d'être* of a woman is maternity. For this and this alone nature has differentiated her from man, and built her up all by all, and organ by organ.' Symbolically, for her, 'the cradle lies across the door of the polling-booth and bars the way to the senate'.[15] The more she herself had failed in achieving the apparent *raison d'être* of her sex, the more loudly she insisted on it as essential to other women, herself remaining an unacknowledged exception to the rule.

Linton's views on women's emancipation changed only slightly between the 1850s and 1890s, and chiefly on the question of the suffrage. In 1870, writing for *Macmillan's*, she reviews 'the late remarkable outbreak of women against the restrictions under which they have hitherto lived', and concludes that some of their claims are in fact reasonable. Ambivalent about their first point, the cry for work, she concedes surprisingly: 'the second demand of the modern revolters is surely just – their right to the franchise'.[16] She also favoured married women's property reform, which in 1870 had been partly addressed. Her whole article is far more friendly to women's rights than most of her work, apparently recognizing that there are women like herself without family responsibilities and restrictions on their outside activities. As early as 1859, however, Linton had distrusted women's meddlesome involvement with politics, even behind the scenes. In 'Woman's Mission' for the *Saturday Review*, she imagined what would happen if politicians' wives came together and plotted a secret strategy.[17] She was terrified of women interfering in the conduct of the British Empire, and was convinced that giving women the vote would destroy the peace of the British home. In ' "The Wild Women" as Politicians', she painted an image of the French Revolution to fortify her alarmist argument:

> Women are both more extreme and more impressible than men, and the spirit which made weak girls into heroines and martyrs, honest women into yelling *tricoteuses* of these blood-stained saturnalia of '92, still exists in the sex; and among ourselves as elsewhere. (p. 81)

Women's demand for political rights she saw as being the 'most anti-Christian that can be named – the more destructive of home peace and conjugal union, of family solidarity and personal love' (p. 82), an oddly-worded protest from one who by this time was an agnostic, a separated wife, and essentially a single woman with few close family ties.

Favouring divorce reform, Linton opposed women's higher education – most notoriously in her novel *The One Too Many* (1894), where her girl graduates are pictured smoking and swearing, but also in her periodical articles such as 'The Higher Education of Woman', written for the *Fortnightly Review* in 1886. Although she always favoured work for women who were genuinely in need of it and were unlikely to marry, she assumed that the norm must be marriage and motherhood, for which an elaborate higher education, possibly damaging to the health, was largely irrelevant. But Linton went further than other propagandists for the health lobby, by insisting that individualism, fostered by university education, was a dangerous and unnecessary characteristic in women. 'Women ought to be individual, not for themselves but for others,' she explains, in an echo of Sarah Ellis's description of women as 'relative creatures'; 'and in that individualism there ought to be the injustice inseparable from devotion.' This argument lies at the heart of

Linton's objection to political rights for women. She believed that motherhood and devotion to the family made them incurably partisan and emotional. Motherhood, for her, cancelled out the individual's claim for her own rights and privileges. 'The ordinary woman cannot be got to see', she complained, 'that she is not only herself but also a member of society and part of an organization; and that she owes, as a duty to the community, the subordination of her individualism to that organization.'[18]

Again, this was an odd and inconsistent stance for someone as individual as Linton to take, particularly as her novels reveal an underlying contempt for weak, submissive women such as Moira in *The One Too Many*. Women like Moira, and even the more worthy Isola in *Sowing*, allow selfish and sadistic men to pursue their outrageous intentions unchallenged. Indeed Linton's comments on marriage, both within her novels and in journal articles, show that she was under no illusions about its dangers and disappointments for women, as she knew herself from her own unsuccessful marriage to Linton. In 'Our Civilization', a bitter survey of contemporary life, written for the *Cornhill* in 1873, Linton criticizes the lavish display common at funerals and especially weddings. 'Marriage being at the best but a lottery,' she adds, 'with more blanks than prizes, it seems a little unnecessary to call the world to take note how the drawing is begun.' More grotesquely, she fulminates against those who marry without due regard for the risk of inherited diseases:

> Women sold for a settlement, and men selling themselves for a fortune; the scrofulous mated with the insane, and neither the mental nor the moral development of the family taken into account as a basis of calculation for the future.[19]

Sounding like a crude summary of an Ibsen play, or of Max Nordau's argument in *Degeneration* (1895), Linton's tirade exposes a subversive protest against what she elsewhere assumes to be women's normal destiny, marriage. Read carefully, her articles reveal an undercurrent of distaste for the very institutions she recommends her sex to enter unquestioningly. Domestic life itself she had little reason to exalt; nor does she do so in her novels, where her heroines are bored and frustrated unless they go out to work, or can lose themselves in motherhood. In an article for *Temple Bar* in 1862, she gives a negative picture of English home life as dull and empty.

'I do not believe in happy homes,' she confesses flatly; 'why, then, swear that the mirage is living water?'[20]

Why indeed? Yet Linton continued to urge women back into the home, and to assume that most women were mothers with all-encompassing and happy domestic responsibilities. Her views hardened in the 1890s, when it was clear that women had advanced on several key fronts: higher education, the widening of employment opportunities, married women's property ownership, and improved access to divorce. Linton rarely discusses these issues in any detail, but clings on to a handful of reiterated principles: that women are designed by nature for motherhood, that they must retain their 'sweetness' and femininity (as men must their strength and masculinity), and that they must eschew anything that will blur the distinction between the sexes. There are several apparent explanations for Linton's tenacity in the face of obvious failure. The simplest is her stubbornness: the common human characteristic that the more one's position is undermined, the more determinedly one clings on to it, and the louder one shouts. Another, going more deeply into Linton's past, is that she had herself been a loud insurgent, and before that, a self-deprecating woman along the lines she recommended to others. In *My Literary Life* she explains that in her early days in London, she was quiet and nervous:

> I was intensely shy, and the sound of my own voice frightened me. Also, I had been brought up on the old lines of childish effacement and womanly self-suppression, and taught that I ought to have no opinion of my own, or if being unfortunate enough to have one, I ought to keep it to myself, and neither talk glibly nor argue freely. (p. 36)

Yet in those days she was also a rebel against the established order, and 'despised all that was old and proved in favour of all that was new and untried' (p. 31). Linton thus reveals herself as split between womanly self-effacement, even fear of her own voice, and a desire to destroy the status quo: a split that was never healed, and which inclines her towards self-punishment in her novels and articles. Whereas in the former, her sympathy for active and independent girls is close to the surface and easily detectable, in her articles it is repeatedly driven underground or twisted into a backlash against the very freedoms she herself valued and practised. Moreover, she had always valued the approval of her father-substitute,

Walter Savage Landor, whose views on women 'were emphatically those of the old school. Women were ladies to him, and aught that touched the very fringe of their delicacy was anathema maranatha' (p. 54). The psychological configurations of Linton's past were therefore exceptionally complicated, each stage of her life adding a further layer of confusion to her sexual identity. Torn between wanting to please Landor, and rebelling against her real father, between speaking out and self-silencing, between contempt for passive, feminine women, and guilty dislike of emancipated 'masculine' ones, she took refuge in the systematic mockery of easily identifiable types, whom she continued to vilify, regardless of social change.

One of her earliest articles along this line was 'Passing Faces' in *Household Words* (1855), in which she noticed the resemblance of human faces, especially women's, to those of animals. Nancy Fix Anderson has suggested that Linton was influenced by Dickens's conservative attitudes to women, and that the 'catalyst for her conversion was her association with Charles Dickens and *Household Words*'.[21] Whether or not this was so, she was eager enough in 1855 to compare women with rabbits, lurchers, setters and cows; the 'lurcher woman' being 'the strong-visaged, strong-minded female, who wears rough coats with men's pockets and large bone buttons, and whose bonnets fling a spiteful defiance at both beauty and fashion'.[22] The notorious 'Girl of the Period' followed in 1868:

> The Girl of the Period is a creature who dyes her hair and paints her face, as the first articles of her personal religion – a creature whose sole idea of life is fun; whose sole aim is unbounded luxury; and whose dress is the chief object of such thought and intellect as she possesses.[23]

The 'G.O.P.', as she came to be called, spawning controversy, imitators, and mementoes, disturbed Linton because she saw her as the disrupter of clearly defined boundaries: those between different countries, and at home, those between respectability and what she called the 'demi-monde'. If, as Carole Pateman has argued, women are traditionally perceived as 'potential disrupters of masculine boundary systems of all sorts', the Girl of the Period was, for Linton, the epitome of this chaotic potential.[24] She was a loose cannon, rolling through society and scattering its well-ordered systems of classification, freeing other women from man-ordained roles into a life of self-indulgence and vulgarity. The G.O.P. was the natural enemy of the fair young English girl with her modest ways and deference to men, and therefore threatened to destroy the distinctive characteristics of the race: a point Linton reiterated in many of her later articles during the imperialist years.

In her criticism of the G.O.P., Linton focused largely on her dress, and her tasteless exaggeration of current fashions. 'Nothing is too extraordinary and nothing too exaggerated for her vitiated taste; and things which in themselves would be useful reforms if let alone become monstrosities worse than those which they have displaced so soon as she begins to manipulate and improve.' Worse still, the G.O.P. had placed herself beyond the pale of masculine respect, scorned all but the most mercenary of marriages, and made the English womanly ideal a thing of the past. For Linton there was no alternative to the English rose or the slang-drawling hoyden, no middle ground of independence and intelligence: a woman who held fast to her own opinions, as Linton did herself, earned her own living, and yet whose manners were something above the level of the men's locker-room. Linton's weakness, as a polemicist, was her failure, not only to accept the existence of other models, but also to look around her and develop her ideals. She reissued *The Girl of the Period* in 1883, without softening or retracting a line of what she had written fifteen years earlier: 'I think now, as I thought then, that the sphere of human action is determined by the fact of sex, and that there does exist both natural limitation and natural direction' (p. viii). Since a pamphlet of the G.O.P. essay sold forty thousand copies for one printer alone, there were clearly plenty of readers who found her attack on contemporary womanhood at least worth reading, whether or not they agreed with it; and Elizabeth Helsinger, Robin Lauterbach Sheets and William Veeder have gathered an awesome quantity of evidence that the 'G.O.P. controversy', as they call it, was 'a major cultural moment'.[25] It brought to the surface increasing tension about the behaviour of women (aired, for example, in the 'sensation novel' of the 1860s), and inspired a heated, emotional reaction from those who resented Linton's attacks on womanhood: a pattern of response that recurred over her later, less notorious articles as well.

The Girl of the Period is perhaps best viewed as another aspect of 1860s 'sensationalism': a woman such as Magdalen Vanstone in Wilkie Collins's *No Name* (1862) or Lucy Graham in Mary Braddon's *Lady Audley's Secret* (1862), who schemes for her own advancement in society, and rejects the womanly ideals of passivity and resignation.

Linton's articles reproduce the dichotomy between the pushing, aggressive woman whom she described as 'this loud and rampant modernization' (p. 9), and the quiet and modest ideal of English womanhood. Although there is no doubt that Linton truly disliked the modern woman, she fails, in her novels, to make the idealized model of the past anything more than a doormat, weakly submitting to be kept a prisoner in her own home, or to observe her husband's tastes in dress and deportment. In her articles, the good girl hovers in the background, as abstract as Wilkie Collins's description of Laura Fairlie, the pale and passive heroine of *The Woman in White*, whose meekness contrasts so vividly with the strongly delineated contours, physical and moral, of the anti-feminist Marian Halcombe. Eliza Linton herself becomes a Marian Halcombe figure: strong-jawed and contemptuous of women because she has remained vigorous when others have collapsed into nervous indecision. Linton's 'Girl of the Period' articles went on to catalogue the follies of a whole host of women, including 'Ideal Women' (who vary from country to country) and 'Little Women', where she dismisses the heroines of sensation novels as 'small-limbed yellow-headed criminals', with an 'angel's face and demon's soul' (p. 49). Besides satirizing 'Gushing Men' and other contemptible masculine types, she pitches into 'Modern Man-Haters', who are in revolt against 'the natural, the supremacy of men' (vol. II, p. 173). Her articles reveal a powerful reaction against all blurring of natural differences: feminine men coming in for as much invective as mannish women.

Linton's articles on women developed over the next twenty years after the 'G.O.P.' controversy into an apocalyptic scenario of sexual chaos. With titles such as 'The Future Supremacy of Women' (*National Review*, September 1886), 'The Threatened Abdication of Man' (*National Review*, July 1889), 'The Modern Revolt' (*Macmillan's*, December 1870), 'The Wild Women' (a series of articles in *Nineteenth Century*, 1891), and 'The Decay of Discipline' (*Temple Bar*, June 1894), Linton signalled the plunging of an ordered society into irreversible breakdown, or 'Modern Topsy-Turveydom', as she called it in an 1890 article for the *New Review*. 'Monarchy, religion, the laws, public opinion, the home, the relations between the sexes, politics, personal habits – nothing is at this moment in a state of stable equilibrium,' she proclaimed at the end of this article.[26] She came increasingly to take the side of men whose sexuality was being policed by the 'New Woman', herself sexually unstable as she oscillated between chastity and open expression of sexual feelings. By 1891, the Girl of the Period had grown into a Wild Woman, one of the 'shrieking sisterhood', whom Linton dismissed as 'excrescences of the times, products of peace and idleness'. She began to wonder if a national disaster might help: 'Who knows? Storms shake off the nobler fruit but do not always beat down the ramping weeds. Still, human nature has the trick of pulling itself right in times of stress and strain.'[27]

It was not only the 'Wild Women' themselves that Linton deplored, but also their supporters, their male and female 'Partisans', whom she attacked in a separate article of March 1892. By this time, Linton was not so much anti-feminist as anti-decadent, seeing the dissolution of sexual difference as part of a much wider programme that was rapidly undermining the moral probity of the country. Her article, which had been scanty on detail even in her calmer days, now boiled over with images of conspiracy and betrayal. The Partisans, she claimed, 'prefer emotion to reason: they champion the individual as against the law and community'; they 'eulogize and uphold the pronounced enemies of our country. They would give the keys of our foreign possessions into the hands of Russia or of France; they brand patriotism as jingoism; and they teach all who will listen to them to break the laws, to despise our national institutions, to ridicule our national traditions, to dishonour our national flag.'[28] Linton thus revives the old eighteenth-century fear (expressed by Jane West, for example) that the breakdown of separate spheres for men and women and distinct sexual characteristics will cause a similar breakdown in national differences, and facilitate the invasion of foreign states. Because the New Women and Men were anti-imperialist and pro-peace, she felt they would surrender the national identity, and all the traditions that go with it.

It is difficult to gauge the response of ordinary middle-class readers to Linton's articles, and to ascertain how far her views were accepted; but the literary response was both antagonistic and popular. Her catch-phrases caught on, and those who disagreed with her opinions were stung into defensive action. Among these was the novelist Mona Caird, who replied, in the *Nineteenth Century*, to the 'Wild Women' articles, by insisting that there was room for all types of woman, and not simply the one idealized model of whom Linton approved. She particularly attacked Linton's emphasis on maternity as the destiny of woman, besides pointing out the inconsistencies of her arguments. 'There is, according to Mrs Lynn Linton, no medium between Griselda and a sublimated Frankenstein's monster, which we have all so often heard of and seldom seen.'[29] Nancy Fix Anderson has catalogued the series of indignant responses to Linton's anti-feminist articles, showing that, if nothing else, they forced both men and women to redefine the role of women, and reconsider whether her allegations were at all just. Responses were divided, and attributed blame for women's behaviour, where it was found to be objectionable, to many different factors in their lives. Men were frequently blamed for encouraging tasteless manners in women, or else for treating them as what Linton called 'the Sacred Sex'.[30] What she failed to acknowledge was that she had led them in this direction, surrounding femininity with images of motherhood and gentleness designed to set them apart from the rough traffic of the outside world.

In fact, Linton often declared that women were morally inferior to men, as she did in *Ourselves*, a series of essays on women collected from *Routledge's Magazine* (1869), which appeared while her anonymous *Saturday Review* articles were continuing. At this stage, authorship of those articles was thought to be by a man, a fiction Linton fostered by referring, in the preface to *Ourselves*, to a 'literary friend of ours' who was bludgeoning women for their own good in the *Saturday*. Linton thus enjoyed the privilege of castigating women both in her own name and anonymously, as a man and as a woman: though there is little difference in the resulting approach. In her book, Linton began by attacking the 'Angel in the House', and women's idea of their own quasi-sacredness; she then exposed their emotional confusion, arguing that women find it particularly difficult to achieve moderation of temper and behaviour. She felt they needed the kind of self-restraint men practised:

> But women get so 'mixed up' by emotion, desperation, passion, and defiance, that no after-restraint is possible when once the curb is slackened; so that, unless they are held in subjection by the fear of God, the world, or the devil, they go headlong to destruction, and neither reason nor philosophy touches them.[31]

This is typical of Linton's approach to women's issues: a sweeping generalization about the emotional make-up of women, which takes no account of individual differences or social change. Despite passing references to higher education, the suffrage and employment, Linton makes no attempt to investigate what these changes meant to the next generation of young women with time on their hands and intellectual ambitions. In *Ourselves* and elsewhere, Linton continued to insist that women *had* jobs already: 'what exquisite beauty and improvement, through the aid of science, might not an intelligent woman incorporate into the management of her house and children!' (p. 70). Those who still wanted to do something different might, she insisted; only their own 'supineness' kept them bound (p. 76). Women who were prepared to stay quietly at home and do what she advised she nicknamed 'Doves': a term implying good-natured contempt on Linton's part, and certainly a lack of originality.[32]

Linton's articles are mostly vituperative and negative. She clearly preferred attacking what was wrong with women to suggesting popular alternatives, other than the time-worn images of the gentle mother and the sweet, home-loving English girl. Perhaps the possibility of a positive image became remote to her, as the century veered towards decadence and increased freedom for both sexes: at any rate, Linton turned towards the past for her ideals, writing a series of articles on the women of Greece, Rome and the Middle Ages. Ancient Greece strongly appealed to her as a period of marked sexual differentiation and graceful manners. 'The men were essentially virile, yet not rude; the women were essentially feminine, yet not weak.' In a companion article she praised Iphigeneia as the epitome of female virtue: 'where can we find anything more pure, more beautiful, more honourable to the ideal of womanhood?' Omitting to see the implications of this – that heroic sacrifice like Iphigeneia's leads to death – Linton argued that woman's virtues 'have ever been those of the stiller, gentler, more patient and more self-sacrificing kind'.[33] Yet in her second novel, *Amymone* (1848), she had praised the liberal outlook of Pericles's mistress Aspasia, whose 'unusual learning and independent life were crimes to the conservatism of social Athens'.[34] Throughout her life, Linton was all too aware of the counterarguments to her position, often admitting them unconsciously into her writing, but failing to confront them openly.

Similarly, she idealized the British past, attributing to its women old English virtues that she castigated in their modern form, disliking anything that smacked of boldness, while praising the courage of women in history. As so often, Linton rested her case on comfortable clichés: 'womanliness in the bower, dignity in the hall, courage in the castle – that was the whole duty of these noble women of a rude but manly age', she concluded in 'The Characteristics of

English Women' (1889). The English Reformation she associated with far nobler female virtues than were to be found in France and Italy, countries she always saw as being essentially feminine, while England was more uncouth, but also more manly. Linton felt that women dominate savage societies; their rule 'becomes the precursor, as it is the sign, of general decay'.[35] She hoped that England would regain its masculine leadership and hence its power in the wider world.

Linton's methods, in her articles, were clear and straightforward. She relied on techniques of caricature, repetition, cliché, generalization, exaggeration and over-simplification, which were also essentially the techniques she used in her novels, though in her articles there was less room for a penumbra of doubt surrounding her main arguments. The self-contradiction which was undoubtedly there arose more from the entangled nature of her attacks on almost every variety of man or woman who could be implicated in the debate. Pitching into man-haters and mutually antagonistic women, into womanish men and mannish women, into the 'angel in the house' and the cigarette-smoking 'New Woman', into 'Grim Females' and 'Dolls', 'The Fashionable Woman' and 'The Shrieking Sisterhood', Linton left few female images unscathed, and herself little leeway for constructive argument. Her approach was based on ever-deepening dyes of calumny, which allowed no turning back and no compromise: her method becoming her form and purpose. It remains the most strident articulation of the fear underlying social change in the second half of the nineteenth century.

MARGARET OLIPHANT: 'EQUALITY IS THE MIGHTIEST OF HUMBUGS'

Reviewing 'New Books' for *Blackwood's* in 1870, Margaret Oliphant attacked both the Girl of the Period and *Ourselves* as productions that treated women as a 'sect', a separate interest group, in a way that was never applied to men. 'Women themselves are chiefly to blame for the strange and humiliating notion that they are a sect, a party, an oppressed nationality as it were, and not an integral part of the race.' Disguising her own voice as male ('Some of us drink, and smoke, and swear, and make ourselves hugely disagreeable not only to our wives but to everybody concerned'), Oliphant insisted that the affinity between two women could never be so close as that which unites husband and wife. She also complained that the interests and behaviour of men and women were judged only in relation to their being designed for marriage, omitting, for example, the bond between parent and child. Throughout her journalism, Oliphant objected to a concentration on the sexual relationships between men and women; she also rejected what she loosely denominated 'theory', on the grounds that its focus was too narrow, and it overlooked common-sense, matter-of-fact reasons why men and women behave the way they do.[36] Whereas Linton's tone is usually opinionated, scornful and sarcastic, Oliphant's is more measured and ironic, though she avoids caricature, and indeed accuses others of it. Her appeal is always to the sensible, normal reader, who knows that nothing untoward is really happening in the relations between husbands and wives. Whereas in her novels she tends to be cynical about human nature, in her journal articles she is more conventional. As one of few women 'regulars' for *Blackwood's*, she perhaps felt obliged to be steady.

Oliphant's correspondence with *Blackwood's* shows her hesitantly proposing new articles, and not banking on their continued acceptance. There had been intervals in her association with them when her work had been rejected (for example, soon after her husband's death in Rome, when she returned to Scotland with her children), and she continued to feel that some subjects might not be considered suitable for a woman. Writing to John Blackwood in 1855, proposing a piece on Pepys and Evelyn, she took care to phrase her request respectfully: 'I am afraid a feminine critic must find but a limited orbit possible to her – but I should greatly like this piece of work if it would answer you.'[37] Seven years later, she told Isabella Blackwood that she read everything in the Magazine except the politics: 'I am a Radical, you know.' Her mother, as a 'fervent Liberal', had been 'completely opposed' to *Blackwood's*, and Oliphant, who idolized her mother, was likely to feel the same way about its political stance.[38] As it happened, most of her contributions were literary – either reviews or biographies – apart from a succession of articles, unconnected (unlike Linton's), on the various debates about women. She responds more directly than Linton does to specific issues, such as John Stuart Mill's *Subjection of Women*, the reform of the married women's property laws, the suffrage, wife-beating, and employment. From the outset, she regarded women's physical limitations as a major obstacle to equality between the sexes, and felt that legislation could do little to help the situation of the average married woman. In any case, she believed the formal legal position of women had little bearing on the actual relations between husbands and wives who were on good terms. In most households, there was no reason for men and women to be at loggerheads, or to need a legal ruling on their respective rights. However true this might have been, this led Oliphant to skate over the marital disputes that did arise, and to minimize the importance of pro-feminist agitation for those with a serious grievance. Not looking at specific cases, as she did in her novels, Oliphant became more complacent about the general situation.

Her biographer, Merryn Williams, has suggested that Oliphant's views, which had 'always been more complicated than simple anti-feminism', changed after her article on Mill, 'The Great Unrepresented', in 1866. Initially, she had believed in the 'separate spheres' philosophy, and had reacted against feminism because it 'appeared to undervalue the work which women were already doing'.[39] Williams is right to suggest that Oliphant was personally indifferent to political privileges, but it is less easy to detect a softening of tone in favour of women's-rights agitation. Although she had some sympathy with Mary Wollstonecraft, whose *Vindication* she read in 1882, and discussed in her *Literary History of England*, Oliphant saw feminism as an irritant which society was as yet incapable of judging. Feminists themselves she dismissed as 'women compelled by hard stress of circumstances to despise the men about them'.[40] In some ways this had been Oliphant's own position. She had never known a strong man, and both her brothers and her sons, as well as her father and husband, had given her little reason to think well of the opposite sex. Nevertheless, Oliphant clung loyally to the image of the well-ordered Victorian home with the father as head of the family, and the wife taking a subordinate, though still vitally important role, in the running of the household. Like Linton, she refused to see her own situation as anything more than anomalous, and therefore irrelevant to the issue.

Why she did this, in the face of so much evidence to the contrary, remains problematic. Where Linton was male-identified, of lesbian sympathies, and angry with her mother for dying young, Oliphant was a devoted mother whose attempts to build a secure family life failed dramatically. She knew women could be forced into situations where they had to work in order to save their children from destitution, and she knew that much of the serious heroic work for the family was as often done by women as by men. Her novels show that she was sceptical about family life, and knew it often failed: not only through death or financial collapse, but also because parents were inadequate or children disappointing. It is clear from novels such as *Phoebe Junior* and *The Curate in Charge* that Oliphant was under no illusions about Victorian domesticity: yet in her articles, she continued to insist that all was well – at least in most houses – and that further legislation was unnecessary. In fact, she thought the existing legislation, on women's property, for example, was irrelevant to the actual situation that prevailed in most marriages: she believed it was 'a mere trick of words to say that the woman loses her existence, and is absorbed in her husband'.[41] The fact that this particular article, 'The Laws Concerning Women' (1856), was written using a male persona, implies that Oliphant saw no reason to dissent from the male perspective on property laws. Quite simply, among reasonable people, she felt this should never become an issue.

Oliphant was also deterred from identifying herself with the women's movement by ladylike feelings of reticence and modesty, which increased to active distaste for the publicity involved in campaigning. In an article of 1880 for *Fraser's Magazine*, 'The Grievances of Women', Oliphant explained her reasons for not attending a suffrage meeting, or any like it:

> We are so weak as to be offended deeply and wounded by the ridicule which has not yet ceased to be poured upon every such manifestation. We shrink from the laugh of rude friends, the smile of the gentler ones. The criticisms which are applied, not to one question or another, but to the general qualities of women, affect our temper unpleasantly.

Confessing to a 'poverty of spirit and timidity of mind' of which she was ashamed, Oliphant nevertheless attributes it collectively to her generation, and reiterates that the physical superiority of men will 'keep women in subjection as long as the race endures'.[42] This was another of Oliphant's unalterable beliefs which made her at best neutral on the possibility of change in women's long-term prospects for greater independence, and at worst convinced there was no point in trying to alter the existing situation. Moreover, many of her objections to the wide airing of women's issues boiled down to sexual reticence on her part. The relations between men and women, which are reviewed ironically in her novels, were to her an essentially private matter, which should not be examined by outsiders. By 1880, she was embarrassed by the open conflict between the sexes, and the painful exposure of views held by both sides.

Oliphant's articles suggest that the public debates about the suffrage and marriage laws were not, to her, the real issues between men and women. Others, which received less publicity, troubled her more deeply, which may be another reason why she resisted the noisier onward sweep of the pro-feminist women's movement. In her 1880 article for *Fraser's* she admits that most women do harbour a sense of injustice about their role in marriage, covering both practical and theoretical issues. Referring to women's greater sufferings (she implies, in childbearing, but is too reticent to name it), she complains that 'neither for these extra pangs do we receive sympathy, nor for our work do we receive the credit which is our due' (p. 700). Her main grievance was that the basic inequalities in women's lot were underestimated, and men rarely gave women credit for the amount of hidden work they performed. At times, her protests amount to a fundamental discontent with the biological condition of being a woman, for which there is no legal redress; at others, she asks more for a change in attitude than for any basic alteration in the law. Like many other Victorian novelists, especially Dickens, George Eliot and Elizabeth Gaskell, she appealed to her readers' sense of decency and humanity, urging a change of heart rather than an overhaul of the marriage laws. Ultimately she believed 'the sentiment of men towards women is thoroughly ungenerous from beginning to end, from the highest to the lowest' (p. 710).

In 1866, writing about the suffrage campaign and Mill, Oliphant took a more ironic line, in keeping with that of the novels (such as *Miss Marjoribanks*) she was writing at the time. Her line in 'The Great Unrepresented' is simply that she has 'got used to' being a woman, and does not find the condition too oppressive. As for not having a vote, 'We have got used to it, and bear the humiliation with the meekness which is truly characteristic of our sex.'[43] As in other articles, such as the *Fraser's* review of women's grievances in 1880, Oliphant detaches herself from the younger generation of activist women, and prefers to play the part of unemotional ironist, complacently accepting men's weaknesses, and rising above the angry indignation of the younger generation. 'We have public opinion in our hands to a considerable extent already,' she pleaded. If all women had the vote, 'the chaos would be too comically bewildering for any ordinary imagination' – though she does not explain why this should be the case any more than if all men were to have the vote (p. 373). Oliphant explicitly rejects Mill's logical approach, on the grounds that intuition is a more appropriate method of dealing with an unreasonable real world. Her final position in the article is that the vote is irrelevant, and that where women have wanted to do something generally reserved for men, they have, in most cases, been able to do it – 'heaven be praised!' (p. 379).

Oliphant's method, in these articles, is anti-logical, idiosyncratic, ironic and personal: an alternative voice to that of the conventional male-authored, authoritarian review normally associated with Victorian periodicals. Her manner in the 1866 article is even coy and flirtatious, revelling in her own femininity, and disrupting the serious flow of reasoned argument. By treating the subject with detached humour, she was able to defuse it of danger, and deal good-humouredly with one of the most controversial issues of the day. When she comes to handling Mill's *Subjection of Women*, in a substantial review for the *Edinburgh* in 1869, she specifically declares his judgement to be 'sometimes warped by theory', and sounds impatient with the attention given to merely practical problems, or 'sentimental grievances' as she saw them. Her objection to the suffrage is stated clearly as a conviction that it was wrong to give the two halves of the marriage unit, husband and wife, whom she saw as one, separate voices. 'We cannot explain how it is, but we know that it is.'[44] Oliphant was honest enough to find single women the exception to her general rules for married women, recognizing their need to work, and even their entitlement to the vote, but this was rarely for her the main point at issue. Once again, she argues from the assumption that most women are married, that man and wife are one unit, that their problems are for them to work out privately, and that legislation can do little to alter the balance of strength between them. Although men were, in her view, often foolish and even pitiable, she bases her analysis of the marriage laws almost entirely on the fact of man's physical superiority to woman: a point Mill himself rejected as sufficient foundation for the subjection of the weaker sex.

Since the 1850s, Oliphant had also believed that the stability of society was dependent on the continued existence of marriage as the norm: hence her reluctance to support the movement for easier divorces. 'The business of a righteous and rational law is not to provide facilities for escaping,' she argued in an article of 1856, 'but to rivet and enforce the claims of that relationship upon which all society is founded.'[45] Her language in the 1850s is certainly blunter and harsher than it was subsequently: here, the notion of handcuffing recalcitrant wives to their husbands reflects Oliphant's impatience with all attempts to undermine the sanctity of the marriage bond. As far as Oliphant was concerned, marriage was a voluntary state, entered into willingly by both parties, on the understanding that the interests of husband and wife would become identical. Once the contract was signed, the wife had to accept the conditions, which, in any case, were not normally oppressive. Oliphant took two further lines when she discussed the so-called difficulties of the married state: one was that men suffered as well, though in a different way; and the other was that women actually gained the power of special legislators when they became queens over their own empires, a view Ruskin also expressed in 'Of Queens' Gardens' in *Sesame and Lilies* (1865).

As Oliphant had never thought well of men, it was a natural progression for her to acknowledge their sufferings and see them as living at the mercy of stronger wives. She believed that the husband's superior physical strength, combined with the economic supremacy inherent in his earning power, made him the naturally dominant partner of the marriage; but his responsibility for his wife's shopping bills, for example, ensured that he too suffered from the restrictions of matrimony. In her 1869 article on Mill, Oliphant characteristically made an ironic joke of the situation: 'While we write, a sense of pity for man comes over us. And he behaves very well on the whole under the circumstances' (p. 587). In an article on 'the Condition of Women' for *Blackwood's* in 1858, when her approach was less subtle, she discussed the problems encountered by single women in finding work, and argued, taking the Brontë family as an example, that the situation was worse for Branwell than it was for his sisters: men, as natural breadwinners, were likely to find unemployment or demeaning work far more humiliating than women, who were unused to having dignified, paid employment. At this stage, Oliphant already favoured the widening of employment opportunities for women: a position she continued developing to take account of single women's needs. But in 1858 she was still capable of declaring vehemently:

> Equality is the mightiest of humbugs – there is no such thing in existence; and the idea of opening the professions and occupations and governments of men to women, seems to us the vainest as well as the vulgarest of chimeras. God has ordained visibly, by all the arrangements of nature and providence, one sphere and kind of work for a man and another for a woman.[46]

'Man goes out to his work and labour till the evening. Woman prepares for him, waits for him, serves him at home,' she insisted in her 1869 article (p. 585). Despite all her personal experience to the contrary, it was difficult for her to accept anything else as the norm for the majority of the population.

Like Sarah Ellis and Ruskin, Mrs Oliphant also – intermittently – created a fantasy scenario of the wife as a mini-queen in her own home, as she does at the end of *Miss Marjoribanks*. Lucilla is clearly the dominant partner in her marriage to Tom, and has already ruled her father's house as a personal empire. Writing about the suffrage campaign in 1866, the year of the novel's publication, Oliphant again dismissed the intellectual powers of men as negligible: 'Men are full of prejudices and prepossessions on this subject, which obscure the little judgement which they may be allowed to possess by nature.'[47] Oliphant felt women were certainly competent to vote, but that their political skills were better employed in the running of their own homes. In 'The Laws Concerning Women' (1856), she argued that the wife is normally the 'Chancellor of the Exchequer' (p. 386): 'And, indeed, to tell the truth, women are the only born legislators, let them complain of their position as they will.' She cites the example of the young bride, a child half an hour before, 'now a law maker, supreme and absolute; and yet, most despotic and unconstitutional of monarchs, you hear them weeping over infringed rights and powers denied'.

Oliphant's shift from referring to women as 'they', to identifying with them as 'we', which occurs from the 1860s onwards, indicates a growing knowledge of the legal disabilities suffered by women, and some sympathy for certain categories who were uncatered for by marriage. Her change of heart seems to have been effected not only by the loss of her own husband, but also by her distaste for the *Saturday Review*'s anti-feminist stance (fuelled by Linton) in 1868: 'swearing blaspheming, and tearing its hair in a blast against all women'.[48] In the 1850s, she had used a male persona to attack the campaign for equality, disguising her voice more fully than she was to do later in the century. Either she believed this would give her views more authority, or she felt uncomfortable about criticizing women in her usual tone of voice. Harriet Martineau, conversely, had adopted a male persona in her influential article 'Female Industry' for the *Edinburgh Review* in 1859, to attract attention to the vast increase in middle-class women looking for work, even though she was sufficiently well known and respected to secure an audience in her own right. Oliphant's use of the male voice in the 1850s sounds crude and self-conscious, as it still does in 1870, the year of the drinking–smoking–swearing image she projected of herself in the 'New Books' section quoted at the start of this discussion. When she uses a male disguise, it is generally that of a married man, who has absorbed his wife's opinions and therefore already knows what women think about a particular issue: 'Which of us', she asked in 'The Laws Concerning Women', 'does not carry our wife's thoughts in our brain, and our wife's likings in our heart, with the most innocent unconsciousness that they are not our own original property?' (p. 381). Even here, however, her tone is sarcastic at the expense of the complacent male, silently taking over his wife's views and presumably retailing them as his own.

Because of the rhetorical strategies and subterfuges, Oliphant's own views are often difficult to arrange in any kind of coherent order. Her attitude to the suffrage is perhaps the most shrouded in irony, as she argues sometimes in favour of women's political abilities, sometimes against; sometimes suggesting that there is no real reason why she should not have the vote, and at others adopting the standard anti-suffrage line that men are already taking care of the few remaining inequalities in the law, and guarding women's interests as well as any female politician could do. She also conceded that there were some anomalies in the marriage law (on property, and the custody of children, for example), but felt their effects were too limited to be worth a disproportionate degree of agitation.

The one area where it is possible to see a clear change of heart is in the issue of employment. Although Oliphant did not envisage married middle-class women regularly going out to work, she began to accept that a significant proportion of female adults fell outside this relatively privileged group. Her 1858 article on 'The Condition of Women' anticipates much of Martineau's argument the following year, as she points out the anomaly between the numbers of women in need of work, and the decrease in openings and opportunities for them. Although she never saw this as an argument for equality between the sexes – indeed in this article she strongly urged women against concerning themselves with anything of the kind – she submitted that if 'half of British women' have to support themselves by means of a handful of limited occupations, 'a little watchmaking, book-keeping, or jewellery, additional thereto, would be a very inadequate remedy' (p. 146). By 1869, she was particularly concerned about single women – 'They are as strong, as courageous, as clever as their masculine contemporaries' – and admitted that objections to their emancipation were unanswerable (p. 591). By 1880, she thought men were actively resisting the idea of the professions being opened to women, and suspected they feared competition. 'My own opinion is that the advantage to women of having a woman-doctor to refer to is incalculable' (*Fraser's*, May 1880, p. 707). Far from using a male persona, Oliphant was by now signing such articles with her initials: evidence of her increased confidence in her own opinions, as well as the move away from anonymous journalism.

Having two intelligent nieces, one of them an artist, also made Oliphant think more, not only about women's employment, but also about their education. She had no doubt that she wanted the best for her boys, and worked all the harder to send them to Eton, living nearby so that they could sleep at home instead of boarding. As far as women were concerned, however, she was at first quite prepared to dismiss the subject of education without much thought, as she does in 'The Condition of Women' in 1858: 'We do not profess to be very learned in the question – the mysteries of a female college have never been penetrated by our profane eyes' (p. 148). All the evidence she could see showed that it turned out women able to cope with their existing duties. Unlike George Eliot, she rarely focuses in her novels on the shortcomings of female education, and makes her heroines less intellectual and more purely practical than Eliot's Maggie Tulliver or Dorothea Brooke. Oliphant's heroines usually make their first appearance at the point where they have left school and are looking for something to do in the domestic sphere before they marry: their social activities then resulting in marriage to a man less intelligent than themselves. Women in Oliphant's novels seem to have a natural quick-wittedness that needs no further training, and unlike Eliot's heroines, they rarely make mistakes in their assessment of the social scene and its all too evident limitations. Oliphant never really interested herself in the issue of women's education to the extent that she did in employment and the suffrage, but when her nieces grew up, she conceded that they might think of attending one of the newly-formed women's colleges.[49]

Oliphant remained convinced that an active working life for women was in most cases incompatible with the demands of marriage and childbearing. She felt celibacy was the only way round this problem, even if it was something unrequired of men, and doubted whether legislation could do much even for those who needed to work. 'Legislation may help the surplus,' she allowed in her 1869 article on Mill, 'the exceptional women ... but for the majority, legislation can do little and revolution nothing at all' (p. 599). Her views for much of her life were representative of the traditionalists of her generation, though always destabilized by her rhetorical strategies. At times, particularly over the suffrage, these strategies seemed to mask her own indecision about the subject. In 1880, she thought it 'highly absurd' that she should not have a vote if she wanted one – 'a point upon which I am much more uncertain' (*Fraser's*, May 1880, p. 708). A more pessimistic character than Linton, Oliphant was also perhaps more honest, occasionally admitting to moments of genuine bafflement and confusion. Ultimately, she both doubted whether anything could be done, and disliked the way the modern generation was talking openly about sex. In a particularly despondent article on Ruskin's *Time and Tide* in 1868, she paints a nightmare image of a society reeling towards self-destruction, very like Linton's: 'Our world is full of sordid sins, of shameless follies, of mean and shortsighted perversity. Whole classes among us bellow for freedom one moment, and bind themselves under a voluntary system of slavery the next.'[50] Feeling that history lurched from crisis to crisis, she believed that the special sin of the time was lawless selfishness, for which Ruskin could offer but a 'childish panacea'.

The fashion among Oliphant critics now is to see her as more feminist than anti-feminist. Her bibliographer, John Stock Clarke, for example, refers to the 'unmistakable feminism of Mrs Oliphant's work', and cites her 1880 *Fraser's* article as recording her change of view. By the time she came to review Sarah Grand's novel *Ideala* in 1889, she was, according to Clarke, 'by conversion – a sympathizer with all the claims made by the women's movement'.[51] The article undoubtedly acknowledges that there have been major changes in women's situation, and that daughters are now as keen to be independent as sons. Characteristically, however, it seems to me that

Oliphant fails to commit herself entirely to the cause. She neither condemns, nor wholeheartedly applauds. She feels a new 'atmosphere' is breathing through every educated household in the land, but ends on a strangely ambiguous note, suggesting that woman in her own right is to be the new Messiah, not merely the mother of one, like Joanna Southcote.[52] Perhaps this was a way of indicating that women of the latest generation felt it was not enough to be mothers and watch the development of their children (especially as Oliphant's own daughter, Maggie, had died in 1864, leaving her without a 'woman-child' to care for): they wanted to be active doers themselves. While Oliphant's voice is clear enough in open condemnation of developments she deplored, she is both reticent and ironic in situations where she can understand women's impatience with the limitations imposed on them, but is uneasy about the threat of a permanent alteration in their role. It is rare to find her openly welcoming a change of direction in women's lives, though unlike Linton, she avoided caricaturing the new woman. She protected herself behind her own rhetorical strategy, by now perfected to shield her from direct involvement with the details of the debate.

MRS HUMPHRY WARD: 'WHAT ARE THESE TREMENDOUS GRIEVANCES?'

At the beginning of Ward's novel *Delia Blanchflower* (1915), the hero, Mark Winnington, has just been reading an article on 'Contemporary Feminism' in the *Quarterly Review*. 'The sketch of an emerging generation of women, given in the *Quarterly* article, had made a deep impression upon him. It seemed to him frankly horrible.' The article tells him that women everywhere are 'turning indiscriminately against the old bonds, the old yokes, affections, servitudes, demanding "self-realization," freedom for the individuality and the personal will'.[53] Although Mark Winnington has a profound sympathy for women, and even knows some suffragists, he is Ward's spokesman for a sense of regret felt at the departure of the old chivalrous image of women as selfless and emotional: a view to which Ward clung throughout her life. In making a male character voice her feelings, at this stage of her career, Ward was perhaps admitting that they would sound more convincing coming from a man. They would have more authority spoken by an athletic young Conservative, a lawyer and a traditional Englishman; or maybe this is an unconscious admission that such words would be more contentious if spoken by herself as narrator, or by a woman character in the novel. Whatever her reasons, Ward begins her novel with the recognition that the debate about women has reached even the *Quarterly*, and its disturbing implications are affecting every home and family.

Mrs Ward's own articles are less easy to trace through the journals and periodicals of the day. Much of what she wrote for *The Times, Saturday Review, Pall Mall Gazette,* and other papers came out anonymously, while those articles which have been safely attributed to her, for example in the *Fortnightly Review* and *Macmillan's Magazine,* were mostly on English and European literature, history and religion. According to her daughter, Janet Penrose Trevelyan, Ward was committed to the broadening of women's educational opportunities, but disliked any form of organized agitation which seemed to be 'anti-man'. She believed that men and women should work together to effect such reforms as still needed to be introduced. By 1889, she was, in any case, asking her sister-in-law:

> What *are* these tremendous grievances women are still labouring under, and for which the present Parliament is not likely to give them redress? I believe in them as little as I believe now in the grievances of the Irish tenant. There *were* grievances, but by the action of the parties concerned and their friends under the existing system they have been practically removed.[54]

Like Oliphant and Linton, she was also discouraged by the image of the feminists themselves: in her case, as a later figure, specifically by the suffragettes and their supporters. Marion Kathleen Jones, in a B.Phil. thesis on 'Mrs Humphry Ward and Feminism', suggests that Ward became disenchanted even with the movement for women's higher education, and was more concerned with their general moral and social education, as she is in her novels.[55] Like George Eliot, she preferred the notion of duty, or service, to that of 'rights', as far as they motivated women's actions.

Nevertheless, she was reluctant to be actively involved in the anti-feminist, anti-suffrage campaigns of the early twentieth century, though she gave in to pressure from Lords Cromer and Curzon, who wanted someone other than an aristocrat to launch a counter-attack. Ward did this in *The Times* of 12 June 1908, as she had, helped by Lord Justice Bowen and J.T. Knowles, for the *Nineteenth*

Century in 1889. Her earlier article was 'An Appeal Against Female Suffrage', based on the grounds that women's responsibilities towards the state 'must always differ essentially from those of men, and that therefore their share in the working of the State machinery should be different from that assigned to men'. Ward was always anxious to prevent women from interfering in areas of government, such as foreign policy, imperialism and heavy industry, of which they could not be expected to have had any experience; though she was eager for them to work for women's and children's charities in the East End of London. She believed that the emancipating process for women had gone as far as it needed to by 1889, and that further political involvement would merely turn women into hot-headed partisans. She preferred to see women as a moral force, aloof, dignified, and pursuing their special mission apart from public and parliamentary activity.[56]

This was a view she reiterated in 1908, when, after the *Times* article, she launched the *Anti-Suffrage Review* as organ of the Women's National Anti-Suffrage League. 'Women are citizens of the State no less than men,' Ward conceded in the opening number, 'but in a more ideal and spiritual sense.' She feared above all the outbreak of a sex-war, which would ultimately have disastrous consequences for England. She was still convinced that what she vaguely termed other 'agencies' existed for the furthering of reform, 'without the rash and ruinous experiment of the Parliamentary vote for women', and that if the country went ahead with the suffrage for women, England would be weakened in the eyes of other nations.[57] Mary Ward was the latest in a line of thinkers, stretching back to Jane West and Sarah Ellis, who linked England's strength with the stability and common sense of its women, who remained subordinate to their fathers and husbands. This first issue of the *Anti-Suffrage Review* also carried a report of a speech made by the Countess of Jersey, who argued melodramatically that the 'enfranchisement of women is a step which might end in a national disaster.... The Empire cannot be carried on if you begin by breaking up the homes of the country.'[58] By 1908, however, such dire warnings were less widely accepted than they had been in the days of Jane West and Sarah Ellis.

Ward seems a much more modern figure than Oliphant and Linton, however. She was prepared to see women active campaigners outside the home, and indeed urged them to participate in local government and tackle women's issues at a local level; but she still baulked at the notion of women's involvement in national events long after it was fashionable to do so. Her articles are less easy to deconstruct for inconsistencies and emotional ambivalence, which are readily detected in Eliza Linton's and Margaret Oliphant's writing. Where they begin to have a hollow ring is when they are contrasted with Ward's own public activities (of all the women in this study she was by far the most prominent campaigner and figure of authority, even in the political establishment), or with her women characters' enthusiasm for politics in her novels. Ward herself visited the House of Commons in 1893, when she was researching *Marcella*, and after that regularly included Parliamentary scenes in her novels. *The Coryston Family* (1913) actually opens in the House of Commons, with a description of the crowds in the Ladies' Gallery, and the women of the upper classes eagerly discuss political issues with at least some sign of being reasonably well informed. Ward sounds like one of her own heroines when she writes in a letter of 1909: 'Politics are horribly exciting! I don't like the Budget, mainly because it must so enormously increase the power of bureaucracy in England – but if the Unionists had no alternative, we could only submit –'.[59] With her father, Thomas Arnold, she discussed many events of the day, including Home Rule, speeches by individual politicians, and the behaviour of the Queen ('It would never have done to have had too clever a woman in such a place!').[60]

In 1910, she issued her *Letters to My Neighbours on the Present Election*, in which she explained why there was an election, and discussed such controversial issues as reform of the House of Lords, its role as a revising power, and tariff reform (which she favoured). 'I am not a hot political partisan,' she insisted at the beginning, 'and shall not attempt to rival political speakers and newspapers in violence of language. But I am a Unionist, and you will find that my letters, if you care to read them, take as before the Unionist view. It is in my belief the view that those who love their country *ought* to take at the coming election.'[61] It never seems to have occurred to Ward that this whole exercise was deeply ironic, in view of her own exclusion from the suffrage, or that she, as a mere woman, had no right to be advising male voters about tariff reform or any of the other controversial issues on which she confidently pronounced.

The supremest irony of all was when President Roosevelt invited her in 1915 to write a series of articles for American readers on what the English troops were doing and suffering in the trenches, so that people in his country might be better informed of the just cause. John Sutherland's biography describes the exhausting tours of munitions factories and the rear lines of the French battlefields for the writing of *England's Effort* (1916), which he believes can be 'plausibly credited with doing much to bring [America] into the European fight'.[62] It was followed by *Towards the Goal* (1917), another 'unfeminine' study of the effects of total war, which was essentially a piece of propaganda. At a point when her novels were at last seeming seriously outmoded, Mary Ward had found a new role for herself as war correspondent and political journalist. It was a repetition of the days when Harriet Martineau had been approached by cabinet ministers to explain a difficult economic controversy in her *Illustrations of Political Economy*: an occasion when a woman with no official political voice was nevertheless being appointed to sway the direction of public opinion.

Mary Ward is like Eliza Linton and Margaret Oliphant in accepting herself as an influential voice in the national debate about women's roles (though Ward's political range was much wider than either of theirs) without any apparent sense of discrepancy between what she was saying and what she was doing. Oliphant and Ward, more than Linton or Yonge, recognized that women's roles had changed irrevocably, and that it was necessary to meet these changes half way, and find some point of compromise. If women were unready for political activity (and indeed should always be kept out of it), Oliphant and Ward acknowledged that some women might still work outside the family home, though preferably in an extension of it, such as settlement houses or philanthropy. Ward and Linton, more than Oliphant, cling to the image of a feminine ideal which is essentially emotional and romantic: an image of a beautiful girl brimful of feeling, but untutored and liable to make mistakes; Oliphant, by contrast, has no doubt of women's capacity for almost any role they care to assume, but sees the biological differences between men and women as a permanent and insuperable obstacle to major change. Their rhetorical strategies vary from vituperative anger and savage caricature on Linton's part, to indirection and irony on Mrs Oliphant's, culminating in direct, logical argument on Mrs Ward's. Oliphant was perhaps the most aware of the specific grievances concerning women, but also the most uncertain of her own feelings about them: Linton and Ward found it easier to dismiss needs of which they themselves were not particularly conscious, even though all three had worked in order to keep themselves and their families from a serious shortage of money, all three being married to inadequate earners. They all also reached something of an apocalyptic vision at the end of their lives: Linton and Oliphant fearing that society was plunging into an ugly immorality, while Ward ends her autobiography, *A Writer's Recollections*, with images of the First World War: 'The shadow descends again, and the evening paper comes in, bringing yet another mad speech of a guilty Emperor to desecrate yet another Christmas Eve.'[63]

6
The Anti-Feminist Woman and Religion

'Are women more religious than men?' This was a question asked in *The Christian Remembrancer* in 1864, in an article discussing 'The Use and Abuse of Female Sentiment in Religion'. 'It seems on the face of it as if they must be,' the reviewer decides, on the grounds that women have two superior beings over them, man and God. A woman is more likely to feel her inferiority in the exercise of pure reason and abstract thought. 'Prone to worship, prone to lean, unvisited by doubt, apt to learn, she has a pleasure in submission, in bowing to authority, in the consciousness that her trust outstrips her reason, in a double faith – faith in her religion, and in him that teaches it.'[1]

This kind of statement exemplifies the confidently anti-feminist stance of the traditional mid-nineteenth-century church establishment. Although it was printed five years after the publication of Darwin's *Origin of Species*, it dismisses the possibility that a woman might ever have doubts about religious belief, and seems Miltonic in its image of the woman looking up to man and God. In fact, Victorian literature contains a surprising number of iconoclastic scenes of women (more often young girls) symbolically defying religious teaching, or questioning it with fearless directness: Jane Eyre arguing about sin and punishment with Mr Brocklehurst, and vowing to stay alive so as to avoid the hellfire he says is waiting for her; Tess of the d'Urbervilles baptizing and burying her illegitimate baby when the local priest refuses to do either; Elizabeth Barrett, aged twelve, formulating her own faith, and recording it in her early autobiographical writing ('At this age I was in great danger of becoming the founder of a religion of my own'); and at thirty-three Florence Nightingale noting in her diary: 'I have remodelled my whole religious belief from beginning to end.'[2] Her writings on religion, which are surprisingly extensive, are primarily interrogatory. She constantly questions religious belief and tradition, particularly as they affect women, and in her privately printed

Suggestions for Thought (1860), she repeatedly attacks the inadequacies of the Church of England, which she compares unfavourably with the Catholic Church:

> The Church of England has for men bishoprics, and a little work (good men make a great deal for themselves). She has for women – what? Most have no taste for theological discoveries. They would give her their heads, their hearts, their hands. She will not have them. She does not know what to do with them.[3]

In 1889 she told Benjamin Jowett that when she had originally been planning her future, she had thought not of 'organizing a Hospital, but organizing a Religion'.[4] As it was, she continued to ponder what was unsatisfactory about the Church of England, especially as it affected women members, and in 1873 wrote articles for *Fraser's Magazine* on the future direction of religious belief. In 'What will be our Religion in 1999?' she attacks both 'modern religious women' and the dominant spirit of Biblical criticism, which has done no more than cure religion of 'ugly excrescences', without bringing believers any closer to an understanding of God's real character. Nightingale was particularly struck by Christ's injunction to leave the home and family, and carry out his work: something that seemed highly apposite to her own situation in a conventional and stifling family context.[5]

There were, of course, women who wrote serious theological works, especially those at the two extremes of religious argument: those motivated by total religious belief, such as Christina Rossetti, in *The Face of the Deep: A Devotional Commentary on the Apocalypse* (1892) and *Letter and Spirit: Notes on the Commandments* (1883), or Julia Evelina Smith, who was the first woman to translate the Old and New Testaments; and those impressed by the new scientific criticism, as shown in George Eliot's translations of Strauss and Feuerbach, or the work of her friend, Sara Hennell. In general, however, women were less interested in the doctrinal side of theology, and seem to have concentrated more on the nature of God and his relationship with believers, or on the procedures for teaching religion in Sunday schools, work that traditionally devolved upon women young and old. Maria Grey and Emily Shirreff, writing their *Thoughts on Self-Culture* (1850), planned to 'abstain as much as possible from any approach to doctrinal theology', and instead urged that the motive of religion was simply 'obedience to God's will through love', which women could teach their children by associating religious principles with 'the strongest feelings of our nature'.[6]

Whether or not traditional Christianity is and was liberating or imprisoning to women is a continuing debate. The Bible itself is contradictory on the issue of women's equality with men;[7] and there have long been staunchly-held views on both sides of the argument. For a long time the movement for the ordination of women was held up by the conviction that women priests break the line of unity with historical tradition. As a recent book on the ordination debate puts it, theologies of the essential maleness of the priesthood are 'based upon the idea that the priest – and the bishop, in particular – stands as an "icon" (image, or picture) of Christ to the Church'.[8] This still constitutes a major objection, for many people, to the ordination of women, and is not to be dismissed as simple misogyny or anti-feminism. Even many Anglican sisterhoods were against the movement, although they were themselves 'religious professionals'. In the middle of the nineteenth century, however, women's ordination, as such, was not an issue: the debate was mainly about the extent of women's permitted involvement in church affairs, and it is in this context that the attitudes of the anti-feminist women novelists will be examined.

It is impossible to discuss women's role in the church without reference to their wider status in society. In the nineteenth century, their ambiguous secular position, constantly evolving, was reflected in arguments about their spiritual equality with men and their social subordination. A compromise position was the solution for most church members, allowing women participation in local Sunday schools, philanthropy and committees, while excluding them from the discussion of doctrinal issues or the practice of ministerial functions. Individual sects varied, of course, in their attitudes, and some allowed women to become more directly involved in church activities. The Anglican Church created its Order of Deaconesses in 1862, at a time coinciding with the establishment of Anglican Sisterhoods; while the Methodist Church officially banned women preachers throughout the century, and did not admit women to their ministerial structures until the 1970s. The branch of the church which perhaps did most to welcome women was the Evangelicals, whose emphasis on self-examination, domesticity, humility and gentleness, placed a high value on qualities traditionally associated with women and family life. As with any movement that admires traditional female values, however, the message for feminism was mixed, and in the twentieth century there have been many Evangelical opponents of women's ordination, on the basis of 'their understanding of the relationship between women and men that they see described in Scripture'.[9] Most Victorian novelists who write about women's interest in the church, see it in terms of local parish work, or, more often, the social round of clerical tea-parties, as in Charlotte Brontë's *Shirley* (1849), the fancy-work fêtes and bazaars described in *The Mill on the Floss* (1860) and Charlotte Yonge's novels, or the rousing public preachings which mean so much to Mrs Oliphant's Dissenting congregations. At its most basic level, the church provided women with a social life: a social life with a purpose. It introduced them to respectable friends, filled their otherwise blank days, and in some cases, trained them in the skills of teaching, organizing committees, financial management, and public speaking. For working-class girls, as Charlotte Yonge's novels often indicate, the church offered the chance of social advancement, by teaching them to read, and sometimes promoting them to the role of Sunday school teacher – as happens to Charity Elwood in *The Daisy Chain*. A crippled ex-servant, Cherry is the ideal Cocksmoor schoolmistress: 'She had the lady-likeness of womanly goodness, so as never to go beyond her own place' (p. 278). Having reached a satisfactory social plateau, which is already in advance of her expectations, Cherry will be content with her lot, and her middle-class lady superiors will be relieved of day-to-day responsibility for the school.

Theorists of women's role in the church found themselves beset by an irresolvable conflict between the images of Eve and the Virgin Mary, the two opposite poles of Biblical womanhood. Whereas Eve stood for sensuality and temptation, Mary symbolized the sanctity and devotion of motherhood. It was impossible to view just one of them as representing the role of women, much as it was impossible to reconcile the apparently contradictory views on women's ministry in the New Testament. Similarly, the question of whether the church sanctioned equality or hierarchy seemed eternally contestable. Thus women ostensibly writing about the role of women in the church were inevitably drawn into wider social issues. If the church professed to care for the powerless, might this include women? Might it even empower them, and follow Christ's teaching? Two women caught up in mid-century anxiety about these issues provide interesting case-studies relevant to those of the anti-feminist women novelists.

The first of these is Elizabeth Strutt, author of *The Feminine Soul: Its Nature and Attributes* (1857). Strutt's background is difficult to establish, but she was a married woman who wrote travel literature, novels and poetry, as well as theological treatises of an accessible kind, such as *The Book of the Fathers* (1837), which summarized the lives of celebrated Fathers of the Christian Church and the spirit of their writings. She was liberal enough to believe there were female angels. Her book pitches unflinchingly straight into the heart of the equality debate. If the essence of God is love and wisdom, woman is 'equally with man, created in the image, and after the Likeness of God'. She even accepts Plato's view that man and woman were originally conjoined in one form. The sexes are born in roughly equal numbers, both with God's attributes. 'Here then surely is equality between the sexes,' Strutt reasons: 'Equality which, beginning with creation, must remain the same; unchanged, unchangeable, as long as creation itself shall endure, which is for ever.'[10]

Strutt sounds unshakeable in her egalitarianism, but she quickly collapses into the 'equal-but different' position. She felt that from the time of the Garden of Eden, there was a generic intellectual or spiritual difference between men and women, with Adam embodying wisdom, and Eve love, or the will. This leads Strutt to the familiar conclusion that 'woman is invariably influenced by her affections, rather than by her understanding' (p. 20), although she at least gives Eve a generous motive in wanting to share her newly-discovered good with Adam. Wherever women have achieved anything of note, according to Strutt, whether as monarchs or as scientists, their driving power was love. As her argument progresses, she sugars her anti-feminism with flattery of women's loving nature and innate gentleness, which fits them only for domestic life. One by one, the other options for women are quietly removed, like dangerous weapons. Women are too swayed by their feelings to write History; authorship is 'trying to their sensibility and their health' (p. 95); they are best avoiding higher education, because it takes them away from domestic life, and they should certainly not attempt public speaking or political activity: 'from the nature of the Feminine Soul, it is as impossible for women ever to take the same standing with men, in the duties of political life, as it is for the heat of the sun to supply the functions of his light' (p. 107), a grand natural simile that seemed to settle the matter once and for all.

Elizabeth Strutt is an example of a woman religious theorist who wrote with a high regard for her own sex, and an apparent belief in the spiritual equality of women with men, but who found these arguments unsustainable in the light of social convention and psycho-sexual theory. She represents a sizeable proportion of Victorian Anglicans who thought that women's spiritual qualities could best be used in the home, and that 'would-be-emancipatresses', as she called feminist activists (with deliberate awkwardness), were mistakenly trying to liberate their sex from a way of life eminently suited to them (p. 165). Like Sarah Ellis before her (a woman of Congregationalist origins, married to a missionary), Strutt tries to make domestic life sound emotionally fulfilling, urges women to be cheerful, and, at the risk of bathos, take an interest in the preparation of meals.

The other woman theorist, writing at mid-century, and conscious that in discussing religion she was being drawn into the women's rights controversy, is Anna Brownell Jameson (1794–1860), best known for her travel writing, books on art, and *Characteristics of Women* (1832), a study of Shakespeare's female characters. Her marriage to the lawyer Robert Jameson soon failed; she was a friend of Lady Byron and a correspondent of Harriet Martineau's, besides gaining a reputation for an interest in women's issues. On these, however, her stance was ambiguous, and she often stopped short of an outright espousal of the women's cause. She was perhaps, as Norma Clarke has suggested, too conscious of her public and of the market, which she needed to placate in order to make a living. For example, in her *Memoirs of Celebrated Female Sovereigns* (1831), she concentrated on her subjects' personalities, avoiding any serious political analysis, and concluding that 'the power which belongs to us, as a sex, is not properly, or naturally, that of the sceptre or the sword'.[11] In 1855, Anna Jameson was writing about sisters of charity, beginning with a comparison of men's and women's work, and recommending that women be given more opportunities to employ their talents outside the home. Immediately, however, she feels embarrassed by the implications of her suggestions:

> I am anxious that you should not misunderstand me at the outset with regard to this *'woman-question,'* as it has been called. I have no intention to discuss either the rights or the wrongs of women. I think that on this question our relations across the Atlantic have gone a mile beyond the winning-post, and brought discredit and ridicule on that just cause which, here in England, prejudice, custom, ignorance have in a manner crushed and smothered up. It

is in this country, beyond all Christian countries, that what has been called, quaintly but expressively, the 'feminine element of society,' considered as a power applicable in many ways to the amelioration of many social evils, has been not only neglected, but absolutely ignored by those who govern us.[12]

Instead of discussing it openly, Jameson strays into it by veiled allusions, and reveals her suppressed anger at the ridicule surrounding the women's movement, caused by extreme activism among the Americans. As a woman favouring moderate advancements in the cause, she is sensitive to bad publicity, and while denying any proto-feminist agenda behind her writing, focuses on the best way to use female labour in the work of churches and charities. Like Florence Nightingale, she admired the Kaiserwerth Institution in Germany, which trained women in nursing skills in a pious atmosphere. Also like Nightingale, she understood the pull of the Catholic Church, in giving women something meaningful to do with their lives. Jameson concluded her book by recommending the establishment of an institution where women 'could obtain a sort of professional education under professors of the other sex' (p. 108), and be trained for a variety of roles as teachers, nurses and poor visitors. In Jameson's writing, dissatisfaction with the church's opportunities for women fed her enthusiasm for training schemes sponsored by religious authorities. She was also instrumental in founding *The Englishwoman's Journal* in 1858, and the Society for Promoting the Employment of Women in 1860.

Increasingly during the second half of the nineteenth century, religion came to be discussed as a form of employment for women. Because it was taken for granted that women could have no role in doctrinal issues, their work for practical causes was encouraged. It was also largely voluntary work, carried out under the supervision of clergymen and other women. Even sisterhoods, which were at first resented, as taking young women away from their 'proper' vocation of marriage and motherhood, gradually gained acceptance as providing a home and a purpose in life to women with no obvious domestic role. Dinah Craik, writing in 1886, confessed:

> It is a strange thing to say – yet I dare to say it, for I believe it to be true – that entering a Sisterhood, almost any sort of Sisterhood where there was work to do, authority to compel the doing of it, and companionship to sweeten the same, would have saved many a woman from a lunatic asylum![13]

Craik focuses on the collateral benefits of religion – work and companionship – but proposes one form of institutionalism to save women from another, with 'authority' to compel obedience. Religion traditionally keeps women in their place and under control, as fundamentalists recognize.

The connection between religious orthodoxy and anti-feminism has a long history, which is still unwinding. 'All major world religions are patriarchal,' Marilyn French argues in her recent book on *The War Against Women* (1992). 'They were founded to spread or buttress male supremacy – which is why their gods are male. But there is nothing inherently patriarchal about the religious impulse.'[14] In the second half of the twentieth century, women have been claiming their spiritual rights within the formal structure of the Anglican Church; in the nineteenth, they struggled to define their exact relationship with the institution that was meant to occupy a large proportion of their free time, but which severely limited their participation. Hence the deflection of spiritual experiences into fiction and autobiography, where women felt more at liberty to explore the personal meaning of their fervour.

Female religious experience has traditionally been on the edge of Christian observance: in the form of mystic or visionary episodes unconnected with the formal conduct of ceremonies and sacraments. Anti-feminism in the church has been linked with distrust of female sexuality, and because women are viewed primarily as physical beings, perpetually in biological crisis, they have been considered unsuitable for the higher forms of ministry. One might therefore expect the Victorian anti-feminist women novelists to accept women's subordinate role in the church, and to depict it unquestioningly as reinforcing gender stereotypes. Victorian family life revolved around the church, and was at times (such as family prayers) even merged with it, the father acting as minister to his household, and the wife or mother as a kind of leading parishioner. Sunday observances ordered the family to behave in a particular way, so that home became an extension of church. Few writers, male or female, who reported on domestic life, could afford to ignore the practical and emotional impact of religious habit on women's experiences. A question to be asked in this chapter is whether Christianity was seen by the anti-feminist women novelists as buttressing traditional family values, and therefore performing its role as moral regenerator of society; or whether they had reservations about its relevance. A further issue will be women's religious experience itself. Do they attempt to illustrate this, and distinguish between it and the kinds of personal spiritual growth sanctioned by the male-dominated church establishment? In the past, as Pat Holden has argued, women's relationship with religion has not been a major issue in the women's movement, partly 'because we live in a secular society, but also because religion seems to offer little scope for challenging dominant ideologies'.[15] If this is the case, we should expect this group of novelists to sympathize with the church's restriction of women to a supportive domestic role in the Victorian household.

All four novelists were keenly interested in religion, though from entirely different standpoints. Charlotte Yonge's was Tractarian; Margaret Oliphant's, a Scots Presbyterian background; Mary Ward's, anti-dogmatic, agnostic, yet Christian; while Eliza Linton, towards the end of her life, described her religion as 'the self-respecting, magnanimous, large religion of the Stoics – those men with a stiff backbone who neither grovelled nor truckled – "the religion of ethics"'.[16] Ironically, she was the only one whose father was a clergyman. Each, however, discusses religion specifically in relation to women's lives – the lives of mothers and young brides; and in response to the religious controversies of the age, reformulates the relationship between belief and women's life experience.

CHARLOTTE M. YONGE: 'CHILDHOOD'S HEART'

The dominant religious influence on Charlotte Yonge was the Tractarian poet and theologian John Keble, who not only prepared her for confirmation, but also became a close family friend with whom the novelist discussed her work. 'No one else,' she explained in 1871, 'save my own father, had so much to do with my whole cast of mind.' Keble gave her two warnings about her religious attitudes: 'the one against so much talk and discussion of Church matters, especially doctrines, the other against the danger of loving these things for the sake merely of their beauty and poetry – aesthetically he would have said, only that he would have thought the word affected'.[17] It is therefore not surprising that Keble quickly gained a reputation for being limited in outlook: a contemporary, Tom Mozley, said 'There really was no getting on with Keble without entire agreement, that is submission.'[18] Like Yonge, he had never escaped his father's influence, and seems to have been both submissive to authority, and exacting of submission in others. He was anxious that Yonge should not be spoiled by the success of her writing, and urged her to think of its real inspiration coming from another mind. Her brief memoir of Keble begins with happy memories of school feasts, which followed afternoon church services and brought together all the poor children of the village, supervised by their teachers and social superiors. Yonge's novels celebrate the annual cycle of treats and fêtes in their appeal to children: adults are at their happiest when they can join in without being racked by private reservations and doubts. In *The Daisy Chain*, Ethel May's heartfelt ambition is to build a church for the poor people of Cocksmoor: something she achieves, with family support, by the end of the novel; while her friend Meta marries Norman May and goes out to New Zealand with him as a missionary. In each of their cases, religion offers the lure of excitement and adventure; though Ethel faces the harder challenge of living a courageous life at home, without being first in any other person's life.

The reader who expects Charlotte Yonge's novels to discuss religious dogma, like John Henry Newman's, will search in vain. She fully internalized Keble's views on avoiding discussion of such issues, except in their most generalized forms: so that when she comes to examine doubt in two of her characters, Norman May and Rachel Curtis, the details are deliberately kept vague. Doubt is a serious matter for both sexes: it can ruin a man's professional career, and it can ruin a woman's whole life, making her permanently unhappy, and beyond the pale of Christian middle-class society. In *The Daisy Chain*, the anxious scholar Norman mentions his doubts, first to Meta, his future wife, and then to his sister Ethel. In each case, the two girls are scarcely able to imagine his experiences: all the more so as Norman describes them in horrific metaphors. Like the Lady of Shalott, he is 'half sick of shadows'; he talks of wanderers in the desert, shells, husks, clouds and mirages; until Meta tells him: '"You have read yourself into a maze, that's all –"' (p. 382). '"Don't think I am unfeeling," she said; "but I know it is all a fog up from books, books, books – I should like to drive it off with a good fresh gust of wind!"' Meta stands for an anti-intellectual intuition of belief, the way Yonge suggests women should believe. When he is safely over his doubts, Norman explains to Ethel how he struggled with them, and examined the case for and against belief by careful reasoning. Ethel feels she would have been unequal to the effort, intellectual though she is:

> 'I suppose examination was right,' said Ethel, 'for a man, and defender of the faith. I should only have tried to pray the terrible thought away. But I can't tell how it feels.' (p. 460)

The implication is that the intellect leads people astray, whereas the heart is always to be trusted: this episode makes Norman decide to renounce the world of academic competition, and seek selfless hard work as a missionary in New Zealand.

Whereas Norman's crisis of faith occurred at the height of personal triumph at Oxford, Rachel Curtis's strikes after the humiliation of her failed wood-engraving project to rescue overworked lace-makers. Rachel tells her future husband Alick Keith that she wants to believe, but 'cannot rest or trust for thinking of the questions that have been raised' (p. 275). Her particular temptation, as she realizes in this scene, is 'self-sufficiency', of which she is cured by going to live with Alick's uncle, the blind clergyman Mr Clare, who symbolically needs no eyes to see his way to salvation. The death of Alick's frivolous sister Bessie removes the final traces of Rachel's unbelief. 'She had her childhood's heart again' (p. 316). Helping Mr Clare compose his sermons Rachel is 'drawn up into the real principles and bearings of the controversy' (p. 337), Mr Clare patiently explaining difficulties as they go along. Yonge believed firmly in the importance of personal influence and its superiority to private reading, at least as far as women were concerned. Whereas Norman May disentangles his own doubts, Rachel has hers patiently unwound by a country clergyman. What religion particularly offers Yonge's women is a calm strength which allows them to cope with the domestic crises, the deaths and diseases, with which her novels are rife. They are rarely calm and strong when her novels open: in her most commonly repeated plots, her young women are fearful, foolish or arrogant before they have been tested by experience, and their friends are pleasantly surprised when they assume command or steer a family through temptation.

Two such heroines are Amy Edmonstone of *The Heir of Redclyffe*, and Violet Martindale of *Heartsease* (1854), both young brides and mothers, who nurse weak men through illness and spiritual despair.

Amy's faith helps her survive her husband Guy's death from fever on their honeymoon, followed by the birth of her daughter and the rehabilitation of the new heir, Philip; while Violet, originally dismissed as a disappointing wife for Arthur Martindale, matures through religion and motherhood to be her husband's true mentor: 'where once stood the self-torturing, pining girl, was now the calm trustful woman, – serene beneath the overshadowing Wings, resting on the everlasting Arms, – relying, least of all, upon herself'.[19] This is always the crucial point for Yonge: self-reliance is a mistake for any Christian, who should trust in God, but it is especially inappropriate in a woman. Nevertheless, her actions are praised at the end: 'She has gone about softening, healing, guarding, stirring up the saving part of each one's disposition' (p. 458). Significantly, however, her 'power' is hidden because it is 'too feminine to be recognised'.

In her discussion of women's family roles, *Womankind* (1876), Yonge declares: 'It is only as a daughter of the Church that woman can have her place, or be satisfied as to her vocation.'[20] She felt that Christianity provided a purpose to single as well as married women: thus, in her novels, religion is seen as being so closely interwoven with daily domestic life that there are few extractable discussions of it. People go to church with as much regularity as their children attend school; grown-up children return home to enjoy a traditional family Sunday; and ordinary family events are discussed and reviewed in the light of secure religious feeling. Rachel reads books on childcare when she is not with Mr Clare being disabused of theological controversy. Yonge herself appears never to have wavered. At the end of her life, she wrote thirteen papers for *The Churchwoman* on *Reasons Why I am a Catholic and Not a Roman Catholic* (1901), in an attempt to stem a flood of recent secessions to Rome. She strongly disliked Mariolatry, and regretted the 'perversion of devotion from Him who forbade direct prayer to any save Himself, the One God and One Mediator'.[21] It was typical of Yonge that the woman was always seen as subservient to the male, even where she had spiritual significance of her own, and she preferred a version of Christianity which gave women a clear hierarchical structure under male authority.

Charlotte Yonge's religious conservatism may be taken as a yardstick by which to measure the less conventional attitudes of the other anti-feminist women writers, all of whom were troubled by the contradictions of theology.

MARGARET OLIPHANT: THWARTED CHOICES

If Charlotte Yonge was dominated by John Keble, Margaret Oliphant was increasingly fascinated by the figure of Edward Irving (1792–1834), the Scots preacher who had been in love with Jane Welsh before she married Thomas Carlyle, and whose sermons concentrated on prophecy and the Apocalypse. When a woman in the West of Scotland began speaking tongues in 1830, Irving was stirred by the apparent revival of faith, and kept stubbornly to a course of action that led to his excommunication by the presbytery of London, and his removal from the National Scotch Church of Regent Square. In 1833, he was deposed from the ministry of the Church of Scotland on a charge of heresy. Mrs Oliphant's two-volume biography of him appeared nearly thirty years later in 1862, during a decade in which she was preoccupied with religious matters, perhaps influenced by the deaths of her husband in 1859, and then her daughter Maggie in 1864. In her Preface to *The Life of Edward Irving*, Oliphant stressed that she was interested 'chiefly with the man himself, and his noble courageous warfare through a career encompassed with all human agonies'.[22] For once, she was able to view a subject without the irony she usually brought to her fictional heroes, perhaps because Irving had lost more than one of his children: a tragedy that had already befallen Oliphant with the deaths of two babies in the 1850s, and which was to continue until all her children were dead. In Irving's case, family troubles were compounded by his dramatic rise and fall as a preacher. Oliphant had decided views on sermons: she inveighed against the dull and dogma-ridden orations that were delivered by callow youths with no life experience, and saw the sermon as something that should be emotionally arousing. 'The highest aim of the pulpit', she insisted, 'is to bring all men, in the first place, to such a noble discontent as will stir them to the deepest and most radical of revolutions. The end of preaching is something to be believed, something to be acted upon, something to do.'[23]

In her writing about religion, Oliphant develops an anti-theoretical, anti-dogmatic approach, which focuses on human feeling, and the needs of ordinary parishioners, especially women. Although women in her novels do parish work, as they do in most Victorian novels, she concentrates, like Trollope, on the church as a male profession, and traces the absurdities of male ambition, incompetence, and failure. Her women characters are spectators, whose personal lives are often damaged by the emotional and professional blunderings of their fathers, lovers and husbands. Oliphant's own position in relation to the church was very much a freewheeling one. She was a natural believer, who never lost her faith in God, but she found it difficult to accept that everything that happened to herself and her children was necessarily for the best. Her background was Scots Presbyterian, which made her something of an outsider in English religious contexts; though according to Margaret Guy, she became disenchanted with the narrowness of the Free Church of Scotland, and had 'strong leanings towards the Catholic Church'.[24] She denied this latter impulse in her *Autobiography*, and shows relatively little sympathy for Gerald Wentworth, the Catholic convert in *The Perpetual Curate* (1864), whose terrified wife assumes his future celibacy must make her and the children redundant.

Oliphant was keen to write about religion in *Blackwood's*. 'I want very much to make a sketch of the constitution and forms (or want of forms) of the Church of England,' she told John Blackwood in 1861, recognizing that it was a 'serious subject to trust in my hands . . .'.[25] Five years later she had transferred her interests to Scotland. 'There is nothing I wish so much as to write something on the movement in the Kirk – which seems to me the most important that has begun in Scotland for many a day'.[26] Oliphant in fact confined herself to the less intellectual side of religion, and wrote about sermons, religious memoirs, and, towards the end of her life, her own religious beliefs, which had been sorely tested by the deaths of her sons, Cyril and 'Cecco'. By 1895, she felt it was 'unusual' to be a believer, but also accepted that a modern Christian had considerable freedom in explaining away aspects of theology which had not been clearly established by revelation. This seems not to have troubled her unduly: by then she was viewing the world as an experiment to see what man would do with his freewill. 'This world is not a consistent world, any more than it is a just one,' she decided. Uncertainty was for her the distinguishing hallmark of contemporary life. 'The only thing of which we are sure is, that we are never sure of anything.' The other aspect of human experience, which she emphasizes in 'Fancies of a Believer', is the inextricable connections between individuals, their actions and fates, so that 'their will for good or for evil will often throw all our plans into the wildest confusion, and baffle our hopes and decisions and intentions by the exercise of a will perhaps stronger, perhaps only more fatal, than our own'.[27] This had, in effect, already become Oliphant's philosophy thirty years earlier, when she was writing her series of Carlingford novels.

Oliphant's is a philosophy geared to coping with disappointment. In that respect her novels trace a similar theme to George Eliot's: the adjustment of idealism and aspiration to match lowered expectations, caused by a combination of human error and entanglement. Whether or not she approved of the Dissenters, the religious group who form the background chorus of *Salem Chapel* (1863), is in some respects irrelevant to an examination of Mrs Oliphant's outlook, though at the time of the novel's publication, she was attacked for not understanding Dissent, or its characteristic language.[28] She confessed in a letter of 1855 to disliking English Dissent, but although she preferred the 'English Establishment' to the 'English sectarians', she had more sympathy for the ungrammatical poor, 'than for the chilly intellectualists, who, so often, hold the higher places in dissenting churches'.[29] Eight years later, however, in *Salem Chapel*, Oliphant plainly shows herself to be more offended by the vulgarity of Dissenting congregations, with their lavish teas, plump, pink daughters, and the general atmosphere of cheese and bacon which pervades their social gatherings.

Salem Chapel is full of equivocal figures who are perhaps representations of Oliphant's own 'inferior feminine and lay position', as she described her situation in a letter of 1862 about religious controversy.[30] Few of the characters seem to have a clear social standing or transparent motives for what they do, and the hero, Arthur Vincent, finds himself tossed to and fro between the unappealing Tozers and the glamorous Lady Western. Disappointed by Lady Western's party, because all the guests are unfamiliar, he throws himself keenly into his work: 'It was the natural cry of a man who had entered life at disadvantage, and chafed, without knowing it, at all the phalanx of orders and classes above him, standing close in order to prevent his entrance' (p. 76). With no particular interest in the teleological differences between Dissent and the Establishment (at least not within the pages of this novel), Oliphant focuses on those aspects of Arthur Vincent which are closest to a woman writer's experience. For instance, when he meets the mysterious Mrs Hilyard, the centre of the 'sensation' subplot which many critics have attacked as clumsy and extraneous, he identifies with her, rather than the man in her story, and 'had the habits of a man trained in necessary subjection to circumstances' (p. 175). This is a novel in which sexual feeling is seen as something guilty and mysterious; as if Arthur's repressed passion for Lady Western is magnified and exposed in the revelation of his sister Susan's apparent abduction by or elopement with Colonel Mildmay. Susan's 'white marble arm', which symbolizes her hitherto unsuspected sensuousness, develops into 'glorious proportion' the more enmired her brother becomes in guilty desires of his own (p. 269). Indeed he deludes himself that Lady Western loves him because she has placed her hand in his arm (p. 292), a gesture repeated by Mrs Hilyard (p. 314). Frustrated sexual feeling fuels his powerful sermons, which shock and excite his parishioners. Unlike his sister, he has a natural outlet for expression, and while she lies inert and silent, he storms aloud in the pulpit, trying also to silence Mrs Hilyard, and prevent her from escaping. Although Arthur's function as a minister is important in the novel, Oliphant uses his character and situation to explore the agonies of the 'nonconformist', in the sense of a person who does not fit into society. Even his mother fails to understand him, and Arthur remains essentially alone, and without a confidant. He and Susan are two halves of a complete person, whose instincts are kept down by society's insistence on propriety; both transgress the social rules, and both pay in the manner demanded of their sex: Susan by illness and silence, Arthur by professional isolation.

The 'nonconformist' feels as trapped as a woman. 'Was he actually to live among these people for years – to have no other society – to circulate among their tea-parties, and grow accustomed to their finery, and perhaps "pay attention" to Phoebe Tozer; or, at least, suffer that young lady's attentions to him?' (p. 18). His is essentially the situation of an unmarried middle-class woman, expected to be passively sociable: the only difference being that his congregants want him to 'do them proud' in his work. The climax of the novel occurs on the day of Susan's return home after her disappearance, a Sunday on which Arthur has to give two sermons. His first, spoken before he knows of Susan's innocence, sets forth 'the dark secrets of life with exaggerated touches of his own passion and anguish' (p. 305); his second, preached in an ecstasy because the truth has been revealed, throbs with a sense of the miraculous. 'He was again in the world where God stoops down to change with one touch of His finger the whole current of man's life – the world of childhood, of genius, of faith' (p. 383). Most critics who deal with *Salem Chapel* either attack the split in the novel between melodrama and social comedy, or else try to find a way of reconciling the two.[31]

Arthur's sermons, which offer two contrasting but equally sensational pictures of human experience, bring the language of religious mystery to the world of sexual relationships and small-town scandal. One way of connecting the two contrasting styles of the novel is to see them as representing Oliphant's own two strongest psychological impulses: the tendency to view all human activities ironically, and the instinct towards belief in unfathomable mystery and the drama of conflicting human wills. Arthur's sermons allow the woman novelist, who strongly disliked the sermons she heard in church, to voice the more turbulent interpretation of the unseen that she came to develop many years later in 'Fancies of a Believer'.

Uncertainty is also the distinguishing mark of Frank Wentworth's life in *The Perpetual Curate* (1864), an uncertainty which Oliphant contrasts with the authority of the church. He is the only reliable male character in a novel overflowing with bad sons and emotionally unstable women, and the main themes are not religious, but social: 'the character of a clergyman was almost as susceptible as that of a woman' (p. 255). Like Arthur Vincent, Frank feels that the external world is inexplicable, especially the inequalities between people's lots, and the undeserved sympathy shown to the sinner, rather than the virtuous man. Most of the women in the novel are preoccupied with religion in some way: Lucy Wodehouse, who marries Frank, with High Anglican practices, Frank's aunts with Evangelical principles, and Mrs Morgan, the rector's wife, with her husband's church politics. Apart from Lucy, most of Oliphant's church-going women gain little obvious support from their religion, and many, such as Louisa Wentworth and Mrs Morgan, are exasperated by the effect it has on their husbands. Oliphant, too, implies that the male religious establishment makes clergymen emotionally inept and retards their development, as she shows in the repeated theme of the frigid bachelor cleric.

This theme appears both in *The Rector* (1863) and *The Curate in Charge* (1876), where a middle-aged Fellow, newly released from Oxford, shrinks from his first contact either with women or with commonplace human suffering. The Rector, Mr Proctor, has no idea how to comfort a dying woman, to whom Frank and Lucy, as a young, emotionally vital couple, successfully minister. He is a further example of the clergyman unsuited to his profession, which was a favourite theme of Mrs Oliphant's, and perhaps a criticism of the disconnection between the kind of preparation a man received as a college Fellow, and the work he was asked to perform if he accepted a country 'living'. The characters in *The Curate in Charge* divide into incompetent priests and efficient women, the priests being particularly inept in handling human feeling. Although Mrs Oliphant stops well short of proposing any major reform of the church hierarchy, or even questioning its usefulness as an institution, the impression that emerges from her best-known Carlingford novels is that the church is quaint, decorative, a part of people's lives, but of little practical use, compared with the quiet, unrecognized domestic work performed by the wives and daughters of the clergy. When, in addition to incompetence and emotional frigidity, the clergyman also becomes guilty of petty crime (such as forgery in *Phoebe Junior*), Oliphant seems to be suggesting that true Christian morality has become detached from those who professionally are meant to exemplify it.

In *Phoebe Junior* (1876), the clergyman's son Reginald is offered a sinecure in the church (a wardenship, rather like Trollope's Mr Harding's), while his daughters, Ursula and Janey, wish they could earn money even by scrubbing floors. Here, and in *The Curate in Charge*, the male-priestly-vocation plot runs alongside a female-frustrated-vocation plot, implying that whereas men have a well-trodden route to professional standing, women, who might prove better at the work they undertake, are prevented from even starting it, by social considerations. Ursula sensibly advises Reginald to accept the sinecure, but look for additional voluntary work in the parish; she also takes over the planning of his future home, 'transformed by the instinct of business and management into the leader of the party' (p. 138). Phoebe, meanwhile, discovers that Mr May has forged her grandfather's signature, visits him to discuss the matter, and finding him asleep, waits for him to wake up, 'sole guardian, sole confidant of erring and miserable man' (p. 298). Oliphant generally holds out more hope for the younger clergymen, and, in the Northcote story, returns to the dilemma of the well-bred Dissenter who is pained by the vulgarity of his parishioners and in love with a woman who appears inaccessible, because of his own lowly status. In this case, the love-story has a happy outcome, in that Northcote leaves the Dissenters and marries Ursula May; but no clergyman in this novel, or any other by Mrs Oliphant, is left with much credibility as a saver of souls. Her outlook is similar to Trollope's, but without the redeeming image of a Mr Harding, a decent old clergyman of the pre-reforming days, but honest and gentle, bringing to the profession such natural goodness as cannot be taught or easily learned, without a basic instinct for it.

Nor does Oliphant show the church or religion in general as bringing much spiritual comfort to her characters, especially the women. With one or two exceptions, such as Lucy Wodehouse, they are usually detached from it, concerning themselves with the stuff of real life. Mrs Oliphant gives a characteristic picture of female aloofness from religious practice in a passage from her *Autobiography*, which describes a group of men taking communion at Notre Dame on Easter morning:

> I, more profane, smiled a little, and was a little ashamed of myself for doing so, at the air of conscious solemnity with which most of the men came up to the altar, very devout, but yet with a certain sense of forming part of a very great and ennobling spectacle.[32]

This is very much the way men and women behave in her novels, so that, in a sense, conventional sex roles are reversed. The men perform a largely decorative function, while the women attend to the practical business of running a household; the clergymen are hypersensitive and hemmed in, while the women move about the town more freely, making their own decisions. At her most tolerant, she implies that clergymen are an important luxury in society, provided they have wives or mothers to do the real work in the background.

Writing more seriously about religion in her *Autobiography*, Oliphant tries to come to terms with the deaths of her two adult sons. Her language is steeped in biblical cadences, and she is struck by the fact that her sons were Christ's age when they died; though it was perhaps the death of her ten-year-old daughter Maggie that most severely tested her religious faith. Oliphant is at her most moving when she explores the state of bereaved motherhood and tries to understand how Maggie's loss can have any meaning or serve any heaven-sent purpose. In most editions of the *Autobiography*, this section is cut, but the complete text, edited by Elisabeth Jay, shows how poignant and extensive was Oliphant's spiritual struggle. 'I try to realize heaven to myself, and I cannot do it,' she admits. 'The more I think of it, the less I am able to feel that those who have left us can start up at once into a heartless beatitude without caring for our sorrow' (p. 6). Her one hope was that Maggie might be with her own mother, who had died a few years before;

otherwise she was left in a state of bafflement and incomprehension. Confessing that suffering made her heart harder, not softer, Oliphant prays:

> O Father Almighty. I strive against thee. I reproach thee, I do not submit, but my reasons and my heart alike confess that thou must know thine own purpose best. That thou canst not have sent without reason a calamity so terrible, that somehow all must be well. (p. 8)

Much of the *Autobiography* is an upbraiding of God for having taken her children away; though after she had come to terms with Cyril's death, she felt it was the only solution to his problems. He was unable to hold down any job, and had begun to lounge around the house in much the same way as her own brothers had done. For Maggie, the 'woman-child', she had more heartfelt concern, and her voice in the *Autobiography* is that of a woman, a mother angry with a male God for not understanding how deeply and permanently she was wounded by her loss.

Further into the text, she compares her bereavements with Archbishop Tait's, but feels her family lacked the religious atmosphere of his. 'I think [Cecco] would not have liked it from me, the boys had that impression, got I don't know how, that a woman should not lead in that way – at least I think so' (pp. 84–5). This partly explains why Oliphant rarely spoke directly about her religious feelings, but also why when she did, she expressed a personal viewpoint, and not the conventionally expected one.

The progress of Oliphant's self-evolved faith can be traced both in the fragmented parts of her *Autobiography*, and in the religious articles she wrote for *Blackwood's*. She never abandoned her belief, or her fundamental trust in God, but she concluded that human experience was basically one of thwarted choice: a view represented in her novels, articles and *Autobiography*, where, in each case, what matters most is securing those we love from death or error. Alongside this, theological dogma seemed dry and irrelevant: something for bachelor dons to discuss until a human drama overtook their lives. Ultimately, as she argues in 'Sermons' (1862), 'the heart has still more to do with God's service than the intellect', and therefore worship, not sermonizing, is 'the daily breath of the soul'.[33] Although her novels fail to show women experiencing spiritual fulfilment, she, unlike Yonge, lends little support to the patriarchal system of religious hierarchy, and moves her discussion of the church closer to a 'woman-centred' view of the institution. She largely demonstrates the inadequacy of the church to cope with human crises, because its male professionals are themselves out of touch with their emotions; while those who can respond emotionally, such as Arthur Vincent and Frank Wentworth, suffer the personal restrictions of their liberty more usually experienced by women. Critical detachment from the church as an organization, and urgent searching for an explanation for her private sorrows, ensured that Oliphant's religious wounds were never completely healed. 'I never have had, I fear, a strong theological turn' she concluded in her *Autobiography* (p. 95).

ELIZA LYNN LINTON: 'A PLEA FOR SINCERITY'

Eliza Linton began and ended her conscious religious life as a stoic, which seemed to her a vigorous masculine position. Writing as Christopher Kirkland in her cross-dressed autobiography, which switches the key male and female identities in her life, she recalls as a teenager depriving herself of all luxuries, and despising bed as 'an unrighteous effeminacy'. 'My whole inner life was one of intense religious realization.'[34] Many Victorian women tell a similar story in their autobiographies, emphasizing the fervency of their devotion, their ecstasies and daydreaming. George Eliot and Annie Besant, for example, were both enthusiasts who subsequently abandoned literal belief in the scriptures, and found alternative value systems to satisfy their moral sense. Harriet Martineau passed through an earnest Unitarianism to become a cheerful agnostic; while Annie Besant and Florence Nightingale focused their religious yearnings chiefly on the longing for something useful to do.

Eliza Linton quickly acknowledged the way female piety may be, in reality, a disguised version of something else: a statement of undefined need, always emotional, and frequently sexual. For her, there was something undignified, or rather 'unmanly', about the contortions of language and behaviour imposed on rational beings by the church, and her own deconversion happened rapidly when she began to doubt the Virgin Birth. The family's pregnant servant girl denied the existence of a human father, which led Linton to doubt the Virgin Mary's veracity in a comparable situation. She also noticed the similarities between Greek and other ancient myths, and the stories underlying Christianity: if the first were known to be untrue, why not the second? Having lost her literal belief in the Gospel, Linton, like Harriet Martineau, also condemned the egotism of Christianity, which led the virtuous to do good for the sake of their own salvation: 'the Christian's sanctified egotism', she called it in *Christopher Kirkland* (vol. I, p. 88). When, in 1848, she fell seriously in love with a Catholic doctor, Edward MacDermot, the relationship foundered on their religious differences. Calling MacDermot Cordelia Gilchrist, according to the pattern of reversed sex roles in *Christopher Kirkland*, Linton writes: 'I lost her because I could not lie, nor could she' (vol. II, p. 243). Their names – Christopher Kirkland and Cordelia Gilchrist – pun on images of Christ, the church, and King Lear's saintly youngest daughter, herself an image of Christ-like forgiveness. One reason for the inversion of identities, however, was Linton's belief that agnosticism is essentially masculine, and religion more suited to women's emotional dependency.

Linton's attacks on the church in her novels are as outspoken and virulent as her ridicule of weak men and modern women. She treats religion as a place where power games are played out, and the sexes learn to manipulate each other for their own self-interested purposes. Christianity, as originally conceived, was to her a vigorous and manly discipline, which the young Christopher Kirkland tries to practise, 'helped thereto by the influence and example of the strong old heathen times. I, at least, in my own person would be faithful to the Lord and a man among men' (vol. I, p. 84). His demonstrations of fortitude, such as digging out his tooth with a knife, are, however, more typical of adolescent female masochism, as is his refusal to look at himself in the mirror for six months, after 'a strange and sudden consciousness' of the beauty of his youth and personality (vol. I, p. 85). Linton connects every stage of Christopher's (and her own) religious development with the crises of adolescent coming-to-consciousness, combining his frustrations over Christian practice with his unhappy relationship with his father. 'Clergyman though he was', Christopher remarks, 'all this ebullient zeal and youthful extravagance of aspiration annoyed my father as if the translation of faith into practice had been an impiety, and not an effort of godliness' (vol. I, p. 91). He is taught that normal conformity is all that is required of him, not presumptuous piety, and that to practise Christianity as Jesus taught it, is to be at odds with Victorian society. Soon afterwards his father refuses him a goodnight kiss because he neither believes in, nor respects his son. Henceforward Linton would view Christianity as a force that breaks up normal family relationships.

Perhaps more than any other human failing Linton hated dishonesty, and felt that Christianity, as practised in nineteenth-century society, fostered its growth. Christopher equates Christianity with Republicanism, seeing no 'via media': 'nor could I understand the compromise between faith and practice, consistency and expediency, made by the believing world' (vol. I, p. 82), ideas Linton had pursued in an earlier novel, *The True History of Joshua Davidson* (1872), which meant, she told a clergyman friend, 'simply a plea for sincerity'.[35] It asks what would happen if a man tried to live according to Christ in modern Christendom, and shows that he would be treated as a criminal, or at the least ostracized for eccentric behaviour. Joshua, a Cornish carpenter's son, goes to London and learns of the class antagonism engendered by Christianity. He befriends a burglar and a prostitute and tries to reintegrate them into society. Having experimented with ritualism and rationalism, he decides that Christianity is really communism, and joins the uprising during the Paris Commune of 1871. Surviving this, unlike Mary, the prostitute, he is finally beaten to death at a public meeting, showing that little has changed since Christ was misunderstood and murdered by the reactionaries of his own times. 'Is the Christian world all wrong, or is practical Christianity impossible?' asks the narrator, one of Joshua's own followers, known only as 'John'. 'I cannot,' he concludes, 'being a Christian, accept the inhumanity of political economy and the obliteration of the individual in averages; yet I cannot reconcile modern science with Christ.'[36] The choice is left unresolved, for the reader to work out; but her point is primarily that the tenets of Christianity, as taught by Christ, are incompatible with modern values, especially materialism, class snobbery, and the double standard in dealing with sexual impropriety. Mary is the only important female figure in the novel: a modern Mary Magdalene, forgiven by the Christ-like Joshua, but by no one else, and killed when mistaken for a *petroleuse* during the Commune. Bigotry and incomprehension are Mary's rewards throughout the novel.

W.R. Greg, examining Christianity in the *Contemporary Review*, assumed the anonymous novel, written by a fictitious male narrator, was by a woman: 'for the eager and wholesome, if sometimes rather uncontrolled sympathies, the imperfect knowledge of facts, the superficial acquaintance with political economy, the impulsive haste of what might otherwise be powerful thought, the intellect always at the command and at the mercy of the feelings, the prejudices and the fancy which break out in every page, stamp it unmistakeably as the work of a woman'.[37] The comment is ironic in view of Linton's equation of rugged truth-telling with masculinity, and quavering emotionalism with the kind of femininity she despised.

This is the type of femininity she explores in her most extensive treatment of religious controversy, *Under Which Lord?* (1879). Written in Linton's characteristically outspoken style, this novel recounts how the Reverend Launcelot Lascelles, a ritualist priest in the parish of Crossholme, exerts a powerful and dangerous infuence over nearly all the women characters, ruining either their health or their marriages. Each woman comes to symbolize the risks of religious susceptibility, and one, an hysterical girl called Theresa Molyneaux, who is in love with him, actually dies an excruciating death from a wasting disease which seems a mixture of anorexia and consumption. 'Her very life was consumed by the fervid passion with which she made love to a man under the form of serving the Church and worshipping God,' Linton comments in the narrative.[38] The novel's main heroine, Hermione Fullerton, finds herself increasingly having to choose between the authority of the church, exerted through Lascelles, and the milder authority of her agnostic husband Richard, who also dies after seeing his home and marriage broken up. Richard's manliness, his association with the decent workmen of the parish, whom he attempts to rehouse after they have been evicted by the church, and his loving patience with his fanatical daughter and wife, make him Linton's martyr–hero. He gives public lectures on the 'duties of men', voicing Linton's own views on the inherent egotism of Christianity: 'In contradiction to the theological view of rewards and punishments, of pleasing God and saving our own souls, duty was set forth as self-respect on the one hand and the good of the community at large on the other' (vol. I, p. 182). His daughter Virginia, meanwhile, rejects men altogether, and placing herself under the infuence of Lascelles's sister Agnes as her spiritual mother, flees with her to become a Roman Catholic nun. The only sensible women in the novel are the Nesbitts, mother and daughter, who rate family life at its correct value, above religion. 'The woman who neglects her own family, that she may give her time and energies to a cause, is doing wrong whatever that cause may be,' Mrs Nesbitt asserts (vol. I, p. 130); while her daughter Beatrice marries Virginia's would-be-lover Ringrove Hardisty: 'Surely a better ending to her girlhood than Virginia's immolation or Theresa's self-destruction – the one for devotional enthusiasm, the other for religious excess!' (vol. III, p. 250).

As for Hermione, the main heroine: 'For herself she had lost husband, child, money, place, and the finest flavour of her womanly repute. But she had gained the blessing of the Church which denies science, asserts impossibilities, and refuses to admit the evidence of facts' (vol. III, p. 308). Linton leaves the reader in no doubt that Hermione has thrown away the priceless possession of a happy home to indulge in an unhealthy obsession with a self-seeking clergyman and the atmosphere of sickly piety he creates. Launcelot Lascelles has a special interest in Hermione because she is the wealthiest of his female followers (few men, in any case, succumb to his charms), and when she shows signs of resistance, he has another woman, Edith Everett, placed in her house to prevent backsliding. The women all call Lascelles 'Superior', a sign of the grovelling abjection in which he holds them. Although he is at the opposite end of the religious spectrum to Mr Slope, he is like Trollope's Evangelical chaplain in the influence he exerts over vulnerable women with money, and the antagonism he arouses in breezy, strong-hearted men.

The advancements of science, especially Darwinism, were final proof for Linton that religion was founded on uprovable mythology, and that true democracy lay with agnosticism. According to Evelleen Richards, she 'offered the only documented resistance to Huxley's exclusion of women from the Ethnological Society', writing an eight-page petition on behalf of women visitors in 1868.[39] Ethically, she thought 'duty' was more important than religious observance, and a higher aspiration attainable by all, for the good of the race. Nevertheless, she still makes something of an exception of herself, an unusually resilient woman who could survive without the consolations of Christianity. The choice for her women characters lies not between orthodoxy and agnosticism, but between church and family, those two elements in a woman's life that Charlotte Yonge felt could merge without conflict. Religion was to Linton yet another 'cause' that could take a wife away from her husband or a mother away from her children. Herself a separated childless wife, a stoic, Darwinian agnostic, Linton stopped well short of recommending other women to follow her precise example. She prefers to imagine them at home with their husbands and families, too absorbed in their true womanly role to have time left over for worrying about religious controversy.

MRS HUMPHRY WARD: 'THE NEW REFORMATION'

The opposite is true of Mary Ward, whose novels show wives and mothers continually wrestling, as she did, with the intellectual debates of the age, combining them with the rest of their strenuous routine. The eldest child of a Protestant mother and a father who converted twice to Catholicism, Mary Ward could hardly escape an early consciousness of religion, or of faction, in a house where the girls were brought up in their mother's religion and the boys in their father's. This must have implied a curious connection between gender and belief, their religious practices being decided according to each child's sex. The sense of division between sects and sexes remained with her as she grew up, and became part of her Oxford college social life, first through her father, and then through her husband. At Oxford the Wards adhered to the more forward-thinking party associated with Jowett and Balliol College, which was opposed to the High Church party of Pusey and Liddon at Christ Church. Ward, by marriage, was as much a part of this largely male world of schism and controversy as any fully established college Fellow, and her autobiography, *A Writer's Recollections* (1918), excludes all but a handful of women contemporaries from the debates and dinner-parties that filled her early married life.

Ward was strongly influenced by T.H. Green of Balliol, a Christian humanist, who wanted to retain belief in God while denying the truth of revelation. Ward's own religious struggles were to focus on the gap between the spiritual needs that she felt most people experienced, and the elements of Christianity which a late nineteenth-century rationalist could not accept. Rejecting dogma, she concentrated on personality: the personality of Christ, then of the young men and women she imagined coming to grips with this major upheaval in their lives. The seed of her novels was sown in her anonymous pamphlet of 1881, *Unbelief and Sin* – her angry response to John Wordsworth's Bampton lecture on 'The Present Unsettlement in Religion', which equated 'unbelief' with 'sin'. Seeing the 'Christian problem', as she called it, in terms of literature and history, the accuracy of documents, which it was becoming easier to disprove, she imagined the effect of religious controversy on two young male university students, 'A' and 'C'. Whereas 'A' is strong enough to retain his belief in God as the 'Highest Ideal', while accepting the range of different viewpoints on revelation, 'C's natural timidity reinforces the religious side, and he is never seriously tempted. Ward hoped that the old kind of blind belief in the face of disproof could be replaced by a 'seeing and rational faith' in a new type of Christianity.[40]

She returned to the image of two college friends in 'The New Reformation, A Dialogue', written for the *Nineteenth Century* in 1889 as a reply to Gladstone's criticism of *Robert Elsmere* (1888), which had appeared in the same journal. Here, the two friends are given names: Merriman has postponed his ordination to spend time studying in German, and Ronalds has already taken orders. Merriman decides that 'temperament' is the key factor in the debate. 'I could not master the passionate desire to think the matter through, to harmonise knowledge and faith, to get to the bottom,' he tells Ronalds, adding: 'You might have done it, I think.'[41] Far from being depressed by the new situation, Merriman, like Ward, is excited and stirred: 'passionate' becomes a favourite word with both of them: but the arena is initially open only to men. Ten years later, in another article on the same theme, Ward argued the need for a new kind of clergyman to 'preach to the thinking workman, or the university graduate, or the intelligent girl, in language that really fits their modern needs'.[42] By this stage in her career, she had begun to switch her attention from the inner turmoils of the young Oxford man, to those of the informally educated 'intelligent girl', whose religious dilemmas were generally compounded with her emotional needs.

But in *Robert Elsmere*, her most extensive examination of religious doubt, the woman symbolizes traditional, unquestioning faith in the truth of holy scripture. Catherine Elsmere, though not caricatured, is as earnest as any of Linton's female characters in *Under Which Lord?*, tremulous with spiritual exaltation. She was largely formed by her father, Richard Leyburn, a fanatical Evangelical with a touch of Quakerism. 'He could talk his soul out to her,' the vicar, Mr Thornburgh tells Robert.[43] Stubborn and self-sufficient, Catherine quells the rest of her family, and exasperates them with her unhuman self-control, suggestive, perhaps, of traditional Christianity's refusal to bend in the face of convincing opposition. She is austere and ascetic: qualities at war with her needs as a woman. While Robert feels it is good to be happy, to her, 'life always meant self-restraint, self-repression, self-deadening, if need be. The Puritan distrust of personal joy as something dangerous and ensnaring was deeply ingrained in her' (p. 158). Devoted to her father first, and then to his memory, Catherine is nearly too stubborn to give her romance with Robert a chance. When she does, her sense of his dependence on her at last gives her the happiness Ward feels every wife should experience.

In her portrayal of Catherine Elsmere, Ward stresses the negative effects of religious enthusiasm on her psychological and emotional development. Like Linton, Ward believes that commitment to other human beings – to husbands and families – is ultimately more necessary for a woman than adherence to theory or dogma, and the greatest test for Catherine, therefore, is when Robert abandons his faith and his living, to work in London. Ward asks a new question at this point in the novel: 'Is it possible now for a good woman with a heart, in Catherine Elsmere's position, to maintain herself against love, and all those subtle forces to which such a change as Elsmere's opens the house doors, without either hardening, or greatly yielding?' (p. 363). She resists the temptation to leave him, but like George Eliot's Rosamond Vincy in *Middlemarch*, remains firmly detached from her husband's way of looking at things. In Catherine's case, however, her detachment stems from 'an intolerable fear of what love might do with her if she once gave it an opening' (p. 389) – in other words, destroy her faith. Although she clings to her religion, it offers her little comfort, and their marriage necessarily diminishes. 'He was really more and more oppressed by her intellectual limitations,' Ward reports (p. 392), while she finds it difficult to accept standards different from her own. Nevertheless, before Robert's death, Catherine does change, and move away from the state of self-torture in which she passes the first year of their life in London. Ward sees what has happened to Catherine as being typical of a larger movement of forces in Victorian thought, but also the result of a play of feelings and influences around her:

> Love, and her husband, and the thousand subtle forces of a changing world had conquered. She would live and die steadfast to the old faiths. But her present mind and its outlook was no more the mind of her early married life than the Christian philosophy of today is the Christian philosophy of the Middle Ages. She was not conscious of change, but change there was. She had, in fact, undergone that dissociation of the moral judgment from a special series of religious formulae which is the crucial, the epoch-making fact of our day. (p. 534)

Like George Eliot's heroines, especially Dorothea Brooke, and Dinah Morris (with whom she is specifically compared, p. 493), Catherine gradually becomes humanized by concern for others, especially by the claims of her husband and child. At the same time, Ward sees her as part of a larger clash of old and new, as a tendency of thought personified. The central image, as it is so often in her novels, is of conflict: between men and women, orthodoxy and criticism, dogma and free thought. Despite her 'passionate submission' to her husband (p. 571), Catherine cherishes hope till the last that Robert will recover his faith, if only on his deathbed. Ward, however, gives each victory to Robert, as the man of the future. Urging Catherine to submit, one last time, and let him reach God in his own way, he begs to be released from her prayers. 'She bowed herself again with a quiet burst of tears, and an indescribable self-abasement. They had had their last struggle, and once more he had conquered!' (p. 572). This tableau, of the woman shamed by the man's superior wisdom, becomes Ward's key image of female weakness, used with either a religious or a political dimension. She admires women who can fight for what they believe, but for her, women's haphazard education and emotional instability make them losers every time.

After *Robert Elsmere*, Ward normally reverses the religious allegiances of her men and women, making her rebellious young girls antagonistic to the traditional religious practices of their lovers and husbands. By repeatedly making her women, rather than her men, freethinkers, Ward stresses their detachment from history and tradition: they are second-class citizens, who have never formally belonged to their country's institutions, and who are therefore ashamed of criticizing them, exposing their inconsistencies, and longing to destroy them. They are outside the 'symbolic order', and frequently, in Ward's terms, 'wild' and 'passionate', their response to Nature, Brontë-like, revealing their repressed poetry and sensuality. They belong to a world that is pagan, free, and without regulations. Ward's point, however, is always that institutions are immovably *there*, and difficult to modify, let alone abolish. In *Helbeck of Bannisdale* (1898), Laura Fountain throws herself furiously against the centuries-old traditions of the Catholic Church, half wishes to capitulate, and finally commits suicide because she is up against forces too powerful for her. Robin Gilmour has commented: 'A good case can be made for considering it the finest novel of religious conflict in the period.'[44] What makes it of particular interest to the history of women's writing is Ward's intense consciousness of gender issues as the conflict between Alan Helbeck and Laura Fountain unfolds.

Like Catherine Elsmere, Laura is strongly her father's daughter, although this time brought up without religious teaching. Aware that her father's career as a Cambridge scientist has been impeded by the religious party (much as Mary Ward's father's was when he returned to Catholicism), 'from her childhood it came natural to her to hate bigoted people who believed in ridiculous things'.[45] Laura's objections to religious orthodoxy continue to be expressed in childish, emotional terms, something that weakens the case for free thought in the novel. For example, until she enters Alan Helbeck's chapel she has never seen an altar before, and when she is told that the 'blessed Sacrament' is kept there, she erupts into scornful rage: 'A wave of the most passionate repulsion swept through her. What a gross, what an intolerable superstition! – how was she to live with it, beside it?' (p. 55). Whereas Alan's world is monkish, dark, and interior, Laura, as her other name, 'Fountain', suggests, is happiest out of doors, exploring the Westmorland landscape: a breezy field or hill-top being the favourite image of freedom from religious orthodoxy used by other nineteenth-century women writers, such as Harriet Martineau.[46]

The house itself becomes claustrophobic, like a prison; the Lenten diet, which Laura sometimes observes although she is free to eat normally, like the reduced rations provided for an inmate, or those of a Brontë heroine, whom Laura resembles in her anorexic tendencies and emotional and physical starvation. Her isolation is also emphasized. An orphan from Cambridge, a freethinker in a Catholic house, a woman in a home that has been entirely masculine for years, Laura has no confidante, apart from her old Cambridge friend Molly Friedland, who makes only a brief appearance in the novel. One of Alan's priests, Father Leadham, points out her vulnerability, and softens Alan's sympathies for her. 'There must be a sense of exile', he tells Helbeck, '– of something touching and profound going on beside her, from which she is excluded' (p. 110).

The religious and sexual battles between them proceed inextricably linked. Laura distracts Alan from his Lenten concentration, passion disturbing his attention to the Passion of Christ. Laura, in turn, feels jealous of his religious practices, which take up most of his spare time, while he is afraid that if he gave into his feelings for her, his life would centre in her, and not in the church. The only satisfactory compromise, for him, would be her conversion to

Catholicism, which she strongly resists, despite a masochistic longing to be conquered. Both fantasize about her submission in sexual terms. 'She would sooner die than obey,' Alan acknowledges. 'Unless she loved. Then what an art, what an enchantment to command her! It would tax a lover's power, a lover's heart, to the utmost' (p. 198). Laura, meanwhile, thirsts to submit, but cannot. 'Just as Helbeck could hardly trust himself to think of the joy of conquest, so she shrank bewildered before the fancied bliss of yielding' (p. 316). Ward suggests that her natural temptation to submit is intensified by the effects of Alan's asceticism, and all it stands for in the history of male–female relations. 'In all ages,' she declares, 'the woman falls before the ascetic – before the man who can do without her. The intellect may rebel; but beneath its revolt the heart yields. Oh! to be guided, loved, crushed, if need be, by the mystic, whose first thought can never be for you – who puts his own soul, and a hundred torturing claims upon it, before your lips, your eyes!' (p. 247). This passage reveals a masochistic relish, in Ward's theorizing, for domination and dismissal: a thrilling fantasy of being ravished by a man with his mind on higher things. Because her modern sense of dignity makes the reality of this dream impossible for her, Laura can find no way out of the impasse other than suicide.

She is particularly disgusted by Catholic hagiography, noticing that family values always crumble in the face of religious devotion, as in the story of St Francis Borgia, who let his wife and children die for the good of his soul. She is insulted by the story of St Charles Borromeo, who refused to speak to any woman, 'not even to his pious aunt, or sisters, or any nun, but in sight of at least two persons, and in as few words as possible' (pp. 320–1). Laura takes the passage as a personal insult. Like Jane Eyre standing up to Rochester, she attacks Alan for his silent complicity, rousing him to a 'kind of angry joy, eager at once to conquer the woman and to pierce the sceptic' (p. 348). Ward clearly demonstrates the connection between male piety and aggressive anti-feminism; but to what extent, given Ward's mixed religious background, should this be seen specifically as an *anti-Catholic* novel?

No one could read it as a recommendation of Catholicism, any more than *Salem Chapel* would inspire its readers to sign up as Dissenters. Alan's priests are seen as pleasant, weak, childish men with a sinister intractability; Laura's stepmother Augustina, who resumes her Catholicism after her husband has died, is a querulous, malleable woman; and the nuns are sweet and sickly, without being overdrawn, like Linton's religious fanatics in *Under Which Lord?* Catholic practices themselves are shown to be gloomy and self-absorbing, and the habit of confession as Linton found it, unhealthily prurient. Janet Trevelyan quotes a comment of her mother's on Laura's horror of this ritual, as she planned for her novel to turn on 'the terror of confession – on what would seem to her the inevitable uncovering of the inner life and yielding of personality that the Catholic system involves – and on the foreignness of the whole idea of *sin*, with its relative, penance'.[47] Ward describes the invasion of a woman's spirit as a form of sexual violation, from which Laura recoils: the notion of personality being as sacrosanct as virginity. Linton records a similar disgust in *Under Which Lord?*, with its image of emotionally dependent women queueing to confess their non-existent sins to Launcelot Lascelles; while Charlotte Brontë, in *Villette* (1853), writes of Lucy Snowe's lonely urge to confess, followed by her shamed reaction against the invasiveness of Catholicism. Laura, similarly, dislikes the 'spiritual intrusiveness of Catholicism, its perpetual uncovering of the soul – its disrespect for the secrets of personality – its humiliation of the will –' (p. 319). Given the essential maleness of its hierarchy, and the dominant presence of priests in Alan's house, Laura feels especially vulnerable as a woman about to be married.

Nevertheless, Ward was anxious not to offend her Catholic father when she was writing the novel, and seems to have thought of it primarily as a love-story in unusual circumstances,[48] perhaps even unconsciously influenced by the Paul Emmanuel–Lucy Snowe relationship in *Villette*, which is also a love affair between an older Catholic man and a younger Protestant woman. Apart from her usual interest in the struggle for dominance, Ward highlights the difficulties faced by the new generation of freethinkers, who know they have rejected dogmatism, but are unable to put a convincing case for their own outlook. Catholicism is perhaps best seen as the most dogmatic of religions, against which Ward wished to pit the arguments for free thought; and psychologically, as her father's religion, it was therefore the one she most associated with patriarchy and the daughter's battle to establish her own individuality. Significantly, Catholicism in the novel is constantly viewed through Laura's eyes, with its peculiarities duly exaggerated. A Catholic reviewer, R.F. Clarke, writing in the *Nineteenth Century*, thought 'there never was a more absurd travesty of all things Catholic put before the English reader. From first to last it is nothing more than a gross burlesque.'[49] Similar criticisms were levelled against Mrs Oliphant's picture of the Dissenters in *Salem Chapel*. But accuracy here is less important than the psychological effect on Laura of what she sees. Moreover, by making her very much her father's daughter, clinging to his memory, Ward splits her own mixed feelings about her father, allowing Laura to express loyalty to one image of him, and antagonism to another. Instead of seeing *Helbeck* as an anti-Catholic novel, it might be more fruitful to see it as Ward's exploration of her position as a freethinking daughter of a Catholic father, and by extension, a study of female rebellion against an institution which had the power to influence even the most personal of human relations. Like George Eliot, Ward saw the inviolability of the individual as being of supreme importance, outweighing the religious hierarchies and dogmas of centuries: nevertheless, she was anxious about her own side's ability to defend itself against the attacks of practised tacticians of the establishment's front line.

Ward returned to religious issues in *The History of David Grieve* (1892) and *The Case of Richard Meynell* (1911), in which Catherine Elsmere and her grown-up daughter Mary reappear, and Mary falls in love with a modernist Anglican priest, the Richard Meynell of the title, and theologically, a reincarnation of her father. Ward, presumably hoping for a successful re-run of her earlier novel, also used it as an opportunity to write a sermon, spoken by Richard, arguing her concept of the New Reformation of the Church, as she had done in her *Nineteenth Century* articles. *The Coryston Family* (1913), which was as unsuccessful as *Richard Meynell*, meanwhile returned to the Helbeck theme in the subplot concerning Marcia Coryston and her intensely High Church fiancé Edward Newbury. Lady Newbury is the equivalent of Augustina: a weak, submissive woman who has no difficulties falling in with her husband's views on the subordination of her sex. Marcia, however, is repelled by Edward's religiosity, and the heavy authoritarianism that goes with it: 'And again a sudden terror seized on Marcia – as though behind the lover, she perceived something priestly, directive, compelling – something that threatened her very self.'[50] Again, the religious and the sexual are inextricably combined, in that it is Edward's wish to take a special communion on their wedding morning that especially alienates her, and makes her feel her own spiritual needs are being overwhelmed by his. She rejects the superior authority of the church to regulate her behaviour, and having been left by her family to think for herself, prefers a humanist philosophy of kindness, empathy and feeling. Like Dorothea Brooke after she has apparently lost Will Ladislaw in *Middlemarch*, Marcia breaks with Edward and becomes newly aware of other people and their sufferings: 'Marcia sat there hour after hour, now lost in her own grief, now in that of others; realising through pain, through agonised sympathy, the energy of a fuller life' (p. 304).

Her position is similar to Rachel Curtis's, at the end of *The Clever Woman of the Family*, in that both have learnt through personal sorrow to feel more kinship with others, and to direct their energies towards providing practical help: yet Rachel has arrived at this humanitarian stance by a resolution of her theological doubts, and gentle re-education by her father-substitute, Mr Clare, while Marcia reached hers by rejection of her High Anglican lover, and a sense of greater kinship with other women suffering because of their emotional perplexities. Whereas Charlotte Yonge reveres all but the lower-class or ineffectual kinds of clergyman, both Eliza Linton and Mary Ward attack either clerics themselves, or secular practitioners of a rigid and unbending form of religious observance. The 'anti-feminist view' on the church is therefore as varied as its proponents, and as the range of objections, in the twentieth century, to the ordination of women priests, not all of which can be dismissed simply as 'anti-feminist'.[51] In 1880, the *Nineteenth Century*, which was later to host the debate on the 'New Reformation' between Gladstone and Mary Ward, staged a discussion of 'Agnosticism and Women', which brought out the traditional arguments for and against encouraging women to remain with religious orthodoxy. The debate provides a useful context in which to reach a final analysis of the novelists' stance on women and religion, besides offering a marker in the evolving discussion of the relationship between Christianity and domesticity, which the Victorians traditionally tied together.

The pro-religious side of the argument was taken by Bertha Lathbury, the wife of Daniel Conner Lathbury, who later wrote on Dean Church and Gladstone in a series on 'Leaders of the Church'. She argued that the spread of agnosticism among women 'would tend to make them discontented with the quiet home life which is often their only lot. It would, moreover, increase tenfold the cry of women for the right of employment in the more active lines of life at present denied to them.'[52] Lathbury was keen to protect women from the dangers of unbelief, which would disturb their instinctive love of virtue and domestic affection. 'Intellectual courage is rarely one of their virtues,' she maintained, feeling that women were too restless and excitable to be capable of reliable judgement in theological matters. She was afraid that if they were thrown into more public roles, their integrity would disintegrate, and their judgement of moral issues suffer. She cites the extreme example of women's care for the sick, and fears that agnosticism might lead women towards the practice of euthanasia, with no concern about the afterlife. Above all, she believed that women's happiness lay in their affections, and their benevolent influence over men: a view held throughout the earlier part of the century by writers such as Mrs Ellis. 'Take away Prayer and Hope,' reasoned Lathbury, 'and you take away the very power that enables women to do this cheerfully, and to do it cheerfully is only another word for doing it successfully' (p. 626). She ends by urging women to reconsider their motives for becoming agnostics, and for leading others in the same direction.

The following month, a reply was written by Jane Hume Clapperton, a convinced agnostic, and later author of a novel, *Margaret Dunmore; or a Socialist Home* (1888), and an ethical tract, *Scientific Meliorism and the Evolution of Happiness* (1885). She argued that in compensation for Christianity, agnosticism offers truth, and a clear standpoint from which to develop a clearness of thought. She was concerned about the widening intellectual gap between men, who were willing to face the theological implications of the Higher Criticism, and women, who still clung to emotion and superstition. Lathbury's article, she suggested, implied that the 'essential nature of the sex is unchangeable. But herein agnostics take a different and much more hopeful view. Human nature is to them infinitely modifiable . . . '.[53] Clapperton stressed the optimism of female agnostics as they adapted to evolutionary change in the development of human ethics; noting that there was 'already a considerable band' of them in existence, she insisted that there was nothing aggressive or obstructive about them; nor did they seek work in order to drown thought. This exchange of 1880 between two women, on the question of whether belief or agnosticism was better for their sex, shows that the fundamentals of the debate had changed very little since the earlier half of the century. Religion for women was discussed, not in relation to dogma, but as it affected their domestic lives, and their roles as 'relative creatures'. The issue most at stake was whether or not religion made women better wives and mothers; the assumption, that agnosticism fostered a feminist desire to kick over the traces and find work outside the home.

The anti-feminist woman novelist whose position is closest to this is clearly Charlotte Yonge. In her women characters, participation in family and community-based religious life makes for a more harmonious household, giving wives, mothers and single women a common purpose in attending to the needs of others and overlooking their own disappointments in the process. Of the four writers in this group, however, only Yonge approximates to the traditional model. The others question the value of conventional Christian practice in the lives of wives and daughters, and, through caricature, irony and extensive analysis, expose the inadequacies of the established church. In each case, they focus specifically on the ways in which the church fails women: whether by exploiting their emotional dependency to bolster the egos of clergymen, or by debarring them from an exclusively male atmosphere. 'What a great god Zeus the vicar was!' Linton comments in *Under Which Lord?* – 'how he regulated and marshalled his little world of subordinates and lovers, and made each do as he desired!' (vol. II, p. 57). Linton, characteristically, expresses it more bluntly than the other novelists, but Oliphant is also conscious that clergymen are only men, and as susceptible to vanity and egotism as ordinary male mortals.

Linton and Oliphant together reverse the favourite image of the clergyman–lover, which George Eliot had ridiculed in 'Silly Novels by Lady Novelists' (1856) in the *Westminster Review*. Although Oliphant still concedes that a young cleric is attractive to women (as with Frank Wentworth and Arthur Vincent), the image of the middle-aged, emotionally-inept bachelor (such as Mr Mildmay and Mr Proctor) expresses her sense of the church's failure to answer women's needs. Where a clergyman does achieve passionate empathy with human suffering, as with the real Edward Irving and the fictitious Arthur Vincent, his career is cut short, or he alienates his followers. Mary Ward returns to the attractive clergyman–hero with Robert Elsmere, but in this, and in *Helbeck of Bannisdale*, is primarily interested in the way religion can destroy a relationship between lovers. Unlike Yonge, she sees it as a divisive force, which retards the development of wider sympathies; while Linton sees religious fanaticism as a destroyer of family life, not a healer of relationships. Ward and Linton agree in arguing that the matter of most importance to women, and the only real source of their long-term happiness, is a fulfilling marriage (children are less essential), and this can work only if neither partner has strong theological leanings which exclude the other.

On the other hand, all four novelists shy away from describing in any detail a process of deconversion in their female characters. Linton recounts her own experience in Christopher Kirkland's words, and from a thinly-disguised male angle; Yonge omits details of Rachel Curtis's doubts; Oliphant largely avoids the subject, except where the loss of one of her own children is concerned; and Ward explores Robert Elsmere's doubts, making Laura a convinced freethinker without the intellectual apparatus to investigate other views, except at a purely instinctive level. Although Ward herself had, as a young woman, experienced the full process of doubt, argument, and reconstruction of an alternative value-system, as had George Eliot before her, it was still unusual in fiction to demonstrate the stage-by-stage deconversion in a woman. Perhaps such a story would have been uninteresting in a novel, or too hot for publishers to handle; perhaps few women had the education to appreciate it: at any rate, it was avoided as a theme by the novelists in this group, who nevertheless judged it safe to write in some detail about the male experience of doubt and deconversion. At bottom, rigorous theological debate, though they were aware of it themselves, was still not a subject for the majority of women to investigate.

Religion enhances the lives of their characters – where it does so at all – only in the perpetuation of traditional roles. It is not shown, for example, opening new outlets for self-expression in work (except in Ethel May's church-building), or building women's self-confidence. There is also little attempt to portray an alternative female experience of religion or spirituality, except by Margaret Oliphant, whose treatment of religious issues is constantly influenced by her sufferings as a mother whose children one by one inexplicably die. It would be true to say that these novelists are far more interested in attacking the shortcomings of the church, and in Ward's case, nominating alternative philosophies, than in representing the kind of feminist theology which has gained popularity in the late twentieth century. They had no wish themselves to become deaconesses or enter a sisterhood, and appear to have felt no frustration at not being directly involved in the ministry of the church.

Their image of the clerical father-figure, with its emotional ambiguities, affirms their need for rebellion qualified by some attachment to the old forms of their childhood. Many of these novels contain unreliable priestly father-figures: the forger, Mr May, in *Phoebe Junior*; the inadequate Mr St John in *The Curate in Charge*; the austere Mr Leyburn, Catherine's father, in *Robert Elsmere*; Alan Helbeck, whose sister is Laura's stepmother; and Launcelot Lascelles, who becomes his female parishioners' spiritual father in *Under Which Lord?* Not all of these are priests, but they all represent a religious commitment seen in relation to women's (usually daughters') lives. The close relationship between fathers and daughters is a strong undercurrent in discussion of these novels, whereas mothers are distinctly absent as an influence on their daughters' spirituality. This suggests that rebellion against religion, and against patriarchy as the symbol of religion, was the uppermost concern of these novelists (Yonge excepted), rather than the construction of a woman-centred religion derived from their mothers, or from other close relationships with women – which are significantly lacking in most of these novels, where the heroine passes from emotional dependence on her father to involvement with a lover, without a long intermediate state. In each case, the father-figure (representing religious orthodoxy) impedes his daughter's growth to maturity, keeping her child-like and dependent. In *Helbeck*, Laura is torn between two father-figures: one (her real, freethinking father) frowning from beyond the grave on her hesitant move toward Catholic conversion; the other (Alan Helbeck), having disapproved of his sister's marriage with Stephen Fountain, struggling against the temptation of his attraction to Laura, and then fighting for spiritual domination over her. The father-figure in these novels is rarely seen helping his daughter to fulfil herself, either in work or in marriage, and where this is what he desires, as with Richard Fullerton, for his daughter Virginia in *Under Which Lord?*, his wishes are overturned by others – in this case by Launcelot Lascelles and Lascelles' sister.

Apart from attacking the extremes of religious orthodoxy, this group of novelists to some extent feminize the clergyman's role, where the priest is a more sympathetic figure: Robert Elsmere, Arthur Vincent and Frank Wentworth are good examples. Here, the woman novelist turns herself into a sermon-writer, using the clergyman as a mouthpiece; she also emphasizes the importance of his social work among the poor, the sick and the children of the parish. In a sense, she rewrites his role, leaving out the wrangling over small points of dogma, and making him rise above the petty professional struggles which threaten to engulf him. Eliza Linton speaks through the freethinker Richard Fullerton, as well as through Joshua Davidson and Christopher Kirkland in a similar way. In this respect, the antifeminist women writers resemble the other Victorian women who offer constructive criticism of the church: Dinah Mulock Craik, Frances Cobbe, Anna Jameson, George Eliot, Charlotte Brontë, Florence Nightingale. All were aware of the dangers of complacency and dogmatism in a centuries-old institution such as the church; all had ideas on how aspects of its running could be improved, and in particular made more relevant to the needs of women. But the split remains until the end of the century, with the 'official voice' of public life, in the journals and tracts, reinforcing women's silent, domestic role as Christians, and the novelists questioning the status quo. The linking of emotional and sexual development with religious prohibition and repression reaffirms ancient Christian teaching on the place of women. But then, in 1994, a Lincolnshire vicar, the Rev. Anthony Kennedy, declared: 'Priestesses should be burned at the stake because they are assuming powers they have no right to.... Or I would shoot the bastards if I was allowed, because women can't represent Christ.'[54] In comparison, even Eliza Linton's caricature of a ritualist priest in Launcelot Lascelles seems mild and harmless.

Conclusion

'Women's rights will never grow into a popular agitation,' Mrs Oliphant concluded in 1856, 'yet women's wrongs are always picturesque and attractive. They are indeed so good as to make novels and poems about, so telling as illustrations of patience and gentleness, that we fear any real redress of grievances would do more harm to the literary world than it would do good to the feminine.'[1]

As with many of Mrs Oliphant's urbane throwaway remarks, it is difficult to estimate her views at their proper value, and decide whether this is actually a veiled attack on contemporary sentimentalism and indifference to the real wrongs of women, or an ironic observation on the way contemporary writers (herself included) exploit other people's misery to make good books. Her comment highlights in miniature the problems any critic has in determining the relative positions of all four anti-feminist novelists, and their significance in Victorian literary history – especially given their interest in other issues (particularly religion), and the fact that they wrote primarily to entertain. The point of comparing them has been to stress the range of attitudes loosely consistent with anti-feminism, and the shades of ambiguity that appear in their work, implying, at the least, unconscious reservations about their stance on women. Because their writing is often cruder and more melodramatic than that of their better-known contemporaries, it exposes its critical edge more openly, especially in its treatment of two crucial themes for women: men and marriage.

Mrs Oliphant's cynicism and unsentimental humour about Victorian family life make her an irreverent critic, even of the sanctities of motherhood and the conventional happy ending, but as her *Blackwood's* articles show, she was at heart too much of a traditionalist to contemplate any overthrow of women's domestic role in the family. Eliza Linton, by contrast, contemplated such overthrows all the time, and acted them out in *Christopher Kirkland* and *Joshua Davidson*. Of the four novelists she is the most confused about what she thinks of women and their social purpose. Although her novels portray them as emotional to the point of hysteria, most of her men are equally unattractive, especially the recurrent image of the middle-aged wealthy suitor with a prurient penchant for young girls. Linton's men often turn out to be rigid conformists with a sinister secret, while the worst that can be said of her women is that they are emotionally unstable. Linton's cynicism about marriage is more blatant even than Oliphant's, and without her humour. She frequently depicts proposed or actual marriages which are nothing short of a sacrifice for the woman, and others where serious distrust between husband and wife leads to a permanent estrangement.

Mary Ward's novels both celebrate and criticize the role of women in upper-class English life, contrasting its limitations, even more than Yonge's did, with the freer scope available to men of the same class. Much of this reflects Ward's interest in politics, religion and social welfare, the first two of which were male-dominated areas. Nevertheless, Ward was committed to preserving an image of the gracious lady, beautiful, emotionally susceptible, and childishly liable to go wrong – not from any bad motives, but because she is incomplete without steady male guidance; and more than the other three novelists, perhaps because she was the most influenced by the Brontës, she acknowledged the irresistible complexities of sexual passion, while rarely progressing, in her account of it, beyond a trembling consciousness of the male presence. Ward and Yonge, although at opposite ends of the religious spectrum and widely different in the types of heroine they portrayed, both taught the worth of submission. In a letter to her dying mother, Ward wrote that 'submission brings peace because in submission the heart finds God and in God its rest', an opinion with which Yonge would have concurred.[2] Naomi Wolf, who rejects the theory of innate 'niceness' in girls, argues that this is 'purchased at the price of great control, cruelty and vigilance'. Collaborative girls' groups are 'the training grounds where girls are taught to do something that goes against the grain: to give up power and subvert the will'.[3] Giving up power – such power as they have – is undoubtedly a strong theme in these novels, where girls are required to exchange an unfeminine control over others for a more properly muted 'influence'. In Oliphant's novels, for instance, both Phoebe Junior and Lucilla Marjoribanks find themselves in possession of their community's secrets, which temporarily gives them both power and responsibility. Phoebe feels like a man, 'having, like all other girls, unbounded belief in the independence and freedom possessed by men.... But now that she had it, Phoebe did not like it' (p. 302). Unlike Ward, Oliphant suggests that power in the hands of women rarely goes wrong, but should none the less be curtailed: whereas Ward's Marcella, Marcia Coryston and Delia Blanchflower make serious errors of judgement, much as Rachel Curtis does in Yonge's *The Clever Woman of the Family*.

Of the four, Ward has the strongest faith in marriage: perhaps, quite simply, because her own was successful and supported her writing. Yonge also sees marriage as important, but accords an even higher value to those who manage without it (such as Ethel May), or become widowed and devote themselves to their children and community (such as Amy Edmonstone and Fanny Temple): these are women with a stronger sense of God, untainted by sexuality. Linton and Oliphant are the most cynical in their novels, however strongly they recommend marriage in their journal articles. All four are uneasy about the image of the dominant wife, Oliphant making a joke of it, and the others curbing their heroines' self-will, while often failing to build up the husband as a wholly admirable tower of strength. Like many modern anti-feminists, they are torn between self-castigation and respect for their own sex, simultaneously dismissing women as too unstable to be left on their own, and applauding them as the sensitive and astute consciences of their family or society. All were strongly conscious of the alternative male paradigm, through their admiration for father-figures (John Keble and Walter Savage Landor) or other male career-patterns (Edward Irving, Matthew Arnold, Mark Pattison), and were troubled by the limitations of their heroines' options.

Each of these novelists took as her central theme the popular Victorian story of a young woman's coming-to-consciousness; her perplexity over her life-choices, and her selection of a suitable mate, with all the accompanying setbacks and humiliations that this process entailed. Although this theme was being explored in new ways by James, Hardy and Meredith, the anti-feminist women writers were more aware of the mundane, the sheer monotony of women's lives. No household event is too trivial for Yonge or Oliphant to document, together with its far-reaching nuances; no personal upset too minor for Ward to explore as crucial to a woman's psychosexual development. Life for these novelists' heroines has become more complex than it was for Jane Austen's and even for Charlotte Brontë's. They are more deeply enmeshed in society, and have the potential to do more damage. Ward's heroines visit the Ladies' Gallery in the House of Commons, mix freely at parties, work among the urban poor, wrestle with Roman Catholicism and have stones thrown at them in the street; Linton's get jobs, enter forced marriages, starve themselves and die of religious ecstasy; even Yonge's deal with diphtheria, carriage-injuries, and a baby dying of an opium overdose. Weak in creating convincing heroes, these novelists specialized instead in varieties of female anxiety, sometimes sensationalized, but often treated with a serious desire to understand and relieve. The largest obstacle, for modern readers, is likely to be the novels' endings, which frequently require an act of self-sacrifice that seems unnecessary or exaggerated. The strangest paradox about anti-feminist women's writing in the nineteenth century is the sense of emptiness or waste generated by their use of the traditional marriage plot. If marriage is so important to them, and the only acceptable way out of the heroine's perplexities, why is it not made more attractive?

In fact, few Victorian novelists present established marriage in an attractive light, but equally they are reluctant to leave their heroines working indefinitely for a living, and since most were, in any case, middle-class, the range of employment options was fairly limited. The anti-feminist women novelists certainly gesture towards an alternative image of a woman's life, and are at their most interesting when they show their heroines struggling against the limitations imposed on them by conventional attitudes; but they stop well short of endorsing an escape from the confines of young ladyhood. Whatever their doubts about the real pleasures of marriage, they still have a residual loyalty to its romantic image, its respectability as a conclusion, and its normality. It was the ending most readers still expected from a novel read for entertainment, as Oliphant concedes reluctantly in *The Curate in Charge*. Cicely's decision to be a village schoolmistress 'would be the highest and the best, the most heroical and epical development of the story' (p. 193), but her readers expect Cicely to be rescued by marriage. She is, but on the last page of the novel, frankly tells her rescuer that she is not in love with him, before Oliphant backs off from this dangerous position: and when Mr Mildmay asks: 'Do you love anyone else?' has Cicely respond quaveringly: 'Unless it is you – nobody!' (p. 207). This ending neatly encapsulates Oliphant's problems with the marriage plot and her frustrations with novelistic convention. All four novelists pay lip-service to the happily-ever-after expectations of the marriage plot, but allow their deep-seated reservations free play. When Oliphant leaves Lucilla Marjoribanks unmarried into her late twenties, she admits that her freedom is compromised by loneliness and emotional emptiness. Even her interest in other people's business begins to pall. If this, and many of the other novels, are prepared to consider other options for their heroines, apart from marriage, and acknowledge the gap between the ideology and the reality of middle-class women's lives, they finally lack the courage or originality to depart from the expected line.

Nevertheless, their image of the ideal woman is more positive and energetic than those of Dickens, Thackeray, George Eliot or Elizabeth Gaskell. Their heroines are mostly intelligent, resourceful, independent in outlook, lively and unsentimental: women cut out for work, adventure, and the management of others. They may have other characteristics that partly negate these, such as emotionalism, liability to error or misjudgement, and a tendency to magnify everything that happens to them, but they are certainly not doll-like and vapid; nor are they angelic and sexless. Their views are outspoken, and they are prepared to defy society's conventions in order to refuse marriage proposals, work for money, or make their own (lower-class) friends. Some are even physically different from the idealized heroine – Lucilla, who is plump, and Ethel May, who is gaunt and awkward, a replica of her father – and many are viewed with amusement by their local communities. We see few of them become mothers: love of freedom being their natural element; impatience with young children a common characteristic.

All four of these writers attempted to describe their lives in 'straight' autobiography, as well as fiction. As autobiographical subjects they differ from their heroines in being both independent and successful. Charlotte Yonge was never required to give up her writing and become a full-time housekeeper; Linton found that her various attempts at family life were a failure, and she was happiest as a self-sufficient journalist–novelist, enjoying maternal quasi-lesbian relationships with daughter-substitutes; and Ward, never 'childish', became the main salary-earner of her family, outperforming son and husband, besides being an activist in several fields, ranging from women's higher education to London settlement projects. Even Oliphant, who is more like her over-burdened heroines, struggling for survival, nevertheless combined the full-time roles of novelist, journalist and single mother without succumbing to either re-marriage or invalidism as a means of escape. All the novelists were certainly aware of alternative plots for women, if only from the evidence of their own lives, but like George Eliot, who sent none of her heroines to do what she had done and lead an independent professional life in London, they bowed to convention, and shut off the exits.

It is open to the late twentieth-century woman reader, living through another anti-feminist backlash, to make of these ambivalent texts what she will. Ultimately, she needs to be guided both by the historical context of the work, and by its rhetorical complexity. Her role is not so much to be a 'resisting' reader (in Judith Fetterley's term[4]) – because all written texts depend on a certain level of co-operation and complicity as part of the reading contract – as to be a reader sensitive to the discordances and discrepancies that go into the making of even a relatively minor work. The reading process does not mean that we necessarily assent to what is being said: only that we understand its importance to the writer, and the role it plays in the development of her case. The reader gets more out of a text if she is open to multiple and even self-contradictory possibilities of meaning: the drive towards a single interpretation being particularly unhelpful to any text written at a time of public debate on a controversial issue. The reader who will get most out of a Victorian anti-feminist novel is one who respects the text's historical and ideological 'otherness', yet is also alert to its rhetorical open-endedness; the way, as in Mrs Oliphant's novels in particular, it may even be inviting discussion. Like all social-problem novels of the nineteenth century, these texts are transitional, time-bound, yet vitally alive as a record of uncertainty in class and gender relations.

Overall, the Victorian anti-feminist women novelists may be seen as self-appointed consciences of a confused and anxious society, reflecting in their complex and self-contradictory explorations of women's lives the wavering direction of public opinion as a whole. Although they offer a clearly-stated moral view – that women should not cross the boundary-line between private and public, or seek any form of self-fulfilment outside marriage – their novels reveal a more passionate attraction to the world of work, activity, the lives lived by men, and freedom from the daily trivia of women's lives at home. Because feminism and anti-feminism are themselves inchoate groupings of ideas with much in common, it is difficult to establish a clear dividing-line between expressions of the two viewpoints, especially in an ambiguous medium such as fiction. Where these novels have most to offer literary history is in the public expression of their confusion, itself representative of the unstable state in which gender relations were developing in the final third of the nineteenth century, and in which they remain today, with many women – in an era of what Naomi Wolf calls 'genderquake'[5] – still unsure of the balance in their lives between the private and the public, the personal and the professional.

Biographical Appendix

Eliza Lynn Linton (1822–98)

Born in Keswick on 10 February 1822, Elizabeth Lynn was the youngest child of James Lynn, an Anglican clergyman, and his wife Charlotte, who died five months later, exhausted with giving birth to twelve children. According to Linton's biographer George Somes Layard, James Lynn 'had a strong prejudice against intellectual pursuits for women, and could not away with the learned lady of the period' (Layard, p. 5). In her thinly-disguised fictional *Autobiography of Christopher Kirkland* (1885), in which the sexes are inverted, Linton depicts herself as the passionate and frustrated son of an equally tempestuous father; while her most recent biographer, Nancy Fix Anderson, thinks Linton was angry with women because she resented her mother's early desertion of her by premature death.

After a haphazard education at home, during which she rejected orthodox Christianity, she persuaded her father to let her try a year of independent research and writing in London. This was so successful that it not only produced her first novel, *Azeth the Egyptian* (1847), but set the pattern for her future life as a professional woman writer. From 1848 to 1851 she was a regular paid journalist on the *Morning Chronicle*; she subsequently contributed to many other leading periodicals, but most notoriously to the *Saturday Review*, which carried her 'Girl of the Period' articles beginning in 1868. This series mourned the passing of the pure-minded feminine English girl and satirized her swearing, crude, emancipated successor. Linton thus became identified with the anti-feminist tradition and was perhaps better known for her attack on the 'New Woman' than for any of her numerous novels.

In 1858 she married the twice-widowed William James Linton, political radical and wood engraver, from whom she soon became estranged. For all her insistence on the importance of family life for women, this was something that Linton never achieved successfully for herself. Her happiest relationships were with her father-substitute, Walter Savage Landor ('one of my great spiritual masters', as she explained in *My Literary Life*), and with a series of daughter-substitutes, especially Beatrice Sichel and Beatrice Harraden. Of the four women discussed in this book, Linton was the most overtly anti-feminist, though her novels reveal a more ambivalent attitude to women's work and family life.

Charlotte Mary Yonge (1823–1901)

Charlotte Yonge had the quietest and least turbulent life of the four women in this study. Its 'greatest event', according to her unfinished autobiography, was the birth of her only brother Julian in 1830, and she was the only one of the group not to marry. Her autobiography suggests that her military father was the strongest influence on her life, together with the Rev. John Keble, who prepared her for confirmation. A devout member of the Church of England, Charlotte Yonge never seems to have experienced religious doubts, but devoted her writing career to inculcating strong moral and theological principles in young girls. Her father allowed her to write only on the understanding that her earnings were to be given to charity. Besides producing over 160 books for children and adults, Yonge edited several journals, including the *Monthly Packet* and *Mothers in Council*.

Whereas Mrs Oliphant portrayed women as energetic and efficient managers, Yonge was drawn to the image of woman as invalid: another influence on her writings was Marianne Dyson, an invalid friend twenty years her senior and a likely model for Ermine Williams in *The Clever Woman of the Family*. Yonge herself accepted the Church's teaching on women as irretrievably inferior because of the Fall: 'I have no hesitation in declaring my full belief in the inferiority of woman, nor that she brought it upon herself,' is her uncompromising statement in *Womankind* (1876), her review of women's roles in the church and at home. Unlike Ward, Linton and Oliphant, who were frequent travellers abroad, Yonge largely stayed in Otterbourne, near Winchester, where she had lived as a child. Her novels, more successful than Linton's, remained popular as absorbing family chronicles, sprinkled with deathbeds and protracted illnesses, long after their values had come to seem outmoded.

Margaret Oliphant (1828–97)

Whereas the other three novelists were father-dominated, Margaret Oliphant was devoted to her mother, a model of efficiency and intelligence whose experiences to some extent prefigured her daughter's. Oliphant's mother not only lost children in infancy, but had two problematic sons who were unable to fend very successfully for themselves. Margaret Oliphant's two sons Cyril (1856–90) and Francis (known as 'Cecco') (1859–94) continued the family tradition of idleness, ill-health and lassitude, although she did all she could to have them well educated at Eton. Educated at home, she married her cousin Frank Oliphant in 1852; he died in Rome seven years later, leaving her stranded there with two small children and a third on the way. Although all her children predeceased her, the greatest loss was probably her ten-year-old daughter Maggie (1853–64), her one 'ewe-lamb', again in Rome, where the Oliphants were visiting. She spent the rest of her life writing furiously to support not only her remaining sons, but after 1868, her brother Frank's children, of whom the two youngest, Margaret (Madge) and Janet (Denny) became in effect her adoptive daughters.

A regular contributor to *Blackwood's Edinburgh Magazine*, Oliphant wrote over 100 novels, several biographies, an autobiography, historical sketches, literary histories, and annals of Blackwood's publishing house. The most frequent comment made by critics and obituarists after her death was that she had simply written too much: if she had paced herself more carefully, she might have produced work of a higher standard, a view shared by Oliphant herself. Never remarrying, however, she knew that a large household of dependent children relied solely on her support, and felt she had no choice but to keep writing. Extravagant by nature, she found it difficult to save what she had earned. Margaret Oliphant is the least overtly anti-feminist of the group, but though sarcastic about men ('He was stupid – but he was a man,' her heroine Phoebe Junior says of her lover Clarence Copperhead), she accepted their superior status in the family and in society. Her 'Carlingford' novels (an Oliphantine version of Barchester) frequently hinge on hapless clergymen and lovers being organized by businesslike young women; her favourite tone is ironic and ambiguous, making her real opinions somewhat elusive.

Mrs Humphry Ward (1851–1920)

Considerably younger than her fellow anti-feminists, Mrs Humphry Ward was originally Mary Augusta Arnold, eldest child of Dr Thomas Arnold's second son, Thomas, and therefore Matthew Arnold's niece. Thomas met his wife, Julia Sorell, in Hobart, Tasmania, where he had gone as inspector of schools; they returned to England in 1856, when their first child, Mary, was five, and headed for the Arnold family home in the Lake District. After attending a series of mostly unsatisfactory boarding-schools, Mary Arnold joined her family in Oxford, where she met her husband, Thomas Humphry Ward, whom she married in 1872. The only one of the group to have a conventional home life, Mary Ward produced a family of three long-lived children, Dorothy (1874–1964), Arnold (1876–1950) and Janet (1879–1956), but shared with Margaret Oliphant the experience of raising an apathetic son. She also had a difficult sister, Ethel (1866–1930), whose life was in many ways the polar opposite of Mary's. Never marrying, she harboured ambitions to be first an actress and then a novelist, before finally discovering a talent for photography. Pro-suffrage and possibly lesbian, Ethel frequently required help from Mary, and would have been a constant reminder of the problems caused by invalidish women without any very clear role in life.

Like Linton, Ward enjoyed academic research, and came to novel-writing via an interest in cultural history. Her first breakthrough came with the huge popular success of *Robert Elsmere* (1888), a tale of religious deconversion which caught the mood of the age. Ward herself had retreated from Christian orthodoxy, especially the belief in miracles, but remained fascinated by the emotional appeal of religion. Her father twice converted to Catholicism, which gave her material for *Helbeck of Bannisdale* (1898), and caused considerable upheaval in his personal and professional life. Ward's stance was not entirely anti-feminist: she did a great deal for women's higher education (unlike Linton, who was largely against it), and was instrumental in founding Somerville College, Oxford; but she remained firmly opposed to women's suffrage, against which she mobilized a group of influential friends in 1889.

Her novels convey an excitement about politics which is not altogether in keeping with her views on women's public involvement with parliamentary issues; they also portray an earnestly intellectual generation of young landowners who take their responsibilities as seriously as do her women their personal lives. At her peak, Ward was an enormously successful novelist, but lived to see her ideas outmoded and mocked. Nevertheless, she achieved important results in her settlement work for the London poor, and was even commissioned by Theodore Roosevelt to write Allied propaganda articles for American readers on the First World War. Her novels combine strenuous debate on topical issues with a discreet knowledge of passionate sexual involvement.

Notes

Epigraphs

1. M.E. Braddon, *Miranda* (London: Hutchinson, [1913]), p. 187. I am grateful to Katherine Alcock for introducing me to this novel.
2. Wilkie Collins, *The Woman in White* (1860; repr. ed. Julian Symons, Harmondsworth: Penguin, 1974), p. 60.

Introduction

1. *Guardian*, 23 March 1993, 'Second Front', pp. 2–3.
2. E.M. Forster, *Howards End* (1910; repr. Harmondsworth: Penguin, 1976), p. 87.
3. Martha Vicinus, review of Herbert van Thal's biography of Eliza Lynn Linton, *Victorian Studies* 24 (Spring 1981), pp. 369–70.
4. Nancy Fix Anderson, *Woman Against Women in Victorian England: A Life of Eliza Lynn Linton* (Bloomington and Indianapolis: Indiana University Press, 1987); John Sutherland, *Mrs Humphry Ward: Eminent Victorian, Pre-eminent Edwardian* (Oxford: Clarendon Press, 1990); Elisabeth Jay, *Mrs Oliphant: A Fiction to Herself: A Literary Life* (Oxford: Clarendon Press, 1995).
5. Vineta Colby, *The Singular Anomaly: Women Novelists of the Nineteenth Century* (New York: New York University Press, 1970).
6. 'If a historian is an Anti-Feminist, and does not believe women to be capable of genius in the traditional masculine departments, he will never make anything of Joan . . . ,' *Bernard Shaw: Collected Plays with their Prefaces* (London, Sydney, Toronto: Max Reinhardt, The Bodley Head, 1973), vol. 6, p. 20.
7. Margaret Forster, *Significant Sisters: The Grassroots of Active Feminism 1839–1939* (Harmondsworth: Penguin, 1986), p. 1.
8. Andrea Dworkin, *Right-Wing Women* (London: Women's Press, 1983), pp. 195, 196, 216.
9. Philippa Levine, *Victorian Feminism 1850–1900* (London: Hutchinson Education, 1987), p. 216.
10. Malcolm I. Thomis and Jennifer Grimmett, *Women in Protest 1800–1850* (London and Canberra: Croom Helm, 1982); Linda Colley, *Britons: Forging the Nation 1707–1837* (New Haven and London: Yale University Press, 1992), p. 281.
11. Mary Poovey, *Uneven Developments: The Ideological Work of Gender in Mid-Victorian England* (London: Virago, 1989), p. 3.
12. Forster, *Significant Sisters*, p. 4.
13. In particular, Brian Harrison, *Separate Spheres: The Opposition to Women's Suffrage in Britain* (London: Croom Helm, 1978).

14. Naomi Wolf, *Fire with Fire: The New Female Power and how it will Change the 21st Century* (London: Chatto & Windus, 1993). She is especially critical of French feminist theorists.

Chapter 1: The Anti-Feminist Woman 1792–1850

1. Harold Nicolson, letter of 2 December 1966, quoted in the Oxford English Dictionary's definition of 'anti-feminism'.
2. Neil Lyndon, *No More Sex War: The Failures of Feminism* (London: Sinclair-Stevenson, 1992). The public debate was held on 6 October 1992, and the 'backlash' debate at the Institute of Contemporary Arts on 2 April 1992; Suzanne Moore, 'The Big Question: Is Feminism Finished?', *Elle* (May 1990), pp. 47–51.
3. Janet Todd (ed.), *Mary Wollstonecraft: An Annotated Bibliography* (New York and London: Garland, 1976).
4. *British Critic* 21 (1803), p. 690; *Harriet Martineau's Autobiography*, 3 vols (1877; reissued London: Virago, 2 vols, 1983), vol. I, p. 400.
5. William Thompson, *Appeal of One half the human race, Women, against the Pretensions of the other Half, Men* (London: Longman, 1825; repr. New York: Source Book Press, 1970), p. vii; Mrs Elwood, *Memoirs of The Literary Ladies of England* (London: Henry Colburn, 2 vols, 1843), vol. II, p. 152. She notes, however, that Maria Jane Jewsbury had been planning to remodel the *Rights*, so 'that it would not fail to become again attractive, and she thought useful', p. 153. Unfortunately, Jewsbury died in 1833, before this plan could be effected.
6. Mary Wollstonecraft, *Vindication of the Rights of Woman* (1792; ed. Miriam Kramnick, Harmondsworth: Pelican Books, 1975), p. 153.
7. Lady Theresa Lewis (ed.), *Extracts from the Journals and Correspondence of Miss Berry from the year 1783 to 1852* (London: Longmans, Green, 3 vols, 2nd edn, 1866), vol. II, pp. 91–2; Annette M.B. Meakin, *Hannah More: A Biographical Study* (London: Smith, Elder, 1911), p. 312.
8. Hannah More, *Strictures on the Modern System of Female Education* (London: Cadell & Davies, 2 vols, 1799), vol. I, p. 135.
9. Quoted in Cora Kaplan (ed.), *Aurora Leigh and Other Poems* (London: The Women's Press, 1978), pp. 6–7.
10. Paula R. Feldman and Diana Scott-Kilvert (eds), *The Journals of Mary Shelley 1814–1844* (Oxford: Clarendon Press, 2 vols, 1978), vol. II, pp. 553–5.
11. Jane Rendall, *The Origins of Modern Feminism: Women in Britain, France and the United States 1780–1860* (London: Macmillan, 1985), p. 73.
12. Mrs West, *Letters to a Young Lady in which the duties and character of women are considered, chiefly with a reference to Prevailing Opinions* (London: Longman, Hurst, Rees and Orme, 3 vols, 1806), vol. I, p. 56.
13. Linda Colley, *Britons: Forging the Nation 1707–1837* (New Haven and London: Yale University Press, 1992), pp. 250–1.
14. Mrs West, *Letters to a Young Lady*, vol. I, p. 58.

15. Mrs Ellis, *The Women of England, Their Social Duties, and Domestic Habits* (London: Fisher & Son, 1839), pp. 9, 14.
16. John Stuart Mill, *The Subjection of Women* (1869; repr. London: Virago, 1983, with *The Enfranchisement of Women*, ed. Kate Soper), p. 66.
17. More, *Strictures*, vol. II, p. 23; [Sarah Lewis], *Woman's Mission* (London: John W. Parker, 2nd edn, 1839), pp. 13, 11.
18. Mrs Ellis, *The Daughters of England, their position in society, character and responsibilities* (London and Paris: Fisher & Son, 1842), pp. 3, 126.
19. Flora Tristan, *Promenades dans Londres* (Paris and London, 2nd edn, 1840), p. 301.
20. Harriet Blodgett, *Centuries of Female Days: Englishwomen's Private Diaries* (Gloucester: Alan Sutton, 1989), p. 100.
21. *Journals and Correspondence of Lady Eastlake*, edited by her nephew Charles Eastlake Smith (London: John Murray, 2 vols, 1895), vol. I, pp. 20–1, 22–3.
22. Nina Auerbach, *Woman and the Demon: The Life of a Victorian Myth* (Cambridge and London: Harvard University Press, 1982), p. 188.
23. Arthur Christopher Benson and Viscount Esher (eds), *The Letters of Queen Victoria: A Selection from Her Majesty's Correspondence between the years 1837 and 1861* (London: John Murray, 3 vols, 1908), vol. II, p. 367.
24. Quoted by Margaret Forster in *Significant Sisters*, p. 16.
25. Mrs John Sandford, *Woman, in her Social and Domestic Character* (London: Longman, 1831), pp. 2, 134.
26. *Woman's Rights and Duties . . . By a Woman* (London: John W. Parker, 2 vols, 1840), vol. I, p. 276.
27. [Elizabeth Hamilton], *Memoirs of Modern Philosophers* (Bath: R. Cruttwell; and London: G.G. & J. Robinson, 3 vols, 1800), vol. I, p. 2; vol. II, p. 88.
28. Mrs Opie, *Adeline Mowbray: The Mother and Daughter* (1802; London: Pandora Press, 1986), p. 257.
29. *Memorials of the Life of Amelia Opie, selected and arranged from her Letters, Diaries, and other Manuscripts by Cecilia Lucy Brightwell* (Norwich: Fletcher & Alexander; London: Longman, Brown, 1854), p. 42.
30. Maria Edgeworth, *Belinda* (1801; ed. Eva Figes, London: Pandora Press, 1986), p. 208.
31. E. Lynn Linton, *The Rebel of the Family* (London: Chatto & Windus, 3 vols, 1880), vol. I, p. 79.
32. Quoted by Vivien Jones in *Women in the Eighteenth Century: Constructions of Femininity* (London and New York: Routledge, 1990), pp. 187–8, 190.
33. [Thomas Galloway], 'Mrs Somerville's *Mechanism of the Heavens'*, *Edinburgh Review* 55 (April 1832), p. 1.
34. Susan Levin, *Dorothy Wordsworth and Romanticism* (New Brunswick: Rutgers University Press, 1987), p. 155.
35. Alan G. Hill (ed.), *The Letters of William and Dorothy Wordsworth: The Later Years, Part II, 1829–1834*, vol. V (Oxford: Clarendon Press, 2nd edition, 1979), pp. 4, 157.

36. Ibid., p. 185.
37. Norma Clarke, *Ambitious Heights: Writing, Friendship, Love – The Jewsbury Sisters, Felicia Hemans, and Jane Carlyle* (London and New York: Routledge, 1990), p. 91.
38. 'Miss Martineau's Monthly Novels', *Quarterly Review* 49 (April 1833), 136–52; John Wilson Croker talked of 'tomahawking Miss Martineau in the Quarterly', though it was actually George Poulett Scrope who wrote the article: anecdote told in *Harriet Martineau's Autobiography*, vol. I, p. 205; Moore's song was 'A Blue Love-Song'; William Maginn caricatured her in 'Gallery of Literary Characters', *Fraser's Magazine* 8 (November 1833), p. 576.
39. [H.N. Coleridge], 'Modern English Poetesses', *Quarterly Review* 66 (September 1840), pp. 374–5.
40. [Marian Evans], 'Silly Novels by Lady Novelists', *Westminster Review* 10 (October 1856), p. 460.
41. [Charles Dickens], 'Sucking Pigs', *Household Words* 4 (8 November 1851), p. 145.
42. Charles Dickens, *Bleak House* (1853; Penguin, Harmondsworth, 1971), p. 479.
43. 'Woman's Emancipation', *Punch* (July 1851), p. 3.
44. Nancy Fix Anderson, *Woman Against Women in Victorian England: A Life of Eliza Lynn Linton* (Bloomington and Indianapolis: Indiana University Press, 1987), p. 71.
45. [Eliza Lynn Linton], 'Mary Wollstonecraft', *The English Republic* 3 (1854), pp. 418–24.

Chapter 2: Anti-Feminist Women and Women's Writing

1. Virginia Woolf, *A Room of One's Own* (1929; Panther Books, Granada, 1977), pp. 72–3.
2. Ethel Romanes, *Charlotte Mary Yonge: An Appreciation* (London and Oxford: A.R. Mowbray, 1908), p. 75.
3. Elaine Showalter, *A Literature of Their Own: British Women Novelists from Brontë to Lessing* (Princeton, 1977; London: Virago, 1978), p. 105.
4. Brian Southam, *Jane Austen: The Critical Heritage, vol. 2 1870–1940* (London and New York: Routedge & Kegan Paul, 1987), p. 11.
5. Mary Ward, 'Style and Miss Austen', *Macmillan's Magazine* 51 (December 1884), p. 91; [Mrs Oliphant], 'The Life and Letters of George Eliot,' *Edinburgh Review* 161 (April 1885), p. 542.
6. Romanes, *Charlotte Mary Yonge*, pp. 145–6.
7. [Margaret Oliphant], 'Miss Austen and Miss Mitford', *Blackwood's* 107 (March 1870), pp. 290–313.
8. Margaret Oliphant, *The Literary History of England in the End of the Eighteenth and Beginning of Nineteenth Century* (London: Macmillan, 3 vols, 1882).
9. Mary Ward, 'Style and Miss Austen', *Macmillan's Magazine* 51 (December 1884), pp. 84–91.

10. Oliphant, 'The Life and Letters of George Eliot', p. 518.
11. Joan Riviere, 'Womanliness as a Masquerade' (1929), in *Formations of Fantasy*, ed. Victor Burgin, James Donald, and Cora Kaplan (London and New York: Routledge, 1986), pp. 35–44.
12. Margaret Oliphant to John Blackwood, 30 June [1866], MS 4213, National Library of Scotland.
13. *My Literary Life*, by Mrs Lynn Linton (London: Hodder & Stoughton, 1899), pp. 95–6.
14. Eliza Lynn Linton, *Ourselves: A Series of Essays on Women* (London: G. Routledge & Son, 1869), Preface, pp. iii–iv.
15. 'George Eliot' by Mrs Lynn Linton, in Margaret Oliphant (ed.), *Women Novelists of Queen Victoria's Reign: A Book of Appreciations* (London: Hurst & Blackett, 1897), pp. 112, 114.
16. [Eliza Lynn Linton], 'George Eliot', *Temple Bar* 73 (April 1885), p. 514.
17. 'George Eliot and Her Critics', by the Editor and the Author of 'Charles Lowder', *Monthly Packet* (May 1885), pp. 471–95; Romanes, *Charlotte Mary Yonge*, p. 176.
18. William S. Peterson, *Victorian Heretic: Mrs Humphry Ward's Robert Elsmere* (Leicester: Leicester University Press, 1976), p. 102.
19. Mary Ward, 'Elizabeth Barrett Browning', *Atalanta* (September 1888), p. 708.
20. Beth Sutton-Ramspeck, 'The Personal is Poetical: Feminist Criticism and Mary Ward's Readings of the Brontës', *Victorian Studies* 34, no. 1 (Autumn 1990), pp. 55–75; at p. 56.
21. Mrs Humphry Ward, 'Some Thoughts on Charlotte Brontë', *Charlotte Brontë 1816–1916: A Centenary Memorial*, ed. Butler Wood (London: T. Fisher Unwin, 1917), p. 29.
22. Mrs Humphry Ward, Preface to the Haworth edition of *Villette* (London: Smith, Elder, 1899), p. xxv.
23. Mary Ward, Preface to *Jane Eyre* (London: Smith, Elder, 1899), p. xviii.
24. [Mary Ward], 'Recent Fiction in England and France', *Macmillan's Magazine* 50 (August 1884), pp. 250–60.
25. [Margaret Oliphant], 'Modern Novelists – Great and Small', *Blackwood's* 77 (May 1855), pp. 554–68; at pp. 557–8.
26. [Margaret Oliphant], 'The Old Saloon: The Literature of the Last Fifty Years', *Blackwood's* 141 (June 1887), p. 757.
27. Romanes, *Charlotte Mary Yonge*, pp. 146–7.
28. [Margaret Oliphant], 'Novels', *Blackwood's* 102 (September 1867), pp. 259, 277.
29. Jonathan Culler, 'Reading as a Woman', *On Deconstruction: Theory and Criticism after Deconstruction* (London: Routledge & Kegan Paul, 1983), p. 49.
30. Adrienne Rich, *On Lies, Secrets, and Silence: Selected Prose 1966–1978* (London: Virago, 1980), pp. 157–83.
31. Judith Fetterley, *The Resisting Reader: A Feminist Approach to American Fiction* (Bloomington and London: Indiana University Press, 1978), p. xxii.

Chapter 3: 'Ardour and Submission': Heroines

1. [Margaret Oliphant], 'Charles Dickens', *Blackwood's* 109 (June 1871), pp. 465–6.
2. Virginia Woolf, *A Room of One's Own* (1929; Panther Books, Granada, 1977), p. 93.
3. Elaine Showalter, *Sexual Anarchy: Gender and Culture at the Fin de Siècle* (London: Virago, 1992), ch. 3, pp. 38ff.
4. 'Women's Rights', *All the Year Round*, 18 August 1894, p. 151.
5. Rachel Brownstein, *Becoming a Heroine: Reading about Women in Novels* (New York: Viking Press, 1982), p. 295.
6. Margaret Oliphant, *The Curate in Charge* (1876; Pocket Classics edn, Gloucester: Alan Sutton, 1985), p. 136.
7. Charlotte M. Yonge, *The Clever Woman of the Family* (1865; London: Virago, 1985), pp. 81–2.
8. William S. Peterson, *Victorian Heretic: Mrs Humphrey Ward's Robert Elsmere* (Leicester: Leicester University Press, 1976); p. 49.
9. [Margaret Oliphant], 'Modern Novelists – Great and Small', *Blackwood's* 77 (May 1855), p. 562. Margaret Oliphant, *Phoebe Junior* (1876; London: Virago, 1989), p. 141.
10. 'Women's Heroines', *Saturday Review*, 2 March 1867, p. 259.
11. Christabel Coleridge, *Charlotte Mary Yonge: Her Life and Letters* (London: Macmillan, 1903), pp. 121, 140.
12. Charlotte M. Yonge, *The Daisy Chain, or Aspirations* (1856; London: Virago, 1988), Preface.
13. Yonge, *The Clever Woman of the Family*, p. 215.
14. Florence Nightingale, 'Cassandra' (written 1852; privately printed, 1859), in Ray Strachey, *The Cause* (1928: repr. London: Virago, 1978), p. 398.
15. Ethel Romanes, *Charlotte Mary Yonge: An Appreciation* (London and Oxford: A.R. Mowbray, 1908), p. 99.
16. Catherine Sandbach-Dahlström, *Be Good Sweet Maid: Charlotte Yonge's Domestic Fiction: A Study in Dogmatic Purpose and Fictional Form* (Stockholm: Avhandl, 1984), p. 151.
17. 'George Eliot and Her Critics', *Monthly Packet* (May 1885), pp. 491–2.
18. E. Lynn Linton, *The Rebel of the Family* (London: Chatto & Windus, 3 vols, 1880), vol. I, p. 9.
19. [E. Lynn Linton], 'The Girl of the Period', first appeared in the *Saturday Review* 25 (14 March 1868), pp. 339–40. It was reprinted, with others in the series, in E. Lynn Linton, *The Girl of the Period and other Social Essays* (London: Richard Bentley & Son, 1883).
20. E. Lynn Linton, *Ourselves. A Series of Essays on Women* (London: G. Routledge & Sons, 1869).
21. *Saturday Review*, 20 November 1880, p. 650.
22. Carolyn Heilbrun, *Reinventing Womanhood* (London: Victor Gollancz, 1979), p. 71.
23. Lee R. Edwards, *Psyche as Hero: Female Heroism and Fictional Form* (Middletown, Connecticut: Wesleyan University Press, 1984), p. 16.

24. [Margaret Oliphant], 'Charles Reade's Novels', *Blackwood's* 106 (October 1869), p. 490.
25. Q.D. Leavis, Introduction to *Miss Marjoribanks* (London: Chatto & Windus, 1969), p. 2.
26. For instance [Stephen Gwynn], 'The Life and Writings of Mrs Oliphant', in the *Edinburgh Review* 190 (July 1899), said that 'Motherhood was the soul of her life', p. 47; more recently, Gail Twersky Reimer, in 'Revisions of Labor in Margaret Oliphant's Autobiography', in *Life/Lines: Theorizing Women's Autobiography*, ed. Bella Brodzki and Celeste Schenck (Ithaca and London: Cornell University Press, 1988), focuses on motherhood and images of childbirth in Oliphant's *Autobiography*.
27. Margaret Oliphant, *Miss Marjoribanks* (1866; London: Virago, 1988), p. 25.
28. Margaret Oliphant, *Phoebe Junior* (London: William Blackwood, 1876; repr. London: Virago, 1989), p. 329.
29. Anne M. Bindslev, *Mrs Humphry Ward: A Study in Late-Victorian Feminine Consciousness and Creative Expression* (Stockholm: Almqvist and Wiksell International, 1985), p. 9.
30. Françoise Rives, 'The Marcellas, Lauras, Dianas . . . of Mrs Humphry Ward', *Caliban* XVII (1980), pp. 69–79.
31. Mrs Humphry Ward, *Marcella* (1894; London: Virago, 1984), p. 5.
32. Mrs Humphry Ward, *Sir George Tressady* (London: Smith, Elder, 1896), p. 120.
33. Ward, *Sir George Tressady*, pp. 314ff.
34. Mrs Humphry Ward, *Helbeck of Bannisdale* (London: Smith, Elder, 1898), p. 16.
35. Mary Ward to Thomas Arnold, 9 August 1898, MS, Pusey House, Oxford.
36. Bindslev, *Mrs Humphry Ward*, p. 125.
37. Mary Ward to Mandell Creighton, 20 December 1893, MS, Pusey House, Oxford.
38. Arnold Bennett, *Books and Persons: Being Comments on a Past Epoch 1908–1911* (London: Chatto & Windus, 1917), p. 52.
39. Annis Pratt, *Archetypal Patterns in Women's Fiction* (Brighton: Harvester Press, 1982), p. 41.
40. Heilbrun, *Reinventing Womanhood*, p. 72.

Chapter 4: Heroes

1. Charlotte M. Yonge, 'Authorship', *Monthly Packet* (September 1892), p. 303.
2. Jane Miller, *Women Writing About Men* (London: Virago, 1986), pp. 5–6.
3. Margaret Oliphant to Isabella Blackwood, 1861, quoted in Elaine Showalter, *A Literature of Their Own: British Women Novelists from Brontë to Lessing* (Princeton, 1977; London: Virago, 1978), p. 135.
4. Margaret Oliphant to John Blackwood, 1869, MS 4251, National Library of Scotland.

5. [Margaret Oliphant], 'Historical Sketches of the Reign of George II. No. X: "The Novelists"', p. 268.
6. Elaine Showalter, *A Literature of Their Own*, p. 136.
7. E. Lynn Linton, *The Girl of the Period and Other Social Essays* (London: Richard Bentley & Son, 2 vols, 1883), vol. II, pp. 245–6.
8. Margaret Oliphant to John Blackwood, 1855, MS 4111, National Library of Scotland.
9. Thomas Carlyle, *On Heroes, Hero-Worship, and the Heroic in History* (1840; repr. London: Everyman, J.M. Dent, 1973), p. 250.
10. Michael Roper and John Tosh (eds), *Manful Assertions: Masculinities in Britain since 1800* (London: Routledge, 1991), pp. 2–3, 18.
11. John Tosh, 'Domesticity and Manliness in the Victorian Middle Class', in Roper and Tosh, *Manful Assertions*, pp. 44–73.
12. John Stuart Mill, *The Subjection of Women* (1869; London: Virago, 1983), p. 81; Harriet Martineau, *Household Education* (London: Edward Moxon, 1849), p. 2; Samuel Smiles, *Self-Help* (1859; repr. London: Sphere Books, 1968), ch. XII, p. 232.
13. Mario Praz, *The Hero in Eclipse in Victorian Fiction* (1956; repr. London: Oxford University Press, 1969).
14. Mrs Ellis, *The Women of England, Their Social Duties, and Domestic Habits* (London: Fisher, 1839), p. 222.
15. Charlotte M. Yonge, *The Heir of Redclyffe* (1853; London: Macmillan, 1902), p. 1.
16. Elaine Showalter, *A Literature of Their Own*, p. 138.
17. Norman Vance, *The Sinews of the Spirit: The Ideal of Christian manliness in Victorian literature and religious thought* (Cambridge: Cambridge University Press, 1985), p. 7.
18. [R.H. Hutton], 'The author of Heartsease and Modern Schools of Fiction', *Prospective Review* x (1854), p. 460.
19. George Somes Layard, *Mrs Lynn Linton: Her Life, Letters, and Opinions* (London: Methuen, 1901), p. 131.
20. E. Lynn Linton, *Grasp Your Nettle. A Novel* (London: Smith, Elder, 3 vols, 1865), vol. I, p. 91.
21. E. Lynn Linton, *The Autobiography of Christopher Kirkland* (London: Richard Bentley and Son, 3 vols, 1885), vol. III, p. 299.
22. Marjorie Garber, *Vested Interests: Cross-Dressing and Cultural Anxiety* (New York and London: Routledge, 1992), pp. 10–11.
23. Margaret Oliphant to Madge Valentine, 16 November [1895], MSS 4295, National Library of Scotland.
24. [Margaret Oliphant], 'Edward Irving', *Blackwood's* 84 (November 1858), pp. 567–86.
25. Lucy Poate Stebbins, *A Victorian Album: Some Lady Novelists of the Period* (London: Secker and Warburg, 1946), p. 160.
26. R.C. Terry, *Victorian Popular Fiction, 1860–80* (London: Macmillan, 1983), p. 71.
27. [Margaret Oliphant], 'Novels', *Blackwood's* 102 (September 1867), p. 275.
28. [Margaret Oliphant], 'The Great Unrepresented', *Blackwood's* 100 (September 1866), p. 372.

29. [Margaret Oliphant], 'The Anti-Marriage League', *Blackwood's* 159 (January 1896), p. 148.
30. Margaret Oliphant, *Salem Chapel* (1863; London: Virago, 1986), p. 89.
31. Margaret Oliphant, *The Perpetual Curate* (1864; London: Virago, 1987), pp. 255–6.
32. Margaret Oliphant, 'Sermons', *Blackwood's* 92 (August 1862), pp. 202–20.
33. Mrs Humphry Ward, *Robert Elsmere* (1888; Oxford: World's Classics edn, 1987), p. 127.
34. Anne M. Bindslev, *Mrs Humphry Ward: A Study in Late-Victorian Feminine Consciousness and Creative Expression* (Stockholm: Almquist and Wiksell International, 1985), p. 12.
35. William Lyon Phelps, *Essays on Modern Novelists* (New York: Macmillan, 1910), p. 202.
36. Mrs Humphry Ward, *Delia Blanchflower. A Novel* (London: Ward, Lock, 1915), p. 4.
37. Mrs Humphry Ward, *Lady Rose's Daughter* (London: Macmillan, 1903), p. 199.
38. Mrs Humphry Ward, *The History of David Grieve* (London: Smith, Elder, 1892), p. xviii.
39. Mrs Humphry Ward, *The Coryston Family* (London: Smith Elder, 1913), p. 232.
40. Margaret Oliphant to Frank Wilson, 20 March 1879, in *Autobiography and Letters of Mrs Margaret Oliphant*, ed. Mrs Harry Coghill (1899; Leicester: Leicester University Press, 1974), p. 280.
41. Margaret Oliphant to Principal Tulloch, 1881, ibid., p. 300.

Chapter 5: Journalism

1. Margaret Oliphant, *Annals of a Publishing House: William Blackwood and His Sons* (Edinburgh and London: Blackwood, 2 vols, 1897).
2. John Gross, *The Rise and Fall of the Man of Letters: Aspects of English Literary Life since 1800* (London: Weidenfeld and Nicolson, 1969).
3. Oliphant, *Annals*, vol. I, p. 493.
4. *The Saturday Review*, Opening Manifesto, 3 November 1855, p. 18 (under 'Advertisements').
5. 'Current Criticism', *Saturday Review*, 9 October 1858, p. 349.
6. Merle Mowbray Bevington, *The Saturday Review 1855–1868: Representative Educated Opinion in Victorian England* (New York: Columbia University Press, 1941), p. 116.
7. Nancy Fix Anderson, *Woman Against Women in Victorian England: A Life of Eliza Lynn Linton* (Bloomington and Indianapolis: Indiana University Press, 1987), p. 119.
8. Alison Adburgham, *Women in Print: Writing Women and Women's Magazines from the Restoration to the Accession of Victoria* (London: George Allen and Unwin, 1972).
9. E.A. Bennett, *Journalism for Women: A Practical Guide* (London and New York: John Lane, The Bodley Head, 1898), pp. 83–4, 13, 26.
10. Margaret Beetham, 'Towards a Theory of the Periodical as a

Publishing Genre', in *Investigating Victorian Journalism*, ed. Laurel Brake, Aled Jones and Lionel Malden (Basingstoke and London: Macmillan, 1990), pp. 20, 30.
11. 'The Occupations of Women', *Englishwoman's Review* (15 February 1884), p. 52.
12. E. Lynn Linton, *Sowing the Wind* (London: Tinsley Brothers, 3 vols, 1867), vol. I, p. 23.
13. [Anne Mozley], 'Mr Mill on the Subjection of Women', *Blackwood's* 106 (September 1869), p. 313.
14. Anderson, *Woman against Women*, p. 10.
15. E. Lynn Linton, 'The Wild Women: No. I. As Politicians', *Nineteenth Century* 30 (July 1891), p. 80.
16. E. Lynn Linton, 'The Modern Revolt', *Macmillan's Magazine* 23 (December 1870), pp. 142, 147.
17. [E. Lynn Linton], 'Woman's Mission', *Saturday Review* (9 July 1859), p. 44.
18. E. Lynn Linton, 'The Higher Education of Woman', *Fortnightly Review* 46 (October 1886), pp. 506–7.
19. E.L.L. [signed], 'Our Civilization', *Cornhill Magazine* 27 (June 1873), p. 675.
20. E.L.L. [signed], 'Domestic Life', *Temple Bar* 4 (February 1862), p. 415.
21. Nancy Fix Anderson, 'Eliza Lynn Linton, Dickens, and the Woman Question', *Victorian Periodicals Review* 22 (Winter 1989), p. 134.
22. [Eliza Lynn Linton], 'Passing Faces', *Household Words* 11 (April 1855), p. 262.
23. The 'Girl of the Period' essay first appeared in the *Saturday Review* on 14 March 1868: it was reprinted, with other essays in the series, in E. Lynn Linton, *The Girl of the Period and Other Social Essays* (London: Richard Bentley and Son, 2 vols, 1883).
24. Carole Pateman, quoted by Elaine Showalter, in *Sexual Anarchy: Gender and Culture at the Fin de Siècle* (London: Virago, 1992), p. 8.
25. 'Eliza Lynn Linton and "The Girl of the Period"', in *The Woman Question: Society and Literature in Britain and America 1837–1883*, by Elizabeth K. Helsinger, Robin Lauterbach Sheets, and William Veeder, vol. I, 'Defining Voices' (Chicago and London: University of Chicago Press, 1983).
26. E. Lynn Linton, 'Modern Topsy-Turveydom', *New Review* (November 1890), p. 437.
27. E. Lynn Linton, 'The Wild Women as Social Insurgents', *Nineteenth Century* 30 (October 1891), p. 605.
28. E. Lynn Linton, 'The Partisans of the Wild Women', *Nineteenth Century* 30 (March 1892), pp. 457–8.
29. Mona Caird, 'A Defence of the so-called "Wild Women"', *Nineteenth Century* 31 (May 1892), p. 812.
30. Anderson, *Woman Against Women*, ch. VIII, 'The Saturday Reviler', *passim*.
31. E. Lynn Linton, *Ourselves: Essays on Women* (London: G. Routledge and Son, 1869), pp. 3, 174.
32. 'Dovecots', *Saturday Review*, (10 April 1869), pp. 477–8.

33. E. Lynn Linton, 'Womanhood in Greece, in History and Art', *Fortnightly Review* 47 (May 1887), p. 715; 'Womanhood in Old Greece', *Fortnightly* 47 (January 1887), pp. 121, 123.
34. Eliza Lynn, *Amymone: A Romance of the Days of Pericles* (London: Richard Bentley, 3 vols, 1848), vol. I, p. vi.
35. E. Lynn Linton, 'The Characteristics of English Women: I', *Fortnightly* 51 (February 1889), pp. 254–5; II (March 1889), p. 376.
36. [Margaret Oliphant], 'New Books', *Blackwood's* 108 (August 1870), pp. 174–5.
37. Margaret Oliphant to John Blackwood [1855], MS 4111, National Library of Scotland.
38. Margaret Oliphant to Isabella Blackwood (1862), reprinted in *Autobiography*, ed. Mrs Harry Coghill, p. 185; on her mother's politics, *Annals of a Publishing House*, vol. I, p. 129.
39. Merryn Williams, *Margaret Oliphant: A Critical Biography* (Basingstoke and London: Macmillan, 1986), pp. 106–7.
40. Margaret Oliphant, *The Literary History of England in the End of the Eighteenth and Beginning of the Nineteenth Century* (London: Macmillan, 3 vols, 1882), vol. II, pp. 248–53. She told George Craik that she wanted no more than a 'glance' at Wollstonecraft's work (*Autobiography*, p. 304).
41. [Margaret Oliphant], 'The Laws Concerning Women', *Blackwood's* 79 (April 1856), p. 381.
42. [Margaret Oliphant], 'The Grievances of Women', *Fraser's Magazine* 101 (May 1880), p. 698 [signed 'M.O.W.O.'].
43. [Margaret Oliphant], 'The Great Unrepresented', *Blackwood's* 100 (September 1866), p. 367.
44. [Margaret Oliphant], 'Mill on the Subjection of Women', *Edinburgh Review* 130 (October 1869), pp. 577, 589.
45. [Margaret Oliphant], 'The Laws Concerning Women', p. 382.
46. [Margaret Oliphant], 'The Condition of Women', *Blackwood's* 83 (February 1858), p. 145.
47. [Margaret Oliphant], 'The Great Unrepresented', p. 368.
48. [Margaret Oliphant], 'The Latest Lawgiver', *Blackwood's* 103 (June 1868), p. 679.
49. Quoted by Merryn Williams in *Margaret Oliphant*, p. 115.
50. [Margaret Oliphant], 'The Latest Lawgiver', p. 678.
51. John Stock Clarke, *Margaret Oliphant* (Victorian Research Guides) (University of Queensland, 1986), p. 6.
52. [Margaret Oliphant], 'The Old Saloon', *Blackwood's* 146 (August 1889), p. 275.
53. Mrs Humphry Ward, *Delia Blanchflower. A Novel* (London, Melbourne and Toronto: Ward, Lock, 1915), p. 4.
54. Janet Penrose Trevelyan, *The Life of Mrs Humphry Ward* (London, Bombay and Sydney: Constable, 1923), p. 227.
55. Marion Kathleen Jones, 'Mrs Humphry Ward and Feminism' (B.Phil. thesis, University of Hull, 1975), p. 11.
56. Mrs Humphry Ward, 'An Appeal Against Female Suffrage', *Nineteenth Century* (June 1889), pp. 781–7. See also John Sutherland, *Mrs*

Humphry Ward: Eminent Victorian, Pre-eminent Edwardian (Oxford: Clarendon Press, 1990), pp. 198–9.
57. M.A.W. [signed], opening article, *The Anti-Suffrage Review* 1 (December 1908), pp. 1–2.
58. Report on the Countess of Jersey's speech on 25 November 1908 at King's Hall, Covent Garden, *Anti-Suffrage Review* 1 (December 1908), p. 5.
59. Mary Ward to Louise Creighton, 22 September 1909, Ward Papers, Pusey House, Oxford.
60. Mary Ward to Thomas Arnold, 7 July 1894, Ward Papers, Pusey House.
61. Mrs Humphry Ward, *Letters to My Neighbours on the Present Election* (London: Smith, Elder, 1910), p. 1.
62. John Sutherland, *Mrs Humphry Ward*, p. 350.
63. Mrs Humphry Ward, *A Writer's Recollections* (London: Collins, 1918), p. 372.

Chapter 6: The Anti-Feminist Woman and Religion

1. 'The Use and Abuse of Female Sentiment in Religion', *Christian Remembrancer* 47 (April 1864), pp. 391, 393.
2. Elizabeth Barrett, 'Glimpses into my own life and literary character' (1820), in *Two Autobiographical Essays by Elizabeth Barrett*, ed. William S. Peterson, Browning Institute Studies II (New York, 1974), p. 126; Florence Nightingale, diary entry, 1853, quoted in Sir Edward Cook, *The Life of Florence Nightingale* (London: Macmillan, 2 vols, 1913), vol. II, p. 469.
3. [Florence Nightingale], *Suggestions for Thought to the Searchers after Truth Among the Artizans of England* (London: Eyre and Spottiswoode, 3 vols, 1860), vol. II, p. 102.
4. Quoted in Cook, *Florence Nightingale*, vol. II, p. 367.
5. Florence Nightingale, 'A "Note" of Interrogation', *Fraser's Magazine* (NS 7, May 1873), pp. 567–77; and 'A sub-"Note of Interrogation" I. What will be our Religion in 1999?', *Fraser's Magazine* (NS 8, July 1873), pp. 25–36.
6. *Thoughts on Self-Culture, Addressed to Women*, by Maria G. Grey and her sister, Emily Shirreff (London: Edward Moxon, 2 vols, 1850), vol. II, pp. 234, 276.
7. For a full account of Victorian attitudes to St Paul's teachings on women, Mary and Eve, see chapter 4 of *The Woman Question: Society and Literature in Britain and America 1837–1883*, vol. 2, ed. Elizabeth K. Helsinger, Robin Lauterbach Sheets and William Veeder (Chicago and London: University of Chicago Press, 1983).
8. Susan Dowell and Jane Williams, *Bread, Wine and Women: The Ordination Debate in the Church of England* (London: Virago, 1994), p. 22.
9. Ibid., p. 92.
10. Elizabeth Strutt, *The Feminine Soul: Its Nature and Attributes* (London: J.S. Hodson, 1857), pp. 2, 13.
11. Quoted by Norma Clarke in *Ambitious Heights: Writing, Friendship,*

Love – The Jewsbury Sisters, Felicia Hemans, and Jane Welsh Carlyle (London and New York: Routledge, 1990), p. 93.

12. Anna Jameson, *Sisters of Charity Catholic and Protestant, Abroad and at Home* (London: Longman, Brown, Green and Longman, 1855), p. 11.
13. Dinah Craik, 'On Sisterhoods', in *About Money and Other Things* (London and New York: Macmillan, 1886), p. 160.
14. Marilyn French, *The War Against Women* (London: Hamish Hamilton, 1992), p. 46.
15. *Women's Religious Experience*, ed. Pat Holden (London and Canberra: Croom Helm, and Totowa, New Jersey: Barnes and Noble, 1983), p. 2.
16. George Somes Layard, *Mrs Lynn Linton: Her Life, Letters and Opinions* (London: Methuen, 1901), p. 365.
17. Charlotte M. Yonge, *Musings over the 'Christian Year' and 'Lyra Innocentium', together with a few gleanings of recollections of the Rev. J. Keble, gathered by several friends* (Oxford and London: James Parker, 1871), pp. iv-v.
18. Owen Chadwick, *The Spirit of the Oxford Movement: Tractarian Essays* (Cambridge: Cambridge University Press, 1990), p. 54.
19. Charlotte M. Yonge, *Heartsease, or the Brother's Wife* (1854; London: Macmillan, 1889), p. 442.
20. Charlotte M. Yonge, *Womankind* (London: Mozley and Smith, 1876), p. 8.
21. *Reasons Why I am a Catholic and Not a Roman Catholic*, by the late Charlotte Mary Yonge (London: Wells, Gardner, Daron, 1901), p. 19.
22. Margaret Oliphant, *The Life of Edward Irving* (London: Hurst and Blackett, 2 vols, 1862), vol. I, Preface.
23. [Margaret Oliphant], 'Edward Irving', *Blackwood's* 84 (November 1858), p. 567.
24. Margaret Oliphant, *Selected Short Stories of the Supernatural*, ed. Margaret K. Guy (Edinburgh: Scottish Academic Press, 1985), p. x.
25. Margaret Oliphant to John Blackwood (1861), MS 4163, National Library of Scotland.
26. Margaret Oliphant to John Blackwood (1866), MS 4213, National Library of Scotland.
27. [Margaret Oliphant], 'The Fancies of a Believer', *Blackwood's* 157 (February 1895), pp. 237–55, *passim*.
28. See Valentine Cunningham, *Everywhere Spoken Against: Dissent in the Victorian Novel* (Oxford: Clarendon Press, 1975); also 'Salem Chapel', *The Nonconformist*, 25 February 1863, pp. 157–8; and 'Chronicles of Carlingford', *National Review* 16 (April 1863), pp. 350–62.
29. Margaret Oliphant to John Blackwood [1855], MS 4111, National Library of Scotland.
30. Margaret Oliphant to Rev. R.H. Story, 1862, *Autobiography and Letters*, p. 182.
31. See, for example, Anthea Trodd, *Domestic Crime in the Victorian Novel* (Basingstoke and London: Macmillan, 1989); and Peter Brooker, Paul Stigant and Peter Widdowson, 'History and "literary value": *Adam Bede* and *Salem Chapel*', in *Popular Fictions: Essays in Literature and*

History, ed. Peter Humm, Paul Stigant and Peter Widdowson (London and New York: Methuen, 1986).
32. *The Autobiography of Margaret Oliphant*, ed. Elisabeth Jay (Oxford and New York: Oxford University Press, 1990), p. 113.
33. [Margaret Oliphant], 'Sermons,' *Blackwood's* 92 (August 1862), p. 218.
34. E. Lynn Linton, *The Autobiography of Christopher Kirkland* (London: Richard Bentley and Son, 3 vols, 1885), vol. I, pp. 85, 87.
35. Layard, *Mrs Lynn Linton*, p. 181.
36. E. Lynn Linton, *The True History of Joshua Davidson, Christian and Communist* (London: Strahan, 1872), pp. 276, 278.
37. W.R. Greg, 'Is a Christian Life Feasible in These Days?', *Contemporary Review* 21 (April 1873), p. 680.
38. E. Lynn Linton, *Under Which Lord?* (London: Chatto and Windus, 3 vols, 1879), vol. II, p. 248.
39. Evelleen Richards, 'Huxley and Woman's Place in Science: the "woman question" and the control of Victorian anthropology', in *History, Humanity and Evolution: Essays for John C. Greene*, ed. James R. Moore (Cambridge: Cambridge University Press, 1989), p. 255. I am indebted to Professor Alan Brook for this reference.
40. *Unbelief and Sin: A Protest addressed to those who attended the Bampton Lecture of Sunday March 6* (printed for the author, 1881).
41. Mary Ward, 'The New Reformation, A Dialogue', *Nineteenth Century* 25 (October 1889), p. 461.
42. Mary Ward, 'The New Reformation, II', *Nineteenth Century* 46 (October 1899), p. 671.
43. Mrs Humphry Ward, *Robert Elsmere* (1888; Oxford: World's Classics edn, 1987), p. 78.
44. Robin Gilmour, *The Novel in the Victorian Age: A Modern Introduction* (London: Edward Arnold, 1986), p. 197.
45. Mrs Humphry Ward, *Helbeck of Bannisdale* (London: Smith, Elder, 1898), p. 33.
46. Harriet Martineau described herself, after shedding her religious orthodoxy, as 'a free rover on the broad, bright breezy common of the universe', *Harriet Martineau's Autobiography* (1877; ed. Gaby Weiner, London: Virago, 2 vols), vol. I, p. 116.
47. Janet Trevelyan, *The Life of Mrs Humphry Ward* (London: Constable, 1923), p. 147.
48. Mary Ward to Thomas Arnold, 9 August 1898, Ward Papers, Pusey House.
49. R.F. Clarke, SJ, 'A Catholic's View of "Helbeck of Bannisdale"', *Nineteenth Century* 44 (September 1898), pp. 459–60.
50. Mrs Humphry Ward, *The Coryston Family* (London: Smith, Elder, 1913), p. 290.
51. See Susan Dowell and Jane Williams, *Bread, Wine and Women: The Ordination Debate in the Church of England* (London: Virago, 1994), pp. 82ff, on reasons why feminists oppose the ordination of women (e.g. that the church is a sexist institution which women should be reluctant to join).

52. Bertha Lathbury, 'Agnosticism and Women', *Nineteenth Century* 7 (April 1880), pp. 619–27.
53. J.H. Clapperton, 'Agnosticism and Women: A Reply', *Nineteenth Century* 7 (May 1880), pp. 840–4.
54. Reported in the *Yorkshire Post* of 10 March 1994, p. 6.

Conclusion

1. Margaret Oliphant, 'The Laws Concerning Women', *Blackwood's* 79 (April 1856), p. 379.
2. Quoted by Janet Penrose Trevelyan, *The Life of Mrs Humphry Ward* (London: Constable, 1923), p. 39.
3. Naomi Wolf, *Fire with Fire: The New Female Power and How it will Change the 21st Century* (London: Chatto & Windus, 1993), pp. 275–6.
4. Judith Fetterley, *The Resisting Reader: A Feminist Approach to American Fiction* (Bloomington: Indiana University Press, 1978), pp. xxi, xxii.
5. Wolf, *Fire with Fire*, p. xiv.

Bibliography

1. MANUSCRIPT COLLECTIONS

National Library of Scotland (Oliphant letters)
Pusey House, Oxford (Ward papers)

2. BOOKS BY THE NOVELISTS, IN ORDER OF PUBLICATION

Eliza Lynn Linton

Amymone: A Romance in the Days of Pericles. London: Richard Bentley, 3 vols, 1848.
Grasp Your Nettle. London: Smith, Elder, 3 vols, 1865.
Sowing the Wind. London: Tinsley Brothers, 3 vols, 1867.
Ourselves: Essays on Women. London: G. Routledge and Sons, 1869.
The True History of Joshua Davidson, Christian and Communist. London: Strahan, 1872.
Under Which Lord? London: Chatto & Windus, 3 vols, 1879.
The Rebel of the Family. London: Chatto & Windus, 3 vols, 1880.
The Girl of the Period, and Other Social Essays. London: Richard Bentley and Son, 2 vols, 1883.
The Autobiography of Christopher Kirkland. London: Richard Bentley and Son, 3 vols, 1885.
Freeshooting: Extracts from the Works of Mrs Lynn Linton, intro. G.F.S. London. London: Chatto & Windus, 1892.
The One Too Many. London: Chatto & Windus, 3 vols, 1894.
My Literary Life. London: Hodder & Stoughton, 1899.

Margaret Oliphant

The Life of Edward Irving. London: Hurst and Blackett, 2 vols, 1862.
The Rector and the Doctor's Family. London: Blackwod, 1863; repr. Virago, 1986.
Salem Chapel. London: Blackwood, 2 vols, 1863; repr. Virago, 1986.
The Perpetual Curate. London: Blackwood, 1864; repr. Virago, 1987.
Miss Marjoribanks. London: Blackwood, 1866; repr. Virago, 1987.
Phoebe Junior: A Last Chronicle of Carlingford. London: Hurst and Blackett, 3 vols, 1876; repr. Virago, 1989.
The Curate in Charge. London: Beccles, 2 vols, 1876; repr. Alan Sutton, 1987.
The Literary History of England in the End of the Eighteenth and Beginning of the Nineteenth Century. London: Macmillan, 3 vols, 1882.
The Wizard's Son. London: Macmillan, 3 vols, 1894.
The Victorian Age of English Literature (with F.R. Oliphant). London: Percival, 2 vols, 1892.

Women Novelists of Queen Victoria's Age: A Book of Appreciations (ed.). London: Hurst and Blackett, 1897.
Annals of a Publishing House: William Blackwood and His Sons, Their Magazine and Friends. Edinburgh and London: Blackwood, 2 vols, 1897.
The Autobiography and Letters of Mrs M.O.W. Oliphant, ed. Mrs Harry Coghill. Edinburgh and London: Blackwood, 1899; repr. ed. Laurie Langbauer, London and Chicago: University of Chicago Press, 1988; ed. Elisabeth Jay (complete text), Oxford: Oxford University Press, 1990.

Mrs Humphry Ward

Robert Elsmere. London: Smith, Elder, 3 vols, 1888; repr. World's Classics, Oxford, 1987.
The History of David Grieve. London: Smith, Elder, 3 vols, 1892.
Marcella. London: Smith, Elder, 3 vols, 1894; repr. Virago, 1984.
Sir George Tressady. London: Smith, Elder, 1896.
Helbeck of Bannisdale. London: Smith, Elder, 1898; repr. Penguin, 1983.
Lady Rose's Daughter. London: Smith, Elder, 1903.
The Case of Richard Meynell. London: Smith, Elder, 1911.
The Coryston Family. London: Smith, Elder, 1913.
Delia Blanchflower. London: Ward, Lock, 1915.
A Writer's Recollections. London: Collins, 1918.

Charlotte M. Yonge

The Heir of Redclyffe. London: Macmillan, 1853; repr. 1902.
Heartsease; or, the Brother's Wife. London: Macmillan, 1854; repr. 1902.
The Daisy Chain, or Aspirations. London: Macmillan, 1856; repr. Virago, 1989.
The Clever Woman of the Family. London: Macmillan, 2 vols, 1865; repr. Virago, 1985.
Musings over the 'Christian Year' and 'Lyra Innocentium'. Oxford and London: James Parker, 1871.
Womankind. London: Mozley and Smith, 1876.
Reasons Why I am a Catholic and Not a Roman Catholic. London: Wells, Gardner, Daron, 1901.

3. JOURNAL ARTICLES BY THE NOVELISTS

Eliza Lynn Linton

'Mary Wollstonecraft', *The English Republic* III (1854), 418–24.
'Rights and Wrongs of Women', *Household Words*, 1 April 1854, 158–61.
'One of Our Legal Fictions', *Household Words*, 29 April 1854, 257–60.
'Passing Faces', *Household Words*, 14 April 1855, 261–4.
'Domestic Life', *Temple Bar* 4 (February 1862), 402–15.
'The Girl of the Period', *Saturday Review*, 14 March 1868, 339–40; separately reprinted, with other essays in the series, 1883.

'The Modern Revolt', *Macmillan's* 23 (December 1870), 142–9.
'Our Civilization', *Cornhill Magazine* 27 (June 1873), 671–8.
'Our Duties', *Cornhill Magazine* 28 (August 1873), 216–24.
'George Eliot', *Temple Bar* 73 (April 1885), 512–24.
'The Future Supremacy of Women', *National Review*, September 1886, 1–15.
'The Higher Education of Woman', *Fortnightly Review* 46 (October 1886), 498–510.
'Womanhood in Old Greece', *Fortnightly Review* 47 (January 1887), 105–23.
'The Characteristics of English Women', *Fortnightly Review* 51 (Feburary 1889), 245–60; 52 (March 1889), 363–76.
'The Threatened Abdication of Man', *National Review* 13 (July 1889), 557–92.
'Candour in English Fiction', *New Review*, January 1890, 10–14.
'Literature: then and now', *Fortnightly Review* 53 (April 1890), 517–31.
'Modern Topsy-turveydom', *New Review* 3 (November 1890), 427–37.
'The Wild Women, No. I, "As Politicians"', *Nineteenth Century* 30 (July 1891), 79–88.
'The Wild Woman as Social Insurgents', *Nineteenth Century* 30 (October 1891), 596–605.
'The Cult of Cant', *Temple Bar* 93 (October 1981), 189–98.
'Partisans of the Wild Women', *Nineteenth Century* 31 (March 1892), 455–64.
'The Decay of Discipline', *Temple Bar* 102 (June 1894), 191–7.

Margaret Oliphant

'Charles Dickens', *Blackwood's* 77 (April 1855), 451–66.
'Modern Novelists – Great and Small', *Blackwood's* 77 (May 1855), 554–68.
'Religion in Common Life', *Blackwood's* 79 (February 1856), 243–6.
'The Laws Concerning Women', *Blackwood's* (April 1856), 379–87.
'The Condition of Women', *Blackwood's* 83 (February 1858), 139–54.
'Edward Irving', *Blackwood's* 84 (November 1858), 567–86.
'Sensation Novels', *Blackwood's* 91 (May 1862), 564–84.
'Sermons', *Blackwood's* 92 (August 1862), 202–20.
'The Great Unrepresented', *Blackwood's* 100 (September 1866), 367–79.
'Novels' [Mary Braddon], *Blackwood's* 102 (September 1867), 257–80.
'The Latest Lawgiver' [Ruskin], *Blackwood's* 103 (June 1868), 675–91.
'Historical Sketches of the Reign of George II – No. X, "The Novelists"', *Blackwood's* 105 (March 1869), 253–76.
'Charles Reade's Novels', *Blackwood's* 106 (October 1869), 488–514.
'Mill on the Subjection of Women', *Edinburgh Review* 130 (October 1869), 572–602.
'Miss Austen and Miss Mitford', *Blackwood's* 107 (March 1870), 290–313.
'New Books', *Blackwood's* 107 (May 1870), 628–51.
'New Books' [incl. Linton], *Blackwood's* 108 (August 1870), 166–88.
'Charles Dickens', *Blackwood's* 109 (June 1871), 673–95.
'Harriet Martineau', *Blackwood's* 121 (April 1877), 472–96.
'Two Ladies', *Blackwood's* 125 (February 1879), 206–24.
'The Grievances of Women', *Fraser's* 101 (May 1880), 698–710.

'The Life and Letters of George Eliot', *Edinburgh Review* 161 (April 1885), 514–53.
'The Old Saloon: The Literature of the Last Fifty Years', *Blackwood's* 141 (June 1887), 737–61; 146 (August 1889), 254–75.
'A Commentary from an Easy Chair', *Spectator*, 14 December 1889; 25 January 1890.
'Fancies of a Believer', *Blackwood's* 157 (February 1895), 237–55.
'Men and Women', *Blackwood's* 157 (April 1895), 620–50.
'The Anti-Marriage League', *Blackwood's* 159 (January 1896), 135–49.
'John Gibson Lockhart', *Blackwood's* 160 (November 1896), 607–25.

Mrs Humphry Ward

'The Literature of Introspection', *Macmillan's* 49 (January 1884), 190–201; (February 1884), 264–78.
'Recent Fiction in England and France', *Macmillan's* 50 (August 1884), 250–60.
'Style and Miss Austen', *Macmillan's* 51 (December 1884), 84–91.
'Elizabeth Barrett Browning', *Atalanta* (September 1888), 708–12.
'The New Reformation', *Nineteenth Century* 25 (March 1889), 454–80; 46 (October 1899), 654–72.
'An Appeal Against Female Suffrage', *Nineteenth Century* 25 (June 1889), 781–7.
Opening article, *The Anti-Suffrage Review* I (December 1908).

Charlotte Yonge

'Hints on Reading', *Monthly Packet*, June 1859, 664–5.
'Hints on Reading', *Monthly Packet*, July 1859, 111–12.
'George Eliot and Her Critics', *Monthly Packet*, May 1885, 471–95.
'Authorship', *Monthly Packet*, September 1892, 296–303.

4. SECONDARY READING: BOOKS

Adburgham, Alison, *Women in Print: Writing Women and Women's Magazines from the Restoration to the Accession of Victoria*. London: George Allen & Unwin, 1972.
Anderson, Nancy Fix, *Woman Against Women in Victorian England: A Life of Eliza Lynn Linton*. Bloomington and Indianapolis: Indiana University Press, 1987.
Armstrong, Isabel (ed.), *New Feminist Discourses: Critical Essays on Theories and Texts*. London and New York: Routledge, 1992.
Auerbach, Nina, *Woman and the Demon: The Life of a Victorian Myth*. Cambridge and London: Harvard University Press, 1982.
Baker, Joseph E., *The Novel and the Oxford Movement*. New York: Russell and Russell, 1965.
Banks, Olive, *Faces of Feminism: A Study of Feminism as a Social Movement*. Oxford: Martin Robertson, 1981.

Barbauld, Mrs, *A Legacy for Young Ladies*. London, 1826.
Battiscombe, Georgina, *Charlotte Mary Yonge: The Story of an Uneventful Life*. London: Constable, 1943.
Battiscombe, Georgina, and Marghanita Laski (eds), *A Chaplet for Charlotte Yonge*. London: The Cresset Press, 1965.
Bax, Ernest Belfort, *Essays in Socialism New and Old*. London: E. Grant Richards, 1906.
Bax, Ernest Belfort, *The Fraud of Feminism*. London: E. Grant Richards, 1913.
Bell, E. Moberly, *Octavia Hill: A Biography*. London: Constable, 1942.
Bennett, Arnold, *Books and Persons: Being Comments on a Past Epoch 1908–1911*. London: Chatto & Windus, 1917.
Bennett, Arnold, *Journalism for Women: A Practical Guide*. London and New York: John Lane, Bodley Head, 1898.
Bennett, Daphne, *Emily Davies and the Liberation of Women* (London: André Deutsch, 1990).
Benson, A.C., *Memories and Friends*. London: John Murray, 1924.
Benson, A.C. (ed.), *The Letters of Queen Victoria: A Selection of Her Majesty's Correspondence between the years 1837 and 1861*. London: John Murray, 3 vols, 1908.
Bevington, Merle Mowbray, *The Saturday Review 1855–1868: Representative Educated Opinion in Victorian England*. New York: Columbia University Press, 1941.
Bindslev, Anne M., *Mrs Humphry Ward: A Study in Late Victorian Feminine Consciousness and Creative Expression*. Stockholm: Almqvist and Wiksell International, 1985.
Black, Helen C., *Notable Women Authors of the Day*. Glasgow: David Bryce, 1893.
Blodgett, Harriet, *Centuries of Female Days: Englishwomen's Private Diaries*. Rutgers, 1988; Gloucester: Alan Sutton Publishing, 1989.
Bourne, H.R. Fox, *English Newspapers: Chapters in the History of Journalism*. New York: Russell and Russell, 2 vols, 1966.
Boyd, Nancy, *Josephine Butler, Octavia Hill, Florence Nightingale: Three Victorian Women who Changed their World*. London: Macmillan, 1982.
Braddon, Mary Elizabeth, *Miranda*. London: Hutchinson, 1913.
Brake, Laurel, Aled Jones and Lionel Malden, *Investigating Victorian Journalism*. London and Basingstoke: Macmillan, 1990.
Branca, Patricia, *Silent Sisterhood: Middle Class Women in the Victorian Home*. London: Croom Helm, 1975.
Brightwell, Cecilia Lucy (ed.), *Memorials of the Life of Amelia Opie*. Norwich: Fletcher & Alexander; Longman, Brown, 1854.
Brittain, Vera, *Lady into Woman: A History of Women from Victoria to Elizabeth II*. London: Andrew Dakers, 1953.
Brodzki, Bella, and Celeste Schenck, *Life/Lines: Theorizing Women's Autobiography*. Ithaca and London: Cornell University Press, 1988.
Brownstein, Rachel M., *Becoming a Heroine: Reading about Women in Novels*. New York: Viking Press, 1982.
Caine, Barbara, *Victorian Feminists*. Oxford: Oxford University Press, 1992.
Campbell, Beatrix, *The Iron Ladies: Why Do Women Vote Tory?* London: Virago, 1987.

Carlyle, Thomas, *On Heroes, Hero-Worship, and the Heroic in History*. 1840; London: J.M. Dent, Everyman, 1973.
Chadwick, Owen, *The Spirit of the Oxford Movement: Tractarian Essays*. Cambridge: Cambridge University Press, 1990.
Chapone, Hester, *Letters on the Improvement of the Mind, Addressed to a Young Lady*. London: J. Walter, 2nd edn, 2 vols, 1773.
'Charlotte Elizabeth' [Mrs Tonna], *The Wrongs of Woman*. London: W.H. Dalton, 4 vols, 1843.
Clarke, John Stock, *Margaret Oliphant, 1828–1897: A Bibliography*. Victorian Fiction: Research Guides 11; University of Queensland, 1986.
Clarke, Norma, *Ambitious Heights: Writing, Love, the Jewsbury Sisters, Felicia Hemans and Jane Carlyle*. London: Routledge, 1990.
Colby, Vineta and Robert A. Colby, *The Equivocal Virtue: Mrs Oliphant and the Victorian Literary Market Place*. New York: Archon Books, 1966.
Colby, Vineta, *The Singular Anomaly: Women Novelists of the Nineteenth Century*. New York: New York University Press, 1970.
Coleridge, Christabel, *Charlotte Mary Yonge: Her Life and Letters*. London: Macmillan, 1903.
Colley, Linda, *Britons: Forging the Nation 1707–1837*. New Haven and London: Yale University Press, 1992.
Cook, Sir Edward, *The Life of Florence Nightingale*. London: Macmillan, 2 vols, 1913.
Craik, Dinah, *About Money and Other Things*. London and New York, 1886.
Cranfield, W.T. (ed.) *Journalism as a Career*. London: Sir Issac Pitman & Sons, 1930.
Crosby, Christina, *The Ends of History: Victorians and the 'woman question'*. New York and London: Routledge, 1991.
Culler, Jonathan, *On Deconstruction*. London: Routledge & Kegan Paul, 1983.
Cunningham, Gail, *The New Woman and the Victorian Novel*. London and Basingstoke: Macmillan, 1978.
Cunningham, Valentine, *Everywhere Spoken Against: Dissent in the Victorian Novel*. Oxford: Clarendon Press, 1975.
Davidoff, Leonore, and Catherine Hall, *Family Fortunes: Men and Women of the English Middle Class 1780–1850*. London: Hutchinson, 1987.
Davis, Philip, *Memory and Writing: From Wordsworth to Lawrence*. Liverpool: Liverpool University Press, 1983.
Delamont, Sara, and Lorna Duffin, *The Nineteenth Century Woman: Her Cultural and Physical World*. London: Croom Helm, 1978.
Dinnerstein, Dorothy, *The Rocking of the Cradle and Ruling of the World*. 1976; London: Condor Books, Souvenir Press, 1978.
Dowell, Susan, and Jane Williams, *Bread, Wine and Women: The Ordination Debate in the Church of England*. London: Virago, 1994.
Drummond, Andrew L., *The Churches in English Fiction*. Leicester: Edgar Backus, 1950.
Dworkin, Andrea, *Right-Wing Women*. London: Women's Press, 1983.
Edgeworth, Maria, *Belinda*. 1801; London and New York: Pandora, 1986.
Edwards, Lee R., *Psyche as Hero: Female Heroism and Fictional Form*. Middleton, Connecticut: Wesleyan University Press, 1984.
Ellis [Sarah Stickney], Mrs, *The Women of England, Their Social Duties, and Domestic Habits*. London: Fisher, Son, 1839.

Ellis [Sarah Stickney], Mrs, *The Daughters of England, their Position in Society, Character and Responsibilities*. London and Paris: Fisher, Son, 1842.
Elwood, Mrs Anne, *Memoirs of the Literary Ladies of England*. London: Henry Colburn, 2 vols, 1843.
Evans, Richard J., *The Feminists: Women's Emancipation Movements in Europe, America and Australasia, 1840–1920*. London: Croom Helm, 1977.
Feldman, Paula R., and Diana Scott-Kilvert (eds), *The Journals of Mary Shelley 1814–1844: Vol. II, 1822–1844*. Oxford: Clarendon Press, 1978.
Fernando, Lloyd, *'New Women' in the Late Victorian Novel*. University Park and London: Pennsylvania State University Press, 1977.
Fetterley, Judith, *The Resisting Reader: A Feminist Approach to American Fiction*. Bloomington: Indiana University Press, 1978.
Firestone, Shulamith, *The Dialectic of Sex: The Case for Feminist Revolution*. 1971; London: Women's Press, 1979.
Forster, Margaret, *Significant Sisters: The Grassroots of Active Feminism 1839–1939*. 1984; Harmondsworth, Middlesex: Penguin, 1986.
French, Marilyn, *The War Against Women*. London: Hamish Hamilton, 1992.
Friedan, Betty, *The Feminine Mystique*. 1963; London: Pelican Books, 1982.
Garber, Marjorie, *Vested Interests: Cross Dressing and Cultural Anxiety*. New York and London: Routledge, 1992.
Gosse, Sir Edmund, *Silhouettes*. London: Heinemann, 1925.
Gould, F.J., *Chats with Pioneers of Modern Thought*. London: Watts, 1898.
Grey, Maria G., and Emily Shirreff, *Thoughts on Self-Culture, Addressed to Women*. London: Edward Moxon, 2 vols, 1850.
Gross, John, *The Rise and Fall of the Man of Letters: Aspects of English Literary Life since 1800*. London: Weidenfeld and Nicolson, 1969.
Guy, Margaret K. (ed.), *Margaret Oliphant: Selected Short Stories of the Supernatural*. Edinburgh: Scottish Academic Press, 1985.
Gwynn, Stephen, *Mrs Humphry Ward*. London: Nisbet, 1917.
Hamilton, Elizabeth, *Memoirs of Modern Philosophers*. Bath: R. Cruttwell; and London: G.G. & J. Robinson, 3 vols, 1800.
Hardwick, Elizabeth, *A View of My Own: Essays in Literature and Society*. London: Heinemann, 1964.
Harrison, Brian, *Separate Spheres: The Opposition to Women's Suffrage in Britain*. London: Croom Helm, 1978.
Harrison, Ethel B., *The Freedom of Women: An Argument against the proposed Extension of the Suffrage to Women*. London: Watts, 1908.
Heilbrun, Carolyn G., *Reinventing Womanhood*. London: Victor Gollancz, 1979.
Heilbrun, Carolyn G., *Writing a Woman's Life*. 1988; London: Women's Press, 1989.
Hellerstein, Erna Olafson, Leslie Parker Hume and Karen M. Offen (eds), *Victorian Women: A Documentary Account of Women's Lives in Nineteenth Century England, France, and the United States*. Brighton: Harvester Press, 1981.
Helsinger, Elizabeth K., Robin Lauterbach Sheets and William Veeder (eds), *The Woman Question: Society and Literature in Britain and America 1837–1883*. Chicago: University of Chicago Press, 3 vols, 1983.
Hill, Alan G. (ed.), *The Letters of William and Dorothy Wordsworth, V: The Later Years*, Part II, 1829–34, 2nd edn. Oxford: Clarendon Press, 1979.

Holden, Pat (ed.), *Women's Religious Experience*. London and Canberra: Croom Helm; Totowa, New Jersey: Barnes & Noble, 1983.

Humm, Peter, Paul Stigant and Peter Widdowson, *Popular Fictions: Essays in Literature and History*. London and New York: Methuen, 1986.

Ireland, Mrs Alexander (ed.), *Selections from the Letters of Geraldine Endsor Jewsbury to Jane Welsh Carlyle*. London: Longman, Green, 1892.

Jameson, Anna, *Sisters of Charity, Catholic and Protestant, Abroad and At Home*. London: Longman, Brown, Green and Longman, 1855.

Jay, Elisabeth, *Mrs Oliphant: A Fiction to Herself: A Literary Life*. Oxford: Clarendon Press, 1995.

Jones, Enid Huws, *Mrs Humphry Ward*. London: Heinemann, 1973.

Jones, Marion Kathleen, 'Mrs Humphry Ward and Feminism', B.Phil. thesis, University of Hull, 1975.

Jones, Vivien (ed.), *Women in the Eighteenth Century: Constructions of Femininity*. London and New York: Routledge, 1990.

Kaplan, Cora (ed.), Introduction to Elizabeth Barrett Browning, *Aurora Leigh*. London: Women's Press, 1978.

Keating, Peter, *The Haunted Study: A Social History of the English Novel 1875–1914*. London: Secker & Warburg, 1989.

Kirkham, Margaret, *Jane Austen, Feminism and Fiction*. Brighton: Harvester Press, 1983.

Klein, Renate D. and Deborah Lynn Steinberg, *Radical Voices: A Decade of Feminist Resistance from Women's Studies International Forum*. Oxford: Pergamon Press, 1989.

Kowaleski-Wallace, Elizabeth, *Their Fathers' Daughters: Hannah More, Maria Edgeworth, and Patriarchal Complicity*. Oxford and New York: Oxford University Press, 1991.

Layard, George Somes, *Mrs Lynn Linton: Her Life, Letters, and Opinions*. London: Methuen, 1901.

Leavis, Q.D., Introduction to Margaret Oliphant, *Miss Marjoribanks*. London: Chatto & Windus, 1969.

Leavis, Q.D., Introduction to Margaret Oliphant, *Autobiography and Letters*. Leicester: Leicester University Press, 1974.

Levin, Susan M., *Dorothy Wordsworth and Romanticism*. New Brunswick and London: Rutgers, The State University, 1987.

Levine, Philippa, *Victorian Feminism 1850–1900*. London: Hutchinson Education, 1987.

[Lewis, Sarah], *Woman's Mission*. London: John W. Parker, 1839.

Lewis, Lady Theresa (ed.), *Extracts from the Journals and Correspondence of Miss Berry from the year 1783 to 1852*. London: Longmans, Green, 2nd edn, 3 vols, 1866.

Lyndon, Neil, *No More Sex War: The Failures of Feminism*. London: Sinclair-Stevenson, 1992; Mandarin Paperbacks, 1993.

Maison, Margaret M., *Search Your Soul, Eustace*. London and New York: Steed and Ward, 1961.

Mangan, J.A., and James Walvin, *Manliness and Morality: Middle-Class Masculinity in Britain and America 1800–1940*. Manchester: Manchester University Press, 1987.

Mare, Margaret, and Alicia C. Percival, *Victorian Best-Seller: The World of*

Bibliography

Charlotte M. Yonge. London, Sydney, Toronto and Bombay: George G. Harrap, 1947.
Meakin, Annette M.B., *Hannah More: A Biographical Study*. London: Smith, Elder, 1911.
Mendus, Susan, and Jane Rendall (eds), *Sexuality and Subordination: Interdisciplinary Studies of Gender in the Nineteenth Century*. London and New York: Routledge, 1989.
Mill, John Stuart, *The Subjection of Women*. 1869; ed. Kate Soper, with *The Enfranchisement of Women*, London: Virago, 1983.
Miller, Jane, *Women Writing about Men*. London: Virago, 1986.
Mineka, Francis E., and Dwight N. Lindley, *The Later Letters of John Stuart Mill 1849–1873*. Toronto: University of Toronto Press; and London; Routledge & Kegan Paul, 1972.
Mitchell, Juliet, and Ann Oakley, *What is Feminism?* Oxford: Basil Blackwell, 1986.
Moore, R. (ed.), *History, Humanity and Evolution: Essays for John C. Greene*. Cambridge: Cambridge University Press, 1989.
More, Hannah, *Essays on Various Subjects*. London: J. Wilkie and T. Caddell, 1777.
More, Hannah, *Strictures on the Modern System of Female Education*. London: T. Caddell, Jun. and W. Davies, 2 vols, 1799.
Morgan, David H.J., *Discovering Men*. London and New York: Routledge, 1992.
Morgan, Thais E. (ed.), *Victorian Sages and Cultural Discourse: Renegotiating Gender and Power*. London and New Brunswick: Rutgers University Press, 1990.
Mulock, Diana, *A Woman's Thoughts about Women*. London: Hurst and Blackett, 1858.
Murray, Janet Horowitz, *Strong-Minded Women*. 1982; Harmondsworth: Penguin Books, 1984.
Newsome, David, *Godliness and Good Learning*. London: John Murray, 1961.
Nightingale, Florence, 'Cassandra', in Ray Strachey, *The Cause*. London: G. Bell and Sons, 1928.
Nightingale, Florence, *The Institution of Kaiserwerth on the Rhine* ... London: 1850.
Nightingale, Florence, *Notes on Nursing: What It Is, and What It Is Not*. London: Harrison, 1860.
Nightingale, Florence, *Suggestions for Thought to the Searchers After Truth among the Artizans of England*. London: Eyre & Spottiswoode, 3 vols, 1860.
Norton, Caroline, *A Letter to the Queen on Lord Chancellor Cranworth's Marriage and Divorce Bill*. London: Longman, Brown, Green & Longmans, 1855.
Opie, Amelia, *Adeline Mowbray: The Mother and Daughter*. 1802; Intro. Jeanette Winterson, London: Pandora Press, 1986.
Paglia, Camille, *Sexual Personae: Art and Decadence from Nefertiti to Emily Dickinson*. Yale University Press, 1990; Harmondsworth: Penguin Books, 1991.
Peterson, William S., *Victorian Heretic: Mrs Humphry Ward's Robert Elsmere*. Leicester: Leicester University Press, 1976.

Phelps, William Lyon, *Essays on Modern Novelists*. New York: Macmillan, 1910.
Poovey, Mary, *Uneven Developments: The Ideological Work of Gender in Mid-Victorian England*. London: Virago, 1989.
Pratt, Annis, *Archetypal Patterns in Women's Fiction*. Brighton: Harvester Wheatsheaf, 1982.
Praz, Mario, *The Hero in Eclipse in Victorian Fiction*. 1956; London and Oxford: Oxford University Press, 1969.
Rendall, Jane, *The Origins of Modern Feminism: Women in Britain, France and the United States 1780–1860*. London: Macmillan, 1985.
Rendall, Jane (ed.), *Equal or Different: Women's Politics 1800–1914*. Oxford: Basil Blackwell, 1987.
Reynolds, Kimberley, and Nicola Humble, *Victorian Heroines: Representations of Femininity in Nineteenth-Century Literature and Art*. London and New York: Harvester Wheatsheaf, 1993.
Rich, Adrienne, *On Lies, Secrets and Silence*. London: Virago, 1979.
Richards, Janet Radcliffe, *The Sceptical Feminist: A Philosophical Enquiry*. 1980; London: Pelican Books, 1982.
Richards, John Morgan, *The Life of John Oliver Hobbes*. London: John Murray, 1911.
Ritchie, Anne Thackeray, *From the Porch*. London: Smith, Elder, 1913.
Roberts, William, *Memoirs of the Life and Correspondence of Mrs Hannah More*. London: R.B. Seeley and W. Burnside, 3rd edn, 4 vols, 1885.
Roiphe, Katie, *The Morning After: Sex, Fear, and Feminism*. 1993; London: Hamish Hamilton, 1994.
Romanes, Ethel, *Charlotte Mary Yonge: An Appreciation*. London and Oxford: A.R. Mowbray, 1908.
Roper, Michael, and John Tosh (eds), *Manful Assertions: Masculinities in Britain since 1800*. London: Routledge, 1991.
Rowbotham, Judith, *Good Girls Make Good Wives: Guidance for Girls in Victorian Fiction*. Oxford and New York: Basil Blackwell, 1989.
Rowbotham, Sheila, *Hidden from History: 300 Years of Women's Oppression and the Fight Against It*. London: Pluto Press, 1973.
Ruskin, John, *Sesame and Lilies*. 1865; in E.T. Cook and Alexander Wedderburn, (eds), *The Works of John Ruskin*, vol. XVIII. Library Edition, 1905.
Sandbach-Dahlström, Catherine, *Be Good Sweet Maid: Charlotte Yonge: Domestic Fiction: A Study in Dogmatic Purpose and Fictional Form*. Stockholm: Avhandl, 1984.
Sandford, Mrs John, *Woman in her Social and Domestic Character*. London: Longman, Rees, Orme, Brown and Green, 1831.
Sewell, Mrs S.A., *Woman and the Times We Live In*. London: Simpkin, Marshall; Manchester: Tubbs & Brook, 2nd edn, 1869.
Shanley, Mary Lyndon, *Feminism, Marriage and the Law in Victorian England 1850–1895*. Princeton: Princeton University Press, 1989.
Shattock, Joanne, and Michael Wolff (eds), *The Victorian Periodical Press: Samplings and Soundings*. Leicester and Toronto: Leicester University Press and University of Toronto Press, 1982.
Showalter, Elaine, *A Literature of Their Own: British Women Novelists from Brontë to Lessing*. 1977; London: Virago, 1978.
Smith, Charles Eastlake (ed.), *Journals and Correspondence of Lady Eastlake*. London: John Murray, 2 vols, 1895.

Smith, Esther Marian Greenwell, *Mrs Humphry Ward*. Boston: Twayne, 1980.
Southam, Brian (ed.), *Jane Austen: The Critical Heritage: Vol. 2 1870–1940*. London and New York: Routledge & Kegan Paul, 1987.
Stassinopoulos, Arianna, *The Female Woman*. London: Davis-Poynter, 1973.
Stebbins, Lucy Poate, *A Victorian Album: Some Lady Novelists of the Period*. London: Secker & Warburg, 1946.
Strachey, Ray, *'The Cause': A Short History of the Women's Movement in Great Britain*. London: G. Bell & Sons, 1928.
Strachey, Ray (ed.), *Our Freedom and the Results, by Five Women*. London: Hogarth Press, 1936.
Strutt, Elizabeth, *The Feminine Soul: Its Nature and Attributes*. London: J.S. Hodson, 1857.
Stubbs, Patricia, *Women and Fiction: Feminism and the Novel 1880–1920*. 1979; London: Methuen, 1981.
Sutherland, John, *Mrs Humphry Ward: Eminent Victorian, Pre-eminent Edwardian*. Oxford: Clarendon Press, 1990.
Terry, R.C., *Victorian Popular Fiction 1860–1880*. London and Basingstoke: Macmillan, 1983.
Thal, Herbert von, *Eliza Lynn Linton: The Girl of the Period*. London: George Allen & Unwin, 1979.
Thompson, Dorothy, *Queen Victoria: Gender and Power*. London: Virago, 1990.
Thompson, William, *Appeal of One half the human race, women* ... London: Longman, 1825; repr. New York: Source Book Press, 1970.
Thomson, Patricia, *The Victorian Heroine: A Changing Ideal 1837–1873*. 1956; repr. Westport, Conn.: Greenwood Press, 1978.
Tillotson, Geoffrey, and Kathleen Tillotson, *Mid-Victorian Studies*. London: Athlone Press, 1965.
Todd, Janet (ed.), *Mary Wollstonecraft: An Annotated Bibliography*. New York and London: Garland, 1976.
Tomalin, Claire, *The Life and Death of Mary Wollstonecraft*. 1974; repr. Harmondsworth: Penguin, 1985.
Trevelyan, Janet Penrose, *The Life of Mrs Humphry Ward*. London: Constable, 1923.
Tristan, Flora, *Promenades dans Londres*. Paris and London, 1840.
Trodd, Anthea, *Domestic Crime in the Victorian Novel*. Basingstoke and London: Macmillan, 1989.
Vance, Norman, *The Sinews of the Spirit: The Ideal of Christian Manliness in Victorian Literature and Religious Thought*. Cambridge: Cambridge University Press, 1985.
Vicinus, Martha, *A Widening Sphere: Changing Roles of Victorian Women*. London and New York: Methuen, 1980.
Vicinus, Martha, *Independent Women: Work and Community for Single Women 1850–1920*. London: Virago, 1985.
Vicinus, Martha, and Bea Nergaard (eds), *Ever Yours, Florence Nightingale: Selected Letters*. London: Virago, 1989.
Wakefield, Priscilla, *Reflections on the Present Condition of the Female Sex; with suggestions for its improvement*. London: 2nd edn, Darton, Harvey and Darton, 1817.
Walters, J. Stuart, *Mrs Humphry Ward: Her Work and Influence*. London: Kegan Paul, 1912.

Wardle, Ralph, *Mary Wollstonecraft: A Critical Biography*. London: The Richards Press; and Lawrence: University of Kansas Press, 1951.
Webb, Beatrice, *The Diary of Beatrice Webb, Vol. 2, 1892–1905: 'All the Good Things of Life'*, ed. Norman and Jeanne Mackenzie. London: Virago, 1986; Vol. III, *'The Power to Alter Things'*. London: Virago, 1984.
Webb, Beatrice, *Our Partnership*, ed. Barbara Drake and Margaret T. Cole. London, New York, Toronto: Longmans, Green, 1948.
Wells, H.G., *Boon*. London: T. Fisher Unwin, 1915.
West, Jane, *Letters to a Young Lady*. London: Longman, Hurst, Rees and Orme, 3 vols, 1806.
Wheeler, Michael, *The Art of Allusion in Victorian Fiction*. London: Macmillan, 1979.
Williams, Merryn, *Margaret Oliphant: A Critical Biography*. Basingstoke and London: Macmillan, 1986.
Wolf, Naomi, *Fire with Fire: The New Female Power and How it will Change the 21st Century*. London: Chatto and Windus, 1993.
Wolff, Robert Lee, *Gains and Losses: Novels of Faith and Doubt in Victorian England*. New York: John Murray, 1977.
Wollstonecraft, Mary, *Vindication of the Rights of Woman*. 1792; ed. Miriam Brody Kramnick, Harmondsworth: Pelican Books, 1975, 1978.
Woman's Rights and the Wife at Home, by a Womanly Woman. London: Robert Hardwicke, 1872.
Wood, Butler (ed.), *Charlotte Brontë: 1816–1916: A Centenary Memorial*. London: T. Fisher Unwin, 1917.
Woodham-Smith, Cecil, *Florence Nightingale*. Edinburgh: Constable, 1950.
Woolf, Virginia, *A Room of One's Own*. 1929; repr. Panther Books, Granada Publishing, 1977, 1978.
Woolf, Virginia, *The Question of Things Happening: The Letters of Virginia Woolf 1912–1922*, ed. Nigel Nicolson and Joanne Trautmann. London: The Hogarth Press, 1976.

5. SECONDARY READING: ARTICLES

Anderson, Nancy Fix, 'Eliza Lynn Linton, Dickens, and the Woman Question', *Victorian Periodicals Review XXII*, no. 4 (Winter 1989), 134–41.
Bellringer, Allan W., 'Mrs Humphry Ward's Autobiographical Tactics: A Writer's Recollections', *Prose Studies* 8 (December 1985), 40–50.
Bentley's Miscellany, 'A Contrast' (review of *Amymone*), 24 (1848), 248–59.
Caird, Mona, 'A Defence of the so-called "Wild Women"', *Nineteenth Century* 31 (May 1892), 811–29.
Christian Remembrancer, 'The Use and Abuse of Female Sentiment in Religion', 47 (April 1864), 378–400.
Clapperton, J.H., 'Agnosticism and Women: A Reply', *Nineteenth Century* 7 (May 1880), 840–44.
Clarke, R.F., 'A Catholic's View of "Helbeck of Bannisdale"', *Nineteenth Century* 44 (September 1898), 455–67.
[Coleridge, H.N.], 'Modern English Poetesses', *Quarterly Review* 66 (September 1840), 374–418.

Collister, Peter, 'Mrs Humphry Ward, Vernon Lee, and Henry James', *Review of English Studies* 31 (1980), 315–21.
Collister, Peter, 'Portraits of "Audacious Youth"': George Eliot and Mrs Humphry Ward', *English Studies* 64 (1983), 296–317.
Contemporary Review, 'Christianity and the Equality of the Sexes', 46 (August 1884), 224–34.
Cox, R.G., 'The Reviews and Magazines', in Boris Ford (ed.), *The New Pelican Guide to English Literature*, vol. 6: *From Dickens to Hardy*, Harmondsworth: Penguin, 1982.
Creighton, Louise, 'An Appeal Against Female Suffrage: A Rejoinder', *Nineteenth Century* 26 (August 1889), 347–54.
[Dallas, E.S.], 'Popular Literature – The Periodical Press', *Blackwood's* 85 (January 1859), 96–112.
Dennis, Barbara, 'The Two Voices of Charlotte Yonge', *Durham University Journal* LXV: 2 (March 1973), 181–8.
Dickens, Charles, 'Sucking Pigs', *Household Words* 4 (8 November 1851), 145–7.
Fawkes, Alfred, 'The Ideas of Mrs Humphry Ward', *Quarterly Review* 217 (July 1912), 1–20.
[Galloway, Thomas], 'Mrs Somerville's *Mechanism of the Heavens*', *Edinburgh Review* 55 (April 1832), 1–25.
Gaskell, Catherine Milnes, 'Women of Today', *Nineteenth Century* 26 (November 1889), 776–84.
[Greenwell, Dora], 'Our Single Women', *North British Review* 36 (February 1862), 62–87.
Greg, W.R., 'Is a Christian Life Feasible in These Days?', *Contemporary Review* 21 (April 1873), 680–700.
Gwynn, Stephen, 'The Life and Writings of Mrs Oliphant', *Edinburgh Review* 190 (July 1899), 26–47.
[Hutton, R.H.], 'The Author of Heartsease and Modern Schools of Fiction', *Prospective Review* X (1854), 460–82.
James, Henry, 'Mrs Humphry Ward', *English Illustrated Magazine* (February 1892); repr. in *Henry James, Literary Criticism: Essays on Literature, American Writers, English Writers*. New York: The Library of America, 1984.
James, Henry, 'London Notes', *Harper's Weekly*, 21 August 1897.
Knoepflmacher, U.C., 'The Rival Ladies: Mrs Ward's "Lady Connie" and Lawrence's "Lady Chatterley's Lover"', *Victorian Studies* 4 (December 1960), 141–58.
Lathbury, Bertha, 'Agnosticism and Women', *Nineteenth Century* 7 (April 1880), 619–27.
Leavis, Q.D., '"Femina Vie-Heureuse" Please Note', *Scrutiny* VII, no. 1 (June 1938), 81–5.
Leavis, Q.D., 'Caterpillars of the Commonwealth Unite', *Scrutiny* VII, no. 2 (September 1938), 203–14.
Lederer, Clara, 'Mary Arnold Ward and the Victorian Ideal', *Nineteenth-Century Fiction* 6 (December 1951), 201–8.
[Lister, T.H.], 'Rights and Conditions of Women', *Edinburgh Review* 73 (April 1841), 189–209.
[Lobban, J.H., and William Blackwood], 'Mrs Oliphant', *Blackwood's* 162 (July 1897), 161–4.

Lochhead, Marion, 'Margaret Oliphant: A Half-Forgotten Victorian', *Quarterly Review* 299 (July 1961), 300–10.
Maudsley, Henry, 'Sex in Mind and in Education', *Fortnightly Review* 21 (April 1874), 466–83.
[Millar, J.H.], 'Mrs Oliphant as a Novelist', *Blackwood's* 162 (September 1897), 305–19.
Moore, Suzanne, 'The Big Question: Is Feminism Finished?', *Elle* (May 1990), 47–51.
[Mozeley, Anne], 'Mr Mill on the Subjection of Women', *Blackwood's* 106 (September 1869), 309–21.
[Mulock, Dinah], 'The House of Commons: From the Ladies' Gallery', *Cornhill Magazine* 8 (October 1863), 429–37.
[Mulock, Dinah], 'Sermons', *Cornhill Magazine* 9 (January 1864), 33–40.
National Review, 'Chronicles of Carlingford', 16 (April 1863), 350–62.
Nightingale, Florence, 'A "Note" of Interrogation', *Fraser's Magazine* NS 7 (May 1873), 567–77; 'A sub-"Note of Interrogation" I. What will be our Religion in 1999?', *Fraser's Magazine* NS 8 (July 1873), 25–36.
Nonconformist, The, 'Salem Chapel', 25 February 1873, 157–8.
Nonconformist, The, 'Dissent in Fiction', 5 July 1876, 675.
Offen, Karen, 'Defining Feminism: A Comparative Historical Approach', *Signs* 14 (Autumn 1988), 119–57.
O'Mealy, Joseph H., 'Mrs Oliphant, *Miss Marjoribanks*, and the Victorian Canon', *The Victorian Newsletter* 82 (Fall 1992), 44–9.
Page, Norman, 'Hardy, Mrs Oliphant, and *Jude the Obscure*', *The Victorian Newsletter* 46 (Fall 1974), 22–4.
Palmegiano, E.M., 'Feminist Propaganda in the 1850s and 1860s', *Victorian Periodicals Newsletter* II (February 1971), 5–8.
Palmegiano, E.M., 'Women and British Periodicals 1832–1867: A Bibliography', *Victorian Periodicals Newsletter* IX (March 1976).
Paston, George, 'A Censor of Modern Womanhood', *Fortnightly Review* 70 (September 1901), 505–19.
Purcell, E., 'The Rebel of the Family', *The Academy*, 19 February 1881, p. 131.
Rives, Françoise, 'The Marcellas, Lauras, Dianas ... of Mrs Humphry Ward', *Caliban* XVII (1980), 69–79.
Roberts, Yvonne, 'Is This the Face of Feminism?', *Elle* (April 1994), 67–70.
Saturday Review, 'Current Criticism', 9 October 1858, 349–51; 'Certain Uses of Light Reading', 19 April 1862, p. 434; 'Women's Heroines', 2 March 1867, 259–61; 'The Curate in Charge', 5 February 1876, 179–80; 'Phoebe Junior', 22 July 1876, 112–13; 'The Rebel of the Family', 20 November 1880, p. 650.
Skelton, John, 'A Little Chat about Mrs Oliphant', *Blackwood's* 133 (January 1883), 73–91.
Smith, J. Norton, 'An Introduction to Mrs Humphry Ward, Novelist', *Essays in Criticism* 18 (1968), 420–28.
Spectator, 'Mrs Oliphant', 20 May 1899, 627–8.
Stone, Donald D., 'Victorian Feminism and the Nineteenth Century Novel', *Women's Studies* I (1972), 65–91.
Sturgis, Howard Overing, 'A Sketch from Memory', *Temple Bar* 118 (October 1899), 233–48.

Sutton-Ramspeck, Beth, 'The Personal is Poetical: Feminist Criticism and Mary Ward's Readings of the Brontës', *Victorian Studies* 34 (Autumn 1990), 55–75.
Tweedie, Mrs Alec, 'A Chat with Mrs Lynn Linton', *Temple Bar* 102 (May 1894), 355–64.
Vicinus, Martha, review of Herbert von Thal's *Eliza Lynn Linton*, *Victorian Studies* 24 (Spring 1981), 369–70.
Watson, Kathleen, 'George Eliot and Mrs Oliphant: A Comparison in Social Attitudes', *Essays in Criticism* 19 (October 1969), 410–19.

Index

Adam, 164
Adburgham, Alison, 128, 218
Albert, Prince, 22, 108
Alcott, Louisa May, 69
All the Year Round, 57
Allen, Grant, 57
Amiel, Frederic, 37
Anderson, Elizabeth Garrett, 4
Anderson, Nancy Fix, 33, 44, 104, 132, 137, 140, 206, 210, 213, 218, 219
anti-feminism
  active, 32
  ambivalent, 34
  backlash, 1, 3, 6, 11, 17, 32, 204, 211
  beginnings, 12
  and Britishness, 16–17
  caricatures, 11, 24–7, 28–9, 30–1
  changes in, 32, 35
  and the church, 160, 167, 193, 196
  definitions of, 2–3, 5–6
  and domesticity, 17–20, 62, 63, 73, 165, 203
  and feminism, 2–3, 5–6
  history of, 10–35
  inconsistencies in, 6, 7, 8
  and insecurity, 132
  male-authored, 11, 27–32
  as the 'norm', 3
  passive, 32
  personalities, 7
  reading anti-feminist texts, 2, 8–9, 204–5
  varieties of, 3, 5–6, 31–2
Anti-Suffrage Review, 156
Arnold, Ethel, 208
Arnold, Frances (Fan), 47
Arnold, Julia, 200, 208
Arnold, Dr Thomas, 95, 208
Arnold, Thomas, 115, 119, 157, 185, 189, 191, 208, 216, 223

Athenaeum, 127
Auerbach, Nina, 22, 212
Austen, Jane, 8, 34, 37, 46, 53, 56, 91, 201
  admired by men, 37
  anti-feminist women and, 37–40, 52
  Emma, 78
  letters, 38
  Mansfield Park, 74
  passion, lack of, 38, 39
  Pride and Prejudice, 37, 38
Austen-Leigh Memoir, 37, 38

Bagehot, Walter, 127
Baillie, Joanna, 27
Barbauld, Anna Laetitia, 26
Barrett, Elizabeth, 14, 160, 211, 214, 221
Beetham, Margaret, 129, 218–19
Bennett, Arnold, 86–7, 129, 130, 216, 218
Berry, Mary, 13, 211
Benson, Edward White, 95
Besant, Annie, 180
Bevington, Merle, 128, 218
Bible, 161–3
Bindslev, Anne M., 79, 86, 115, 216, 218
Blackwell, Elizabeth, 14
Blackwood, Isabella, 144, 220
Blackwood, John, 42, 94, 144, 173, 216, 217, 220, 222
Blackwood's Edinburgh Magazine, 37, 38, 49, 51, 52, 55, 92, 108, 109, 112, 126, 127, 129, 132, 143, 144, 149, 173, 179, 199, 207
Blodgett, Harriet, 22, 212
Bloomer, Amelia, 30
bluestockings, 27
Bodichon, Barbara, 6
Bowen, Lord Justice, 155
Brabourne, Lord, 38

240

Index

Braddon, Mary Elizabeth, 51, 55, 56, 57, 59, 104, 109, 138, 210
Brontë, Branwell, 51, 149
Brontë, Charlotte, 8, 27, 29, 34, 37, 38, 44, 46, 52, 53, 55, 56, 79, 82, 86, 88, 149, 189, 201
   Jane Eyre, 22, 30, 38, 47, 48, 49, 51, 52, 53, 55, 56, 57, 59, 71, 80, 88, 91, 93, 96, 104, 105, 123, 160, 190, 214
   Shirley, 48, 50, 56, 88, 96, 163
   Villette, 47, 51, 56, 84, 96, 191, 214
   Oliphant on, 49–51
   Ward on, 46–9
Brontë, Emily, 47, 48, 50, 91
   Oliphant on, 50
   Ward on, 48
Browning, Elizabeth, *see* Barrett, Elizabeth
Browning, Robert, 41
Brownstein, Rachel, 58, 215
Byron, Lady, 165
Byron, Lord, 39

Caird, Mona, 140–1, 219
Carlingford, Chronicles of, 37
Carlyle, Jane Welsh, 172
Carlyle, Thomas, 94–5, 172, 217
Caroline, Queen, 17
Carter, Elizabeth, 26
Chapman, John, 42
Chapone, Hester, 26
Christian Remembrancer, 160, 221
Christianity, 14, 16, 162, 193
Churchwoman, The, 171
Clapperton, Jane Hume, 194, 224
Clarke, John Stock, 153, 220, 221–2
Clarke, Norma, 28, 165, 213, 221–2
Clarke, R.F., 191–2, 223
Cobbe, Frances Power, 129, 198
Colby, Vineta, 2, 210
Coleridge, Christabel, 64, 215
Coleridge, Henry Nelson, 29, 213
Coleridge, Sara, 29
Colley, Linda, 4, 16, 17, 210, 211
Collins, Wilkie, 55–6, 57, 59, 91, 104, 138, 139, 210
Contagious Diseases Acts, 5

Contemporary Review, 129, 182–3
Cook, John Douglas, 128, 130
Cornhill Magazine, 129, 135
Craik, Dinah Mulock, 166–7, 198, 222
Creighton, Mandell, 86, 216
Croker, John Wilson, 213
Cromer, Lord, 155
Cross, John, 37, 44, 45
cross-dressing, 107
Culler, Jonathan, 52–3, 214
Cunningham, Valentine, 174, 222

Daily News, 127, 129
Darwin, Charles, 160, 184
Davies, Emily, 4
Desbordes-Valmore, Marcelline, 47
diaries, 21–2
Dickens, Charles, 78, 108, 127, 147, 203, 213
   anti-feminist caricature, 30
   Bleak House, 30, 60
   David Copperfield, 58
   Dombey and Son, 5
   heroes, 97
   influence on Linton, 137
   Oliphant on, 36
   on women campaigners, 30–1
domestic detail, 9, 19, 61–2, 74, 98, 201
Dowell, Susan, 162, 221, 223
duty, 19–20
Dworkin, Andrea, 3, 210
Dyson, Marianne, 207

Eastlake, Elizabeth, Lady, 22, 53, 129, 212
Edgeworth, Maria, 25–6, 36, 212
Edinburgh Review, 127, 129, 148, 151, 212
education, 12–13, 14, 16, 20–1, 24, 25
Edwards, Lee R., 71, 77, 88, 215
Eliot, George, 8, 14, 20, 34
   Adam Bede, 45, 46, 96, 123, 188
   anti-feminist novelists' hostility to, 39
   Cross's *Life* of, 37, 44, 45
   Felix Holt, 42

Index

Eliot, George – *continued*
  heroes, 91–2
  heroines, 203–4
  Linton on, 42–4
  on male reviewers, 29
  Middlemarch, 5, 21, 45, 52, 56, 57, 60, 65, 76, 82, 89, 96, 117, 118, 123, 152, 187, 188, 193
  The Mill on The Floss, 56, 60, 80, 96, 118, 152, 163
  Oliphant on, 40–2
  religion, 174, 180
  reviews, 129
  Scenes of Clerical Life, 74, 96
  'Silly Novels by Lady Novelists', 195, 213
  translations of Strauss and Feuerbach, 161
  Ward on, 46
  Yonge on, 44–5
Elle, 11, 211
Ellis, Sarah Stickney, 17, 18, 20, 21, 22, 33, 97, 134, 150, 156, 165, 194, 212, 217
Elwood, Anne, 12, 211
English Republic, The, 33, 213
Englishwoman's Journal, 166
Evangelicals, 13, 15, 16, 95, 162–3, 176, 186
Eve, 163, 164, 221

Faludi, Susan, 11
family life, 6
  failure of, 6, 135–6, 203, 206
  values, 11
father–daughter relationships, 197
femininity, 5, 11, 28, 31, 40, 41, 44, 63, 95, 115, 132, 136, 141, 158, 183
feminism, 1, 2–3, 5–6, 7, 10, 11, 15, 32, 37, 46, 122, 145, 153, 154, 155, 204, 211
  in *Delia Blanchflower*, 122
  personalities, 6
Fetterley, Judith, 53, 204, 214, 224
Fielding, Henry, 92
Forster, E.M., 1, 88, 210
Forster, Margaret, 2, 7, 210, 212
Fortnightly Review, 129, 134, 155

Fraser's Magazine, 146, 147, 161
French, Marilyn, 167, 222
French Revolution, 3, 12, 16, 50, 134

Garber, Marjorie, 107, 217
Gaskell, Elizabeth, 20, 29, 44, 47, 127, 147
  heroes, 96–7
  heroines, 203
  Mary Barton, 56, 74
  Ruth, 100
'gender crisis', 10, 204–5
Gillick, Victoria, 7
Gilmour, Robin, 188, 223
'Girl of the Period', 69, 70, 71, 126, 137–9, 140, 143, 206, 215, 217, 219
Gladstone, W.E., 37, 115, 186, 193
Godwin, William, 12, 24
Goethe, J.W. von, 39
Grand, Sarah, 110, 153
Green, T.H., 185
Greer, Germaine, 7
Greg, William Rathbone, 182–3, 223
Grey, Maria, 161–2, 221
Grimmett, Jennifer, 4, 210
Gross, John, 127, 218
Guardian, The, 1, 210
Guy, Margaret, 173, 222

Hamilton, Eliza, 28
Hamilton, Elizabeth, 24, 212
Hardy, Thomas, 51, 53, 88
  heroes, 97
  heroines, 201
  Jude the Obscure, 57, 109
  Tess of the d'Urbervilles, 59, 91, 160
Harradan, Beatrice, 106, 206
Harrison, Brian, 210
Hays, Mary, 26
Heilbrun, Carolyn, 71, 88, 215, 216
Helsinger, Elizabeth K., 138, 219, 221
Hemans, Felicia, 28
Hennell, Sara, 161

Index

heroes, 8, 55, 91–8
  decline of, 96–8
  guilt and, 100–1
  weakness of, 125
heroines, 6, 7, 8, 26, 34, 35, 54, 55–60
  broadening role of, 57, 60
  centrality of, 60
  choices of, 201
  crises of, 39
  fruitless self-sacrifice of, 90, 203–4
  disruptive behaviour of, 59–60, 87
  humiliation of, 59, 65, 66, 68, 82, 88, 89
  marriages of, 77, 201, 202–3
  new kind of, 88, 89, 201, 203
  as outsiders, 87
  submission of, 55, 59, 64
heroism, 58, 64, 72, 73, 123
Hogg, James, 127
Holden, Pat, 168, 222
home, ideology of, 7, 15, 16–17, 20, 25
  as extension of the church, 167
  as mini-state, 18, 74–5
  as moral testing-ground, 19–20, 61–4, 73, 125
Household Words, 30, 33, 127, 137
Hutton, R.H., 37, 41, 103, 127
Huxley, T.H., 184

Ibsen, Henrik, 135
Irving, Edward, 108–9, 172, 195, 201, 217, 222

James, Henry, 37, 47, 91, 115, 201
Jameson, Anna, 129, 165–6, 198, 222
Jay, Elizabeth, viii, 2, 178, 210, 223
Jersey, Countess of, 156, 221
Jewsbury, Geraldine, 127
Jewsbury, Maria Jane, 28, 127, 211
Jex-Blake, Sophia, 4
Johnson, Samuel, 36
Johnstone, Christian Isobel, 127
Jones, Marion Kathleen, 155, 220

journalism, 8, 27, 36, 94, 125, 126–59
  women and, 126–30
Jowett, Benjamin, 161, 185

Keble, John, 36, 45, 93, 103, 168–9, 172, 201, 207, 222
Kennedy, Rev. Anthony, 198
Kingsley, Charles, 103, 117
Knowles, J.T., 155
Kowaleski-Wallace, Elizabeth, 36

Landor, Walter Savage, 36, 94, 137, 201, 206
Lathbury, Bertha, 193–4, 223
Lawrence, D.H., 79, 88, 118
Layard, George Somes, 104, 206, 217, 222
Leavis, Q.D., 73, 216
Leopold, King of the Belgians, 23
Levin, Susan, 27, 212
Levine, Philippa, 4, 210
Lewes, George Henry, 37, 39, 40, 41, 43, 45, 47, 68, 127
Lewis, Sarah, 18, 19, 20, 212
Lewis, Lady Theresa, 211
Liddon, Dean, 185
Linton, Eliza Lynn
  agnosticism, 184
  anger at mother's death, 104, 132, 145, 206
  biographical summary, 206
  biographies of, 2, 33, 210
  on Charlotte Brontë, 51
  daughter-figures, need for, 106, 132
  deconversion, 180–1, 196, 206
  on divorce reform, 134, 136
  on dress, 138
  on George Eliot, 42–4, 45, 46, 52, 53, 214
  failed family life, 203, 206
  heroes, 103–7, 123, 124, 125, 200
  heroines, 68–71, 77, 200, 202
  on higher education, 134, 136, 141
  journalism, 126, 127, 128, 130–2, 143, 144, 158–9, 206
  on mad wives, 104, 105

Linton, Eliza Lynn – *continued*
  on marriage, 135, 200, 201
  on married women's property reform, 133–4, 136
  men, knowledge of, 94
  men, satire of, 139
  on motherhood, 132–3, 135, 136, 140, 141
  and religion, 168, 180–4, 193
  and science, 184
  stoicism of, 168, 180, 184
  on the suffrage, 133, 135, 141
  on Mary Wollstonecraft, 33–4, 213
  on women's heroes, 93
  Amymone, 142, 220
  Autobiography of Christopher Kirkland, 105–7, 180, 181–2, 196, 197, 199, 206, 217, 223
  Azeth the Egyptian, 206
  'Characteristics of English Women', 17, 142–3, 220
  'The Decay of Discipline', 139
  'Domestic Life', 135–6, 219
  'Dovecots', 142, 219
  'The Future Supremacy of Women', 139
  'The Girl of the Period', 69, 70, 71, 126, 137–9, 140, 143, 206, 215, 217, 219
  Grasp Your Nettle, 103, 106, 124, 133, 217
  'The Higher Education of Woman', 134, 219
  'The Modern Revolt', 139, 219
  'Modern Topsy-Turveydom', 139, 219
  My Literary Life, 44, 136, 206, 214
  The One Too Many, 105, 134, 135
  'Our Civilization', 135
  Ourselves, 70, 141, 142, 143, 215, 219
  'The Partisans of the Wild Women', 140, 219
  'Passing Faces', 137, 219
  The Rebel of the Family, 26, 57, 60, 68–71, 105, 106, 131, 133, 212, 215
  'The Rights and Wrongs of Woman', 33
  Sowing the Wind, 130, 133, 135, 219
  'The Threatened Abdication of Man', 139
  The True History of Joshua Davidson, 182–3, 197, 199, 223
  Under Which Lord? 183–4, 186, 191, 195, 197, 198, 223
  'The Wild Women', 133, 134, 139, 140, 219
  'Womanhood in Greece', 142, 220
Linton, William James, 70, 94, 104, 105–6, 132, 206
Lockhart, John Gibson, 108, 127
London Review, 128
Longman's Magazine, 129
Lyndon, Neil, 11, 211

Macmillan's Magazine, 38, 129, 133, 155
Maginn, William, 127, 213
Marie Antoinette, 17
marriage, 5, 23, 24, 56, 65, 66, 67, 71, 76, 77, 89, 105, 109, 113, 132, 135, 139, 199, 202–3
Martineau, Harriet, 4, 12, 14, 24–5, 28–9, 47, 70, 96, 127, 129, 151, 158, 165, 180, 181, 189, 211, 213, 217, 223
Mary, Virgin, 163, 180, 221
masculinity, 8, 94–8, 116, 120, 121, 122, 124, 125, 136, 183
  and Christianity, 103
Meakin, Annette, 211
men,
  heroines of, 91
  inferiority of, 21
  novelists on, 48, 89, 199
  women's attitude to, 7
Meredith, George, 201
Mill, John Stuart, 6, 10, 18, 75, 96, 109, 132, 144, 147–8, 149, 152, 212, 217, 219
Miller, Jane, 91, 216
Milton, John, 36, 160

Index

Mitford, Mary Russell, 14, 38
Montagu, Elizabeth, 26
Montalembert, Comte de, 108
Monthly Packet, 44, 46, 68, 126, 128, 207, 214, 215
Moore, Suzanne, 11, 211
Moore, Thomas, 28–9
More, Hannah, 10, 13–16, 18, 19, 20, 26, 36, 211, 212
Morning Chronicle, 130, 206
motherhood, 3, 6, 10, 15, 25, 70, 74, 89, 132–3, 163
Mothers in Council, 207
Mozley, Anne, 129, 132, 219
Mozley, Tom, 168
Mulock, Dinah, *see* under Craik

National Review, 139
Newman, John Henry, 169
New Monthly Magazine, 129
New Review, 139
New Woman, 7, 56–7, 80, 109, 129, 139, 140, 143, 154, 206
Nicolson, Harold, 10, 211
Nightingale, Florence, 4, 7, 14, 166
  'Cassandra', 66, 215
  religion, 160–1, 180, 198, 221
  Suggestions for Thought, 161, 221
Nineteenth Century, 129, 139, 140, 155–6, 186, 191–2, 193
Nordau, Max, 135
Norton, Caroline, 4, 7, 23, 30, 56, 129

Oliphant, Cyril, 107–8, 124, 173, 178, 179, 207
Oliphant, Francis R. ('Cecco'), 107–8, 124, 173, 178, 207
Oliphant, Frank (brother), 207
Oliphant, Frank (husband), 172, 207
Oliphant, Frank (nephew), 108
Oliphant, Margaret,
  anti-feminist? 153, 208
  on Jane Austen, 37, 38, 39, 213
  biographical summary, 207–8
  on Mary Braddon, 51, 55
  on Charlotte Brontë, 49–51, 52, 53
  on Emily Brontë, 50
  on Catholicism, 173
  clergymen characters, 115, 175–8, 180, 195, 197
  on church as male profession, 172, 180
  on Dissenters, 163, 174, 177, 190, 192
  on divorce, 149
  on education, 152–3
  on George Eliot, 37, 39, 40–2, 43, 44, 45, 50, 92, 213, 214
  'empire' vocabulary, 74–5, 149, 150
  on family life, 73–4, 146
  notion of 'genius', 73, 75, 80, 96
  heroes, 107–14, 117, 123, 124, 125
  heroines, 55, 71–9, 88, 152
  irony, 154, 176, 199, 208
  journalism, 41, 126, 127, 143–54
  on Linton, 150
  male persona, 40–1, 49, 52, 143, 146, 150–1, 152
  on marriage, 49, 76, 78–9, 113, 144, 147, 148–9, 151, 201
  on marriage plot, 72, 77–8, 202–3
  on married women's property reform, 144, 146
  on men, 77, 88, 92–3, 94, 107, 109–10, 145, 146, 148, 149, 208
  on modern novels, 50, 51, 61
  on motherhood, 74, 133, 145, 154, 178, 196, 199, 216
  on politics, 74–5, 78
  on religion, 168, 172–80, 195, 196
  on sensation novels, 50–1, 55
  on sermons, 172, 173, 175, 176, 179, 218, 223
  sexual reticence, 146, 153
  on the suffrage, 144, 146, 147–8, 150, 151, 152, 153
  theory, rejection of, 144, 148
  on Wollstonecraft, 220
  on women, 74, 110, 144–5, 147, 158

Index

Oliphant, Margaret – *continued*
  on work, 144, 145, 148
  Annals of a Publishing House, 126, 127, 207, 218, 220
  'The Anti-Marriage League', 110, 218
  Autobiography, 37, 41, 49, 52, 108, 173, 178–9, 180, 216, 220, 223
  'The Condition of Women', 149, 150, 151, 152, 220
  The Curate in Charge, 58, 71–3, 76, 87, 113–14, 146, 176–7, 195, 196, 202, 215
  'Francies of a Believer', 173, 176, 222
  'The Great Unrepresented', 145, 147, 150, 217, 220
  'The Grievances of Women', 146, 147, 152, 153, 220
  'The Latest Lawgiver', 153, 220
  'The Laws Concerning Women', 146, 149, 150, 151, 199, 220, 224
  The Life of Edward Irving, 108–9, 172, 222
  The Literary History of England, 145, 213, 220
  'Mill on the Subjection of Women', 149, 150, 153, 220
  Miss Marjoribanks, 60, 72, 73–7, 78, 111, 113, 114, 147, 150, 200
  'Modern Novelists Great and Small', 49
  'The Old Saloon', 153–4, 220
  The Perpetual Curate, 74, 110–11, 113, 124, 173, 176, 180, 195, 197
  Phoebe Junior, 59, 60, 72, 73, 77–9, 96, 114, 124, 146, 177, 196, 200, 208, 215, 216
  The Rector, 176, 195
  Salem Chapel, 109, 110–13, 174–6, 180, 190, 192, 195, 197, 222
  Women Novelists of Queen Victoria's Reign, 44, 50, 214
Oliphant, Margaret (Maggie) (daughter), 154, 172, 178, 179
Opie, Amelia, 25, 212

Paine, Tom, 18, 25
Pall Mall Gazette, 155
Pankhurst, Emmeline, 6
Pateman, Carole, 137, 219
Pattison, Mark, 36, 46, 115, 201
Peterson, William S., 59, 214, 215, 221
Phelps, William Lyon, 115, 218
Plato, 164
Polwhele, Richard, 26
Poovey, Mary, 5, 210
Pope, Alexander, 74
Pratt, Annis, 87, 88, 216
Praz, Mario, 96, 97, 217
Punch, 30, 213
Pusey, Edward, 185

Quarterly Review, 22, 28–9, 129, 154–5, 213

Raine, Kathleen, 1
Reade, Charles, 36, 51, 55, 73, 216
reader-response theory, 52
realism, 48, 60
religion, 8, 15, 23, 34, 45, 67, 115, 160–98
  and domesticity, 193–4
  religious experience (female), 167, 196
  and female sexuality, 167
Renan, Ernest, 115
Rendall, Jane, 15, 211
Rich, Adrienne, 53, 214
Richards, Evelleen, 184, 223
Richardson, Samuel, 92, 99
Rigby, Elizabeth, *see* under Eastlake, Lady
rights, women's, 13, 15, 18, 25
Rives, Françoise, 79–80, 216
Riviere, Joan, 40, 214
Romanes, Ethel, 45, 67, 213, 214, 215
Roosevelt, Theodore, 157, 209
Roper, Michael, 95, 217
Rossetti, Christina, 161
Routledge's Magazine, 141
Ruskin, John, 18, 75, 124, 149, 150, 153

Sand, George, 38
Sandbach-Dahlström, Catherine, 67, 215
Sandford, Mrs John, 23, 24, 212
Saturday Review, 59, 69, 71, 126, 127–8, 129, 134, 141, 145, 150, 155, 206, 218
sensation novels, 50–1, 55, 59, 90, 104, 110, 111–12, 138, 139, 215
'separate spheres', 4–5, 16, 17, 33, 75, 95, 140, 150
Shaw, George Bernard, 2, 210
Sheets, Robin L., 138, 219, 221
Shelley, Mary, 14, 22, 211
Shirreff, Emily, 161–2, 221
Showalter, Elaine, 37, 93, 100, 213, 215, 216, 217
Sichel, Beatrice, 106, 206
Smiles, Samuel, 96, 97, 217
Smith, George, 46
Smith, Julia Evelina, 161
Somerville College, Oxford, 208
Somerville, Mary, 25, 27, 212
Southam, Brian, 37, 213
Southey, Robert, 27, 28
Spectator, 129
de Staël, Mme, 38
Stanley, A.P., 108
Stebbins, Lucy P., 109, 217
Stephen, Leslie, 46, 127
Strutt, Elizabeth, 164–5, 211
suffrage, 7, 8, 16, 122–3, 141, 144, 146, 147–8, 150, 151, 152, 153, 156–7, 208, 210
Sutherland, John, 2, 158, 210, 220–1
Sutton-Ramspeck, Beth, 46–7, 53, 214

Tait, Archbishop, 179
Tait's Edinburgh Magazine, 127
Temple Bar, 44, 135, 139
Tennyson, Alfred, 108
Terry, R.C., 109, 217
Thackeray, William M., 36, 88, 91, 97, 203
Thomis, Malcolm, 4, 210
Thompson, William, 12, 211
Times, The, 11, 155, 156

Todd, Janet, 211
Tosh, John, 95, 217
Trench, Maria, 44–5
Trevelyan, Janet Penrose, 155, 191, 208, 220, 223, 224
Tristan, Flora, 21, 212
Trodd, Anthea, 222
Trollope, Anthony, 36, 37, 51–2, 96, 111, 114, 124, 172, 177, 184, 208
Tulloch, Principal, 124, 218

Valentine, Madge, 107, 207
Vance, Norman, 103, 217
van Thal, Herbert, 2, 210
Veeder, William, 138, 219, 221
Vicinus, Martha, viii, 2, 210
Victoria, Queen, 7, 17, 18, 22–3, 74, 157, 212
Victorian Studies, viii, 2, 46, 210

Walpole, Horace, 25
Ward, Arnold, 208
Ward, Dorothy, 208
Ward, Janet, *see* Trevelyan, Janet
Ward, Mary Augusta (Mrs Humphry)
　on Jane Austen, 37, 38–9, 213
　on Elizabeth Barrett, 46
　biographical summary, 208–9
　on Catholicism, 185, 188–92, 202, 208
　on Charlotte Brontë, 46–9, 50, 214
　on Emily Brontë, 47, 48, 50
　'childishness' of heroines, 80, 83, 84, 115, 123, 189, 200, 203
　duty, idea of, 155
　on George Eliot, 45–6, 47
　heroes, 114–23, 125
　heroines, 59, 60–1, 79–87, 88, 118, 188, 201
　on higher education, 155, 208
　journalism, 154–9
　manliness, idea of, 119–20
　on marriage, 49, 82–3, 87, 201
　on men, 36, 80, 94, 115
　on politics, 81, 83, 115, 118, 156, 157, 201, 208

Ward, Mary Augusta – *continued*
  on religion, 84, 86, 115, 116, 118, 119, 168, 185–93, 195, 202, 208
  on sexual attraction, 118, 200, 209
  submission theme, 82, 83, 85, 200
  on suffrage, 122–3, 154, 155–6, 208, 220
  womanliness, idea of, 119–20
  on women's writing, 46–9
  'An Appeal against Female Suffrage', 156
  The Case of Richard Meynell, 192
  The Coryston Family, 80, 121–2, 157, 192–3, 201, 218, 223
  Daphne, 60
  David Grieve, 47, 53, 60, 118, 192, 218
  Delia Blanchflower, 60, 83, 115, 122, 154, 201, 218, 220
  England's Effort, 158
  Helbeck of Bannisdale, 84–6, 87, 89, 118–19, 188–92, 195, 196, 197, 208, 216, 223
  Lady Rose's Daughter, 60, 116, 218
  Letters to My Neighbours, 157, 221
  Marcella, 57, 60, 80–3, 84, 85, 86, 89
  Milly and Olly, 116
  Miss Bretherton, 116
  'The New Reformation', 186, 192, 193, 223
  'Recent Fiction in England and France', 48
  Robert Elsmere, 37, 60, 72, 84, 103, 113, 114, 116–17, 186–8, 189, 196, 197, 208, 218, 223
  Sir George Tressady, 83, 89, 119, 216
  Towards the Goal, 158
  Unbelief and Sin, 185–6, 223
  A Writer's Recollections, 159, 185, 221
Ward, Thomas Humphry, 208
Watson, Ellen, 68

Wells, H.G., 47
West, Jane, 16–18, 19, 140, 156, 211
Westminster Review, 29, 195
Williams, Helen Maria, 26
Williams, Jane, 162, 221, 223
Williams, Merryn, 145, 200
Wilson, John, 108, 207
Wolf, Naomi, 9, 200, 205, 211, 224
Wollstonecraft, Mary, 10, 11, 12–15, 17, 18, 24, 25, 26, 28, 31, 32, 33–4, 145, 211, 220
Woman's Rights and Duties, 23–4, 212
women
  and agnosticism, 193–4
  'Angel in the House', 43–4, 141, 143
  Bildungsroman, 87
  deconversion of, 196
  as domestic managers, 41, 61–2, 75, 78, 177
  heroes of, 91–2, 93
  and journalism, 126–30
  ordination of, 162–3, 193, 221
  and politics, 75
  and religion, 160–8, 193
  worship of, 43–4, 141
Women's National Anti-Suffrage League, 156
Wordsworth, Elizabeth, 37
Wordsworth, John, 185
Wordsworth, William, 27–8, 39, 212
Woolf, Virginia, 36, 47, 48, 49, 55, 213, 215

Yonge, Charlotte, M.
  on Jane Austen, 37
  autobiography, 203, 206
  biographical summary, 206–7
  on Charlotte Brontë, 51
  Catholicism, dislike of, 171, 222
  on George Eliot, 44–5, 52
  heroes, 91, 92, 97, 98–103, 115, 123–4, 125
  heroines, 58–60, 61–8, 77, 170, 202
  invalids, 61, 74, 99–102, 125, 126, 207
  on marriage, 66, 68, 201

Yonge, Charlotte, M. – *continued*
  men, dependence on, 36, 67, 168–9
  men, knowledge of, 93–4
  and parents, 36, 206–7
  on religion, 168–71, 179, 195, 207
  on single life, 63–4, 66, 201
  The Clever Woman of the Family, 58, 60, 61–2, 64–7, 68, 80, 81, 89, 100, 102, 103, 126, 127, 169, 170, 193, 196, 201, 207, 215

The Daisy Chain, 14, 59, 61–4, 65, 67, 68, 74, 81, 83, 87, 100–2, 163, 169–70, 196, 201, 203, 215
Heartsease, 36, 59, 103, 170–1, 222
The Heir of Redclyffe, 59, 96, 98, 103, 121, 123, 124, 170–1, 201, 217
Musings over the Christian Year, 169, 222
Womankind, 171, 207, 222